❇ ❇

DEDICATED
IN LOVING MEMORY
OF OUR FATHER

MOSHE BEN ZVI

❇ ❇

├──── DAVID KORETZKY ────┤

❦ ❦

IT'S VERY GOOD
TO POUR OUT YOUR HEART
TO GOD
AS YOU WOULD
TO A TRUE,
GOOD FRIEND.

❦ ❦

├────── REBBE NACHMAN OF BRESLOV ──────┤

TABLE OF CONTENTS

⁂

**IF YOU HAVE AWARENESS,
WHAT DO YOU LACK?**

**IF YOU LACK AWARENESS,
WHAT DO YOU HAVE?**

⁂

—— TALMUD, NEDARIM 41A ——

The title, *Where Earth and Heaven Kiss,* is based on Rebbe Nachman's teaching of the following Talmudic story (*Bava Batra* 74a):

> Rabbah bar bar Chanah recounted:

> The Arab merchant said to me, "Come, I will show you where Earth and Heaven kiss." I went and saw that windows had been made. I took my basket and placed it in Heaven's window. I said my prayer, but afterwards did not find it. "Are there thieves here?" I asked. He replied, "The Wheel of Heaven has turned. Wait till this time tomorrow; you will find it."

Rebbe Nachman says that this teaching refers to the power of prayer. Earth and Heaven are the body and the soul, respectively. Where—and when—they kiss is the inner peace, harmony and tranquility that each of us seeks.

Maharsha comments that it is indeed possible to change the world for the better through prayer and good deeds. Good deeds and kindness are born through honest self-judgment and sincere prayers that one will act benevolently. The setting for this self-judgment and prayer is hitbodedut.

Looking at this story through a Kabbalistic lens, the Ben Yehoyada reminds us that prayer and mitzvot raise the fallen sparks. Each of us needs to elevate certain sparks. Each day one has new sparks to raise, the work of today's prayer completed by tomorrow's.

The peace you make between body and soul, writes Reb Noson, can extend more and more, till it envelops the entire world. Amen. ❋

⊢—— WORDS OF THANKS ——⊣

M ost people just take a quick glance at the acknowledgements page to see if anybody they know is mentioned, and then go on to the rest of the book. But there's more to acknowledgements than the thrill of recognition.

Thanking is an expression of human decency, which is the basis of the Torah. The gratitude underlying a "thank you" imparts value to what we do. Thanking shows that we are all interconnected, that nothing anyone does can be accomplished alone. Rebbe Nachman teaches that this oneness is what the Ultimate Future is all about.

Without any further ado, thanks to:

Peretz Rubel for lighting the fire to get this book started.

Eliezer Shore; one of us had to finish first. You won!

Yaakov Wieder for sticking it to me again and again, unblocking and unlocking, helping things get to where they had to go.

Robbie and Marcella for chilling.

Efraim and Yonah Alexandre of Palo Alto for keeping the ball rolling.

Dave White for insisting that I write.

All the early readers, especially Tal, Zac, Yeshayahu, Daniel, Danny and Diane.

Lee and Laura, my Western lights.

Nissan Soumekh for wielding the royal whip with such precision that it brought me to my knees and to tears, time and time again. I'm sorry that you had to stop, but am consoled that you are in a better place.

Yisrael Yitzchak Speiser for the inspiration for "One-Minute Hitbodedut."

My legal staff: Al, Steve, Herchel, Matt, Mike and Sopher.

Dr. Tzivia Fuld and Rae Ekman; their unsung web efforts in making people aware of hitbodedut have just been sung.

Nachman and Mimi for changing the course of history.

Moshe Stern for riding shotgun whenever the payroll train came through.

Dovid Sears for adopting me as his little brother.

My friends, teachers and—dare I say—colleagues, Moshe Mykoff and Yehoshua Starrett, for setting the bar high, but not too high. And most of all for banishing Complacency from the Kingdom of God.

My dear cousin Seth for combining with me to write this book.

My dear brother Symcha whose calls from the New Jersey Turnpike first piqued my interest in hitbodedut.

My late brother Yehoshua Moshe for insisting on unflinching honesty. I'm getting closer to it.

Mrs. Yonina Hall, editor extraordinaire. She tried so hard to make this book, like, really good, you know? Anything you like about it, thank her. Anything you don't like, blame me.

Chaim Kramer for insisting that I stay when I had one foot out the door. There are bosses and there are bosses, but there's only one Holy Boss.

My sisters-in-law Bev and Leah for teaching me the meaning of "grace under fire."

My late father-in-law Morty Marcus for teaching me the value of simplicity, and my mother-in-law Phyllis for teaching me to hold on to my dreams.

My father who, despite having been in WWII and Siberia, cared and did for all human beings; and for teaching me my first koan: *When I was your age, I was older.*

My mother for teaching me that love means giving whatever you have for the one you love.

My children: *Oyyyy!*

My wife Udel for finding the hope when I had mislaid it and for out-davening me when the chips were down <hmtadlg>.

Reb Shlomo Freifeld, founder and rosh yeshiva of Sh'or Yoshuv Yeshivah, to whom this book is dedicated. On our excursions to the Metropolitan Museum of Art he taught me many lessons, among them: how to read a painting, Nietzsche was wrong, and, "This above all: To thine own self be true."

You, the reader, for spending your precious time reading this book.

Rebbe Nachman for looking across the centuries and choosing me to be a messenger to bring his words to you.

The Blessed Creator for putting His world at my disposal and for nudging and noodging me in the right direction.

To those I've forgotten, forgive me; you're written in *His* book. ❁

OZER BERGMAN

Jerusalem
Sivan 5766/June 2006

❀ *❀*

DEDICATED TO
REB SHLOMO FREIFELD

❀ *❀*

⊢── INTRODUCTION ──⊣

On a recent visit to Manhattan, I was on my way to meet a friend for lunch. As I walked, I relished the spectrum of humanity that I saw: old, young, male, female, working, funning, in-line skaters, strollers, serious, conservatively dressed, outlandishly attired, vacationing, Black, Oriental, "white bread" Americans, Europeans and, of course, Jews. I thought to myself, "What would the world be like if all these people each spent an hour a day talking to God? What would it do for their personal lives? What would it do for the condition of the human race?"

From my own experience, I had a fair idea of some of the things it could do for their personal lives. It would encourage them to be more generous, guide them to make more reasoned, calmer and wiser decisions, and help them to determine what was truly valuable about life and how to live a genuinely valuable life.

What it would do for the human race I wasn't sure, but multiplying the personal results by 10,000 or 50,000 was a good start. I knew that at a certain point, at the critical mass, the results would be exponential and the world would become unrecognizably good.

The idea of talking to God in your own language and your own words is a key teaching of Rebbe Nachman of Breslov, a chassidic master of the early nineteenth century. Rebbe Nachman calls this practice "hitbodedut"—unstructured, spontaneous, individualized prayer—and recommends it as the highest path to self-awareness and God-consciousness. Reb Noson, his main disciple, recalls how Rebbe Nachman first introduced him to the idea:

> Rebbe Nachman put his arm around my shoulder and said, "It's very good to pour out your heart to God as you would to a true, good friend."

Hitbodedut is a versatile practice that lends itself to several applications, or "rooms" of understanding. In the Refuge/ Recovery Room, you can use hitbodedut to improve yourself and your relationship to God. In the Conference Room, you can use hitbodedut to think about and plan for the future. In the Bedroom, you can experience the delight of loving God for no reason. The least-known room is the NoPlace, a silent form of hitbodedut. As you explore each of these "rooms," you will find yourself changing and growing in ways you never thought possible.

This is the power of hitbodedut, that one hour a day of talking to God: It makes you more human, and the world more humane. ❀

⊢—— THE GENIE ——⊣

As he walked wearily through the desert, his unknown destination as far removed as ever, he noticed something gleaming just a few steps away. Probably a mirage, he thought—but in a desert one cannot afford the luxury of despair. He changed direction and went over to investigate. There was something there.

He reached down to pick it up, but it was stuck. He got down on his knees to pull it out. It was buried more deeply than he had thought. Other than the little bit that had reflected the sunlight, whatever it was seemed to be part of the sand itself. The blistering sun made his job harder, but made him more determined to unearth his discovery. He dug his fingers and hands more deeply into the sand, getting his fingers under the box. He leaned in, straining his back and shoulders, and started pulling.

He pulled and he pulled harder, the box beginning to budge, the sand beginning to give way. Breathing heavily and perspiring, he stopped and started again and again until finally—finally!—the box came free. He pulled it up.

The box was totally encrusted with sand. He banged on it once, then twice, and layers and layers of sand fell away. Underneath all the sand was a small rusty tin box, its opening sealed with an even rustier lid. He dug his bleeding fingertips into the rust and clawed hard to remove the lid. He did—and out rushed the genie.

"You have freed me!" the genie roared. Our amazed hero looked at the lion-shaped apparition. "I have been trapped for thousands of years and you have freed me! To show my gratitude, I will grant you one wish, any wish you may ask."

The man thought. He had been in the desert so long. There were so many things he lacked, so much that he needed, so much that he hoped for. Choosing only one thing would not leave him much better off. Was there one wish that he could make that would provide all his needs or fulfill all his hopes, even those he didn't yet know about? Calmly and fearlessly, he gazed at the genie and replied, "My wish is to have a thousand wishes."

We live our lives in a spiritual desert. The heat of the sun of desire is merciless, constantly cooking us: more food, more sex, more money, more power. The sun's glare makes us see what is not there, and blinds us to what really exists. The sand is hollow; it makes walking so difficult and nothing substantial can be built out of it. The desert has no map and no landmarks. We wander aimlessly. That we still hope to make it out of the desert alive is itself a miracle.

By God's grace, we are given a glimmer of hope. Overlooking past disappointments, we break our inertia and change direction, for no good reason, just out of faith. Our desire to find something worthwhile pushes us to humble and lower ourselves so that we'll even dig to find what we're looking for. We'll strain and ache for deliverance.

When success seems to elude us, we'll dig in with our fingernails to get success in our grasp. When the genie is finally set free—when we discover what tools we have—we'll keep our wits about us to use the genie's power in the best possible way.

Tefilah ligt in drert. Prayer lies in disgrace. It's buried so deeply, so hidden from view, that people don't think of it much, nor think much of it. "It's like sand, impractical to build with. It's rusty, a relic of primitive times."

King David, author of the Psalms, said, "I am prayer" (*Psalms* 109:4). Rebbe Nachman echoed those words when he said, "*Gor mein zakh iz tefilah* (My entire mission is prayer)!" (*Likutey Moharan* II, 93).

By opening this book, you have released the genie and put the power of prayer at your disposal. Your wish has become a thousand.

Someone once asked Rebbe Nachman for his advice on how to best approach God. Rebbe Nachman recommended that the man study a particular subject. "But Rebbe, I can't do that. I am unable to learn," the man protested.

Rebbe Nachman responded, "With prayer, one can achieve anything, every sort of good. One can achieve success in Torah study, prayer, sanctity, any type of Divine worship and any and every sort of good on any spiritual plane" (*Likutey Moharan* II, 111). ✿

PAY ATTENTION
⊢── (YISHUV HADAAT) ──⊣

This may be the most important page you ever read in your life.

I know that sounds rather pretentious, but by the end of the page, I hope—and think—you'll agree.

A second is not a very long time. One goes by, followed by another and then another. A minute or two also doesn't seem like a very long time, unless one is suffering or in a state of anticipation. The minutes add up—ten go by, then twenty, and soon half an hour is gone. We don't watch, and time slips away. One day follows another. Life flows by, passing quickly, as in a dream. Before long, one is on his way to a facility for the aged or a retirement community—if he lives that long and doesn't die suddenly.

How many of us, in any of the brief seconds of life that tick away unceasingly, never to return, stop and think, "What am I doing here? What is all this food, money and sex about? Does any of it *mean* anything?"

> One needs a great deal of merit in order to be worthy of settling his mind for an hour each day, to regret what needs to be regretted. Not everyone is worthy of this. The day passes by so quickly that one may not have any time to reflect and settle his mind even once in his lifetime.

If you've read this far, you have enough merit to be informed. If you have—or want—more merit, you'll want to know what it means to settle your mind and how to go about it. Read on.

One needs to be very determined to devote part of his day to reviewing what he does and to considering carefully how he spends his time. "Is what I'm doing how I should be spending my days?"

Perhaps you have already reflected briefly on the meaning and purpose of life. Did that translate into any significant changes in your thinking or behavior? Did it make you a better person? How long did you remain moved by your reflection? How long did any of the changes last? How long did your resolve last? How long was it till you remembered your observations and attempted changes? When was the next time you considered trying again?

> Even if a person does occasionally settle his mind, it doesn't last long—it immediately passes. Nor is it strong. This is why people fail to realize what foolishness life contains.

A lot of life is foolishness. Can you identify the foolishness? Can you then avoid it? You might want to jot down some of your initial answers and compare them to what you perceive later, after you've settled your mind and taken a good, honest look at life in general and your life in particular.

> If a person were to calm his mind in a very strong way, he would see that everything is foolishness and transience.

So, if you've been spending your time on foolishness, here's your invitation to stop and change all that. If you've tried to change in the past, now you have an invitation—and a companion to help you. Rebbe Nachman bids you:

> "Give me your heart and I will lead you on a new path, the ancient path our ancestors walked." ❋

GETTING READY FOR HITBODEDUT

⊢── 1 • What is Hitbodedut? ──⊣

There is no single or simple answer to this question. Hitbodedut takes many forms, moving easily and naturally from one to another, often imperceptibly, and so cannot be described as being only one thing.

That said, hitbodedut is raw, unadulterated prayer. Rebbe Nachman points out that historically, prayer referred to the communication between a person and God, spoken in one's native tongue and one's own words. No prayer book, no formalized or ritualized service—just straight talk from the heart. Hitbodedut.

Reb Noson writes how Rebbe Nachman first introduced him to hitbodedut:

> Rebbe Nachman put his arm around my shoulder and said, "It's very good to pour out your heart to God as you would to a true, good friend."

Now, straight talk from the heart is not always going to be about only one thing, nor will it always be expressed in the same way. We can see this when we talk with a good friend. Sometimes we share our grief, sometimes we express a complaint and sometimes we confide a secret. Our grief may be wet with tears, our complaint painted red, and our secret conveyed in hushed tones. If our good friend is also a significant other, our straight talk will often be lined with love.

Whatever expression our straight talk may take, it must be straight—that is, honest, sincere, genuine and true. Formalized prayers, however extraordinary, are only scripts. The biggest challenge presented by a script is that of reading it as if its words were yours. (Even for one who is fluent in Hebrew and well-versed in the sources of the siddur, and who can appreciate the genius and the poetry of the obligatory prayers, there still exists the danger of being lulled into the unthinkingness of routine.) However, prayer is not theater. Prayer is real life.

It is a serious mistake, if not a spiritually fatal one, to think that the goal of hitbodedut is piety or "to be more religious." The goal of hitbodedut is to plant, nourish and grow your awe, joy and love of God. ❈

2 • WHAT DO I NEED TO DO
⊢—— HITBODEDUT? ——⊣

On the material side, there's not too much that you need for hitbodedut. You need the ability to speak (which we assume you have), and even that is not 100% required. There may be some days that you've got a sore throat, other days that you're at a loss for words, and days that you just don't have the strength or spirit to concentrate on communicating with God. Even at those times, you can still do hitbodedut. We'll talk later about silence.

Most of what you need for hitbodedut is internal. Fortunately, God has already blessed you with at least some measure of each of the characteristics that you will need. They are (not necessarily in any particular order):

Faith in:
- God
- yourself
- tzaddikim (Jewish saints and sages)
- Judaism and Torah
- the practice of hitbodedut itself
- the process

Determination

Courage

Youth (which has nothing to do with how many of your
     birthdays have passed)

Perseverance

Love

A dash (sometimes more) of chutzpah

Simcha (defined more fully later; for now, think of it
     as optimism)

Trust

Patience, patience and more patience

Enthusiasm

FAITH

(IN GOD)

Obviously, if you are engaging in hitbodedut and talking to God, you have to believe that He exists. Nonetheless, there are many times in hitbodedut, as in life, that God seems to vanish, either slowly or suddenly. It is specifically at those times that you have to draw upon—or even create—your own reservoir of faith to bring His presence closer in order to feel it in your heart. This is easier said than done. This can even be said to be the essence of the challenge of life.

(IN YOURSELF)

I believe in you. If I didn't, I wouldn't have invested so many months and so many tears in writing this book. While you and some fellow readers may find this bit of encouragement occasionally helpful, it isn't going to be enough. *You* have to believe in you. You have to believe that you—yes, *you*—are important and precious to God. As before, this is much easier to believe when life is going your way. The trick is to believe it when all the evidence is to the contrary.

(IN TZADDIKIM)

Frankly, I find it surprising that faith in tzaddikim is a notion that some find troublesome. They feel it makes the tzaddik a superman or, God forbid, a god. The latter is certainly not true. As we announce twice a day in the Shema Yisrael: "There is only one God!" A tzaddik may serve many vital roles and functions in the world, but he is neither a creator nor an object of worship. Don't ever think otherwise, even for a moment.

On the other hand, the tzaddik is most certainly a super man and a remarkable chap. Why shouldn't he be? He's devoted years of toil, sweat and tears to prayer, study and kindness, striving to turn his mind and body into vessels of the Divine. We turn to experts when we need expert advice. We acknowledge that an artist or a chef "just knows" when to add something to the mix and when not, even if we (or she!) can't explain why. We have faith in the tzaddik because he has worked to achieve all that he has, and he has been graced with a "something extra" that makes it worthwhile to take his advice. Tzaddik knows best.

(In Judaism)

Many books, including this one, contain wisdom. Yet this is not a wisdom-book. This is a faith-book. This is an unabashed faith-book. Part of the message that this book hopes to convey is the faith-message to which Rebbe Nachman dedicated his entire life: The Torah is the Tree of Life, and that Torah, taught in the time-honored fashion, determines the way Judaism is meant to be lived. This does not mean that you have to change your mode of dress right now or begin observing the Torah as if you were born in the heart of Orthodoxville. It simply means you have to do your best to take your next step.

(In Hitbodedut)

Hitbodedut is, to paraphrase Rebbe Nachman, a wonderful practice. You can take his word for it, but when it comes right down to it, you have to believe that not only is it going to work, but that it is working, even as you're doing it. To merely go through the motions while pretending that hitbodedut has meaning and value to you, is equivalent to not doing it all.

(In the Process)

Another bit of faith that you're going to need is faith in the process. As with any new endeavor, you're probably going to approach hitbodedut with high hopes. You expect that by investing your time and energies into it, you will see clear, positive and permanent results. Lo and behold—you do! It's fantastic, it's wonderful. You cherish your progress and share this wonderful discovery with all your friends ("It's called 'hitbodedut.' It's a teaching of Rebbe Nachman of Breslov. It's great. You should really do it.") And then—WHAM! All of the progress you've made in your personal life, self-control, faith, etc., evaporates, sucked so completely out of existence that it seems as though you merely dreamt it.

That's part of the process. Ups and downs, storms and calm, progress (real and imagined), setbacks (real and imagined), encouraging signs and disappointment. Whichever you experience, be aware that it's only part of the process, only one step on your journey. None of your successes is your final destination—and certainly none of your failures.

DETERMINATION

Making a practice part of your daily life—perhaps even building your schedule around it—is a goal like any other. To make it happen, you've got to do more than wish it to happen. You've got to want to make it happen. In Breslov teachings and tradition, the rule of thumb is that the greater the goal, the greater the obstacles and hindrances that get in a person's way. The purpose of these obstacles is not to discourage you and drive you away, God forbid. On the contrary, the obstacles are placed there by design, to encourage you to increase your determination and drive to achieve your goal.

COURAGE

Some people aren't afraid of anything. There's the proverbial 4' 10" old lady who doesn't hesitate to take on a biker with chains, mano a mano. Then there are the rest of us. We talk a big game, but when push comes to shove, we're quite deferential to the police officer who's writing out a ticket, or flustered when we meet the star we've always idolized. There's a certain point at which we lose our bravado.

So what's going to happen when you want to have a private audience with the All-Powerful, All-Knowing Creator of Everything? Will you be able to muster up the courage to do it? Absolutely, no doubt about it. As great as a person's fear of taking a risk, there are times he realizes that the dangers and negative repercussions of not taking the risk are greater. Life is going to hurt a lot more if you don't talk to God than if you do.

YOUTH

Chronological age has no bearing on hitbodedut. You're never too young or too old to start practicing it. However, you do have to be young at heart. You have to believe that your life can start again *now*, that there's time enough left in your life to grow and to succeed, and that the growth and success you achieve is significant and far-reaching, even world-changing. You have to believe that there is time enough to regret and correct whatever needs to be undone, unsaid or un-thought.

PERSEVERANCE

Being a nudnik is generally considered a deficiency, and rightfully so. There are, however, occasions and situations where nudnik-like qualities are just the ticket. Showing up for hitbodedut day in, day out, and greeting the good Lord day in, day out, is one of those situations.

Even if a person were to do hitbodedut only once in his entire lifetime, it would be a fantastic feat and a noble accomplishment. All the more so if he does it every day, so that its benefits spread further and further, touching more and more of Creation and penetrating more deeply to its core.

LOVE

Love is not only a tender "head in the clouds" blinding emotion. Love is a passionate glue that binds, and an extremely powerful force that propels you into action. It makes you go to places that you never imagined visiting, do things you never considered doable, and say things you never knew you felt—with an eloquence you didn't know you possessed.

Love also makes you jealously protect that which you love. If not, it ain't love. You have to love God and your time alone with Him. Don't let anything get in the way.

A Dash of Chutzpah

Even when you're inside the bank safe, when you've made it past the guards and entered a place you shouldn't be in the first place, you still haven't made off with the loot. Your presence may get you some of what you need and some of what you want, but it's not guaranteed that you'll get all of it.

Some things need to be asked for out loud. Even though God is a mind reader, it's your job to "bring it to His attention" and let Him know what you want. If you don't have the chutzpah to ask for it, you don't deserve it. You wouldn't know how to use it right. If you realized how valuable and practical it would be for you, you wouldn't be too shy to ask for it.

Chutzpah also means thinking big. If you need $100,000, why not ask for $500,000? If you want to find ten more minutes a day for your hitbodedut, why not ask for twenty? It's not harder for God to give you more time or more money.

Simcha

The Hebrew word "simcha" is usually defined as happiness or joy. Both are correct, but it is also good to think of simcha as optimism, enthusiasm, lightheartedness, blitheness, gladness, cheerfulness and… Well, you get the idea *and the feeling* by now.

If you're more familiar with broken-heartedness than with simcha, don't be discouraged. Broken-heartedness is often the heart's training ground for becoming simcha-worthy.[1] Hitbodedut can make it so.

TRUST

God's there. He's listening, but He's not going to reveal to anyone what you've told Him (unless you want Him to). He's listening, even if and even when you don't experience any response: Your material situation may not have improved (it might have even gotten worse!) and you may still be a rotten, creepy anti-saint, a villain of the worst order. In fact, Judaism and Jewishness may be looking less and less attractive as a path in life.

He's listening. Carefully and lovingly. There are two things that are absolutely essential to keep in mind. The first is that not everyone is privy to see all that he is really accomplishing in life. (How you choose to react—emotionally, spiritually and behaviorally—to what's done to you is a significant part of what you accomplish.) The Sfat Emet, the second rebbe of Gur, gave the following analogy to one of his students who lamented that he felt no inner change from his Torah study and mitzvot:

> The farmer gets up in the morning and goes out to the barn. He hitches up his ox, takes him down to the field and plows acre upon acre. After the fields are plowed, he loads the ox with seed and walks beside it up and down the rows, planting seeds. After the crops are grown, they head out again to the fields, the farmer harvesting and loading the wagon which the ox draws behind him. They do this year after year.
>
> The ox remains an ox—but the job gets done.

The second thing to remember is that the frustration, regression and other "negative" results that you may experience

---

[1] A true broken heart leads to simcha because it not only indicates the capacity for containing joy, but it also possesses the humility to treasure every drop of kindness that it receives. Such a heart will not be denied; it will be granted what it seeks. And genuine simcha leads to honest, broken-hearted hitbodedut, because the happy heart, in its humility, understands the need—and also desires—to give more to the Giver, in word and deed.

are really steps forward on the journey that you must take to *your* destiny. As Rebbe Nachman put it, "Every rebuff is an invitation to come closer."

Patience, Patience and More Patience

It's boring to watch grass grow. It's hard to notice any discernible change from one moment to the next or find something to cheer. Yet the grass is busy absorbing water and nutrients from the ground, being refreshed by the dew and soaking up sunlight. At a certain point—it's grown!

Same thing with hitbodedut, says Rebbe Nachman. You can't tell anything is happening. It may look to you like nothing is happening, sort of the same effect as when drop after drop of water falls on a stone. Water is soft. It can't do anything to something as hard as rock. But it will—if you pour enough water over a long enough period of time.

It's the same with a heart of stone, says Rebbe Nachman. Just keep pouring those "soft" words on it, and sooner or later you'll discover how spiritually sensitive you really are.

Enthusiasm

The newer your toy, the more you enjoy playing with it and discovering what it can do. You've been doing hitbodedut for how long now? I've been doing it for longer. As of this writing, I've been doing an hour of hitbodedut every day for more than twenty-seven years. That's 9,855 hours, or 591,300 minutes of hitbodedut. (I was pretty shocked myself when I did the math!) I hope to do some more today and at least another hour tomorrow.

My hitbodedut is new every day. It's not the same now as when I started. Hitbodedut is different at age forty than it was at age thirty, which was different than it was at age twenty. It's different when you're single than when you're married, when you want to become a parent than when you are a parent (of one, of two, of more, of a daughter, of a son, of a healthy child, of a challenged child). Hitbodedut cannot and must not be the same when you're out of a job as when you are employed; when your domestic life is peaceful as when it is contentious.

Your hitbodedut becomes new as you learn more Torah and more about the pain, mysteries and wonders of life. It becomes new as people enter your life and as they leave it. It becomes new as each new day follows each new night. It becomes new as you do. ❀

⊢— 3 • WHERE CAN I FIND THE WORDS? —⊣

"Is that what hitbodedut is about? Just words?"

"Yes," I answered. "And no, not at all."

Where can you find the words? The first place to look is right there in your heart.

Rebbe Nachman states clearly and emphatically that hitbodedut has to be in your native tongue. He is quite explicit in the reasons he gives. The first reason is that you cannot fully explain yourself, discuss every nuance of a problem, or express your deepest emotions in a language that is not yours. If you try to speak in a language that is not yours, you will be more concerned and try harder to say what's right instead of saying what's true.

> In Paris in the 1890's, an assimilated French Jewess lay in her bed, waiting to give birth. Her equally assimilated Jewish husband and the Jewish doctor were waiting in the next room, playing cards until she would need their help.
>
> "*Sacre bleu!*" she cried. Her husband started to get up. The doctor reached out his hand. "Not yet," he said.
>
> A few minutes later they heard a much louder cry. "*Mon Dieu!*" As the husband started to rise, the doctor motioned him back to his seat. "Not yet."
>
> After a few more minutes they heard the expectant mother once more. "*Oy!*" she cried. The doctor threw his cards on the table. "Now!"

In attempting to talk in a foreign tongue, you will be using your head more than your heart. This hobbles your hitbodedut.

The second reason Rebbe Nachman gives for using your natural language is also heart-related. A person is simply not as moved and affected by hearing a message in words that are unnatural to him. If you're not convinced, try this simple experiment: Tell someone near and dear to you, "I love you," first in English and then in Swahili. Notice which elicits a warm smile and which a puzzled look.

Hitbodedut is an affair of the heart. The words have to come from your heart and penetrate your heart. Not only does the language have to be yours, but also the specific choice of words, in order to let your thoughts and emotions flow naturally. For example, one person who feels that he is always failing may ask of God, "Help me not to get so down on myself," while you might express it as, "Support me in my efforts to be less self-deprecating."

Your "native tongue" includes the technical expressions, jargon and slang of your profession, hobbies and social milieu. If a word or expression in Hebrew, Yiddish or Pali comes to you and is "just right" for what you want to say, say it! If a phrase or paraphrase from a song, TV show, poem, book or even the Bible says it best, use it!

How you address God is also your decision. "God," "Lord," "Almighty," "Hashem" ("The Name"), "Father in Heaven," "Great Spirit," "Ribono shel Olam" ("Master of the World"), "Your Highness," "Your Majesty," "Kind One" and "Merciful One" are all options. Technically, you may use God's holy names, but since they are especially sacred, you should think twice before doing so. Uttering any of them under the wrong conditions may have undesired effects.

Even though hitbodedut is meant to be personal, intimate and heart-to-heart, certain terms of address towards the ever-benevolent Creator are never acceptable. "Big Fella" is the only specific example I'm going to offer here.

I'm occasionally asked, "What about invective and scatological terms? Are those ever OK to use in hitbodedut?" Certainly it's far from ideal to use any such words in regular parlance, and ladies and gentlemen would never even think such words, let alone use them. However, for some people, these words don't even register on the "bad word" scale. In fact, for those who grew up in certain less-than-genteel environments, swear words and cussing *are* their native tongue. Such words may be the only way for them to truly express what they need to express.

Even one who does recognize the difference between acceptable and unacceptable language may find herself in a situation for which nothing but a four-letter word will do. Someone in genuine pain is not held accountable if she makes a poor choice of words, even if she says something blasphemous. If invective is a result of true pain, if it is a consequence of "open-heart surgery," then there is nothing wrong in its expression. If, however, invective is used as part of a philosophical or theological diatribe to attack the Shekhinah, it is wrong.[2]

"But whence the words? I'm not a King David. I'm not a poet or an author or an orator. I don't have a way with words. How should I know what to say?"

Hitbodedut is for everyone. You don't need to be a wordsmith in order to speak to God. The actual words you say are not the critical element. The crucial ingredient is the honesty of your words and the broken-heartedness, open-heartedness and guilelessness with which they are spoken.

The Midrash relates that Nebuchadnezzar, the infamous Babylonian king, once began to recite poems in praise of God. These poems were of such beauty and grace that King David's psalms paled in comparison. An angel came and slapped Nebuchadnezzar on the face. Nebuchadnezzar fell silent and could not continue.

The Kotzker Rebbe was puzzled by this Midrash. If someone was praising God so eloquently, why should he be silenced? He answered his own question with this insight: It's not the external beauty of the words that God seeks. It's the heart-to-heart connection to Him that you feel when the going gets rough.

---

[2] Be aware that the words you speak—the ones that actually pass your lips, in any context and without regard to whom they are addressed—express the quality of your soul. Rebbe Nachman bases this teaching on a verse from *Song of Songs* (5:6). Your choice of words may indicate areas of your self that need improvement. Additionally, the Zohar points out that one's trash talk stains the holy words he later speaks (*Zohar* 2:263b).

In this way, hitbodedut is not about words at all. Words are merely tools, and sometimes not even the best ones. Hitbodedut is about improving yourself, your life and the world. Hitbodedut is about expressing yourself and freeing yourself of your demons.

Most of all, hitbodedut is about being connected with God in the closest, most intense way possible. Your feeling of that closeness may be as ecstatic as a first kiss or as warm as a smile or a gentle caress. At an extremely advanced stage of spiritual development, your hitbodedut is not about you at all. At a certain level, hitbodedut is simply and only the One.

When he first introduced Reb Noson to the practice of hitbodedut, Rebbe Nachman urged him, "It's very good to pour out your heart to God as you would to a true, good friend." In addition to implying that you should say what you need to say openly and honestly, without any fear or worry of being judged, there is another message here. Two friends have a shared history with common points of reference and a common language that is specifically theirs. They each know what the other means, even when others do not. ❈

If no words are coming, sing a song, hum lazily.

Let your hitbodedut be kinetic — get up and dance, clap your hands.

Don't force the words to come. Let them come to you. ❈

⊢—— 4 • What Do I Talk About? ——⊣

What would you like to talk about? One of the most powerful features of hitbodedut is that it is all yours. You can do with it whatever you like and take it wherever you want to go. This is what makes it so challenging. You've got to decide what it is you really want and then figure out how to get there.

Sometimes it's not so difficult to figure out what to talk about. If you're getting married soon, or you're about to become a parent, then God has already provided you with plenty of grist for the hitbodedut mill. Even needing something as mundane as a parking space at the mall or a button for your shirt can get you talking and pick up your awareness of God's presence and power. Viewing the Grand Canyon does so as well, in a different way.

Is it summer, spring, winter or fall? What do you appreciate or relate to most in the season at hand? The sand and surf at the beach? The rebirth of the flora? The silence and gestation of winter? The colors of autumn? No matter who you are or what your interests, you have some common ground on which to meet the Creator of all.

Undoubtedly, you've watched sunrises and sunsets in the past. Their beauty and majesty almost defy expression. Did you pierce their beauty and perceive the wisdom built into them—for example, the physics and mathematics of the globe's orbit, or the sunlight's refraction? Did they make you aware of the newness of each day, of God's role in the affairs of nations (as darkness and light continuously struggle, so do nations), of His planting charity into natural events, of suddenly finding yourself out of harm's way, or of being healed?[3]

---

[3] All these ideas are considered in one of the blessings we say before reciting the Shema. Did any of them occur to you on your own?

What sort of music makes you sing? Whose lyrics—and which author's writings—resonate? If you want to talk to God, there are many potential sources for topics. You don't have to go looking very far, and sometimes it's best not to. In fact, once in a while, you get shown the light in the strangest of places—if you look at it right. A flash of inspiration in a motel, a lawyer's office or a rock concert can also be a source for hitbodedut.

Hitbodedut can also be a time to bare your soul, to talk with God not only of your hopes and aspirations, dreams, wishes and plans, but also of your weaknesses and fears. It is the time for you to admit and regret your mistakes. It is the time for you to probe, to put your toe in the water and gird your loins, in order to fix the parts of you that were damaged and stunted by poor parenting, abusive siblings and cruel teachers or classmates. It is the time to reach into your past and find the comfort in the pain you suffered; to find the light that you missed during your trek through the darkness, the fullness in the void, and the life in the crater of Death that almost became your grave. Hitbodedut is the time to ask God, "What was the point?"

Obviously, none of this is easy. Reliving the worst experiences of your life and expressing your anger against the Deity, asking questions that fade into the Emptiness, cutting through echoes of trite platitudes that ring falsely in response, requires the patience and bravery of Job. They are not challenges undertaken lightly. Yet, if you are to live as *you*, this is what must be done.

Though we've focused more or less exclusively on praying for and about *you*, don't make the mistake of thinking that hitbodedut is self-centered. You can—and should—devote some of your hitbodedut to others. As we mentioned previously, there is a *physical* limit to how much you can do. This is true of helping others as well. However, a well-aimed and timely prayer can be of inestimable assistance to untold numbers of people, whether they are alive or have yet to be born.

You can pray for relatives, friends, acquaintances, those whom you'll never meet and those who will never know about you. You may even want to devote some of your hitbodedut to God's "needs."

Sometimes, though, no matter how much you try, you may not be able to focus on any particular Torah topic or subject of life. In that case, talk to God about whatever He puts into your heart. ❀

⊢— 5 • DO I TALK LOUD OR SOFT? —⊣

A sort of inborn reflex takes over when human beings find themselves on their own. Though they can modulate their voices quite capably for an ordinary conversation with another human being (or even a pet), the moment they're alone, they start to whisper. There's nobody there, so who am I talking to?

Of course, you'll lower your voice if you don't want someone to hear or overhear you, but in hitbodedut, when you're by yourself and (usually) out of earshot of the nearest human being, why whisper? What, or whom, are you afraid of? Of course, there's no need for you to shout; God will hear even the trace of your quietest thought. But you're not alone—you believe that and know that. So speak in a normal tone of voice.

When you want to convince God to assist you in planning your next step, carrying it out or bestowing His blessing on its results, a conversational volume—and tone—is certainly proper. Use emphasis and inflection; speak to God as you would to a true, good friend. *However*, if you've lost the key, or the building is burning down, you need to take a hatchet and start breaking down the door!

Sometimes you need to scream in order to break down the barriers between you and the next level of you—the higher awareness and the greater inner-strength that's almost within your grasp. You may have forgotten the combination, or feel compelled to make this next significant step. A request at an ordinary volume works well when addressing a waiter, but not when your soul is in danger!

It is quite possible that you are having troubles because you need to scream. Screaming is part of growing up. (Don't kids make a lot of noise?) Screaming is also part of the birthing process. In order to give birth to new awareness, to get that baby out of the womb, the mother screams!

There is a special type of scream, a silent one. Sometimes it is triggered by any old pain or frustration, and sometimes it is triggered by the frustration of being stymied and stuck, when you have nary a clue of what to do. The first trigger produces a quiet roar that you push from your lungs and send rising higher and higher. As it rises, you hear it getting louder and louder—and louder still—till it fills your mind.

> Rebbe Nachman said: This is a real scream, not just a figment of your imagination. You can scream words in this way, but then it is harder to contain your voice. It is much easier when the scream is wordless.

The second trigger sends a silent scream out of your heart. This type of scream reflects the heart's desperation when it wants to know which direction to take, and seeks guidance to decide what needs to be decided.[4]

On the other hand, in certain situations, screaming is all wrong. When you're cuddling close with someone you love, anything more than a romantic whisper will be as appropriate as a subway train screeching to a halt. It just doesn't fit. ❋

---

[4] Do not confuse the silent scream or the scream from the heart with silent hitbodedut. See Room 4: The NoPlace.

⊢── 6 • WHERE CAN I DO HITBODEDUT? ──⊣

By nature, any personal conversation calls for privacy. The more personal the conversation, the more privacy one will want to have. Rebbe Nachman specifically suggests going outdoors into a natural setting, such as the woods, or dedicating a private room to hitbodedut (and other spiritual pursuits). He was aware, however, that not everybody has either of these options available. Other places where one could practice hitbodedut include: in bed under the covers, enwrapped in a tallit, or while pretending to look into a book (let others think you are studying).

Of course, your own bedroom, a corner of the living room or study, or any room you can peacefully commandeer is suitable, as is a (safe) park bench, a quiet stretch of beach or an unused classroom or office. Be creative. If need be, you should be prepared to be interrupted or otherwise have your hitbodedut curtailed or circumscribed.

These suggestions are for "at home" hitbodedut, when you are in your regular environment. When traveling, one has to be much more creative and motivated to find a conducive setting. It can be done. Where there's a will, there's a way![5] ❋

---

[5] I've done hitbodedut at train stations around the world, on the Metroliner, on a boat crossing the English Channel, and at 37,000 feet on the redeye from LAX to JFK.

┝── 7 • WHEN CAN I DO HITBODEDUT? ──┥

You can do hitbodedut day or night, in the morning, afternoon or evening. You can do hitbodedut shortly after you wake up to start the day, before or after your morning routine, or before or after the sun starts to peek over the horizon. You can do it as the shadows grow longer, as the sun turns red. You can do it at night before tucking yourself into bed. You can rise well before dawn when the world is still asleep. You can do it at any or all of these times.

You can do it whenever you want to, but you can't be haphazard about it. Hitbodedut has to be so important to you that you schedule it into your day. It must be on your to-do list.

It's best if your hitbodedut can be at the same time every day, but it doesn't have to be. Six o'clock in the morning may work for Tuesdays but not for Wednesdays. That's OK. Make it Wednesdays at 6:30. The actual time of day you do hitbodedut is not as important as the fact that you are doing it on schedule. If it's a part of your schedule, you are telling God, "You are so important to me, I'm going to make sure to have some private time with You every single day. I'm not going to leave it to chance." You think God won't be pleased with that? (If you're married with children, your spouse and offspring may also be thrilled to get some private time alone with you at some point during the day!)

It would be ideal if you could build your daily schedule around your hitbodedut, but if you're like most people, you don't have that luxury. When you introduce hitbodedut into your already busy life, you have to give it a place at the table. Make space for it.

Rebbe Nachman highly recommended doing hitbodedut for sixty minutes each day, in one sitting (session). Some people, especially beginners, find this daunting, if not overwhelming. Have no fear! If you can do only thirty minutes a day, or twenty, fifteen or ten, that's perfectly acceptable. The main thing is to make hitbodedut part of your schedule and *show up*! If having two sessions a day for thirty minutes works better for you, then by all means, do it that way. In the Holy Temple in Jerusalem, the kohen gadol brought a daily flour offering in two parts, half in the morning and half in the afternoon.

The best time to do hitbodedut, teaches Rebbe Nachman, is when your corner of the world is asleep. When people are not spending their God-given talents and energies on temporary and temporal pursuits, it's much easier for you to connect to yourself, to the eternal things in life and to God. It's true, certain cities never sleep, yet there are quieter hours in every locale, and those times are the most ideal for hitbodedut. (Bear in mind that it does no good to schedule your session for hitbodedut and then sleep through it. In addition, you also have to be awake during the day to take care of your other responsibilities, so plan accordingly.)

The only time it is definitely *not* good to do hitbodedut is when you are driving or operating any sort of machinery. The Talmud teaches that safety cannot be compromised. Since the purpose of hitbodedut, as of all of Torah and mitzvot, is to enhance and increase life, putting oneself in mortal danger to perform a mitzvah is counterproductive.

Another time that is not conducive to hitbodedut is someone else's time. Extending your lunch hour or taking your employer's time without permission to perform any religious obligations is a no-no. To steal in order to perform a mitzvah is blasphemous. Whether you realize it or not, performing your job honestly is spiritually edifying.

You really shouldn't do hitbodedut while checking your e-mail, surfing the Internet or playing a mindless computer game. Hitbodedut during moments like these may come in handy if you are in particularly bad spiritual shape, but it's not ideal. The Talmud compares reciting a blessing while engaged in some other activity to addressing the king while drunk. It's just not respectable. ❃

8 • WHAT CAN I EXPECT FROM ⊢— HITBODEDUT? —⊣

Angels will descend, filling your room with light and song. They will scatter roses and myrrh at your feet, and you will live happily ever after.

Then the alarm clock will ring.

Hitbodedut is not instant magic. Rebbe Nachman describes hitbodedut in two ways. It is a *path*—that is, an all-encompassing way of dealing with every facet of life, large or small, temporary or long-lasting. It is also a *practice*—namely, one particular tool among many that you can use to deal with life in general or a single challenge in particular. However you decide to use hitbodedut, it won't solve your problems. It *will* help you to identify the issues and challenges you face, let you explore and weigh your options, give you the necessary confidence to decide which choices to make, and allow you to review and readjust to the results of your decision. Most importantly, hitbodedut allows you to enlist God's help at each and every step along the way.

What can you expect from hitbodedut? It will imbue you with a new and well-founded calm and tranquility that will continue to grow as you pursue more hitbodedut. It will also give you a growing awareness of God, an understanding that your life, in *all* its details, has meaning and purpose, and a realization that by partnering with God, you are bringing meaning and purpose to all of Creation. ❈

⊢── 9 • IS HITBODEDUT REALLY FOR ME? ──⊣

It certainly is, and for two very good reasons: You have needs, and you are needed. These reasons are grounded on the bedrock of Judaism: You are important.

You have needs. Even if you think that not all of your needs are adequately met, there are definitely those that are being met. Count your blessings. A lot of love, simcha and trust grow when blessings are acknowledged.

No one lives in this world without experiencing pain and problems. There are things (or situations) you desire, things you need and things that seem right for you. Yet many of them are elusive. You're frustrated, annoyed and angered. That's good. It means you've got a lot of grist for the hitbodedut mill!

You need to feel that you are successful as a human being. Yet you may feel incompetent, frustrated by the lack of progress towards your goals of self-improvement, Jewishly and otherwise. Practicing hitbodedut helps you shed frustration and feelings of incompetency. How?

Let's say you are sitting at a table, absorbed in your reading. Or you are walking down the street, engrossed in some subject that has struck your fancy, and all of a sudden, someone sneaks up from behind and yells, "BOO!" Before your conscious mind is aware of what happened, you react with fright. But how can a person be scared before she's even aware of what occurred? asks Rebbe Nachman.

The answer, he explains, is that the *person* is not scared. Rather, there is an "other" within the person that is frightened. It is this "other" that fears and casts dread into your thinking and emotions. This "other" also usurps control of your cognition and decisions before you know it—when sense-desire has sneaked up and gotten you to nosh those cookies or tell that lie. Can the real you please stand up?

One of the basic assumptions of Jewish nature that Rebbe Nachman teaches and drums into our heads is that a Jew is inherently good. Not only somewhat good, tangentially good or capable of good, but naturally, essentially and intrinsically good. Yes, Rebbe Nachman was fully aware that some Jews steal, cheat, eat non-kosher food, etc., etc. But none of that is the real Jew. The real Jew—the real you—is the one who is generous with his time and money, who helps the less fortunate (and even the more fortunate), who tries honestly to study and understand the Torah correctly, and who conducts himself with proper decorum in the synagogue. The real Jew—the real you—is all the good you've done and all the good you will do.

So who is this "other"? More importantly, can we get rid of him? Rebbe Nachman does not name the "other." He does say, however, that you can easily train your mind/daat to be rid of him. What you need to do is calm your mind, settling it very, very well. Intellectually, you know that the body's pleasures last briefly, that addictions don't benefit you and that the objects of your phobias can't harm you. You simply must choose to get into the habit of dismissing the "other."

By taking the time in hitbodedut to calm your mind, to stop and realize that the crippling fear neither belongs to you nor owns you, to discover that the desire and addiction belongs to an "other," you can easily dissociate from those vices and gain control of your self and your life.

Hitbodedut is the tool to see you through the practical aspects of your problems, as well as the key to understanding why your problems are not hindrances, but stepping-stones (a.k.a. opportunities) for growth. In fact, they are much more than stepping-stones, incidental means to achievement. Grist becomes flour becomes bread, the actual stuff of nourishment.

You are needed. As you look around your neighborhood, walk down the street, gaze out the window of the train or car, or read your newspaper, you become acutely aware that much is wrong in the world. "Each person is required to say, 'The entire world was created for my sake'" (Sanhedrin 37a). Rebbe Nachman teaches that since the world exists for your sake, it is your responsibility. It is up to you to see to it that the world becomes a better place.

However, most of us live our lives thinking about how the world can provide for *our* needs and satisfy *our* desires. Even when we give tzedakah or do a favor, the act is usually brief and the thought and emotion that accompany it—if there are any—are fleeting. Rebbe Nachman teaches that one needs to be proactive in contributing to the betterment of the world. Hitbodedut allows you to open your eye of generosity and see what others need. Even though there is only so much you can do and only so much tzedakah you can give, the force of your words can bring betterment and well-being to people across the globe and to generations yet unborn.

One way you can do that is by making conscious decisions to speak and act wisely. Hitbodedut will help you fend off foolish temptations by enabling you to recognize them and helping you to resist them.

The biblical villain Balaam is a good example of a bad example. He could jinx and damn with the worst of them. The Talmud (Berakhot 7a) tells us that Balaam knew the exact moment in the day in which God's anger was the deciding element of Divine decision. Balaam prepared himself to thoroughly curse the Jewish people at precisely that moment so as to wipe them off the face of the earth, God forbid. What could Balaam have said in such a brief instant that would be so destructive? He could have said, "Annihilate them" (in Hebrew this can be said in one word).

Imagine. The wrong word said by one individual at the wrong moment could utterly affect the lives of millions. What if you say the right word at the right time? If one of the greatest villains had it within his grasp to harm and counter the purpose of God's creation, certainly words that you speak for the betterment of mankind will have a positive impact. ❈

10 • WHY ISN'T ANYONE ELSE I KNOW DOING ⊢—— HITBODEDUT? ——⊣

I n a word, ignorance.

This is true not only of those who are unschooled in things Jewish, but even of those who can confidently swim in the sea of Talmud. As amazing as it sounds, many people have simply never been introduced to the idea of speaking to God! They have been taught—or assumed—that God can only be addressed on a formal basis, with specific set prayers and only at certain times. (Judaism does prescribe three daily prayers, and a fourth on Shabbat and Jewish festivals, but that's a minimum, not a maximum.)

In his lesson on hitbodedut, Rebbe Nachman says, "Many well-known tzaddikim have related that they achieved their spiritual success only through the practice of hitbodedut." Rebbe Nachman himself did hitbodedut every day, even when he was dying of tuberculosis. Often he spent entire days practicing hitbodedut.

Rebbe Nachman's maternal great-grandfather, Rebbe Yisrael, the Baal Shem Tov, the founder of Chassidut, was known to practice hitbodedut. So was Rebbe Aharon Karliner, one of the early chassidic masters. Even the latter-day sage, Rabbi Yisrael Meir Kagan, author of *Sefer Chofetz Chaim* and *Mishnah Berurah*, would spend an hour a day alone in his room or in the woods of Lithuania, speaking to God in his own words. Even the Sages of the Talmud did hitbodedut![6]

Some people are aware of hitbodedut, but get sidetracked or distracted and forget what they gained and could have gained from the practice. Reb Yitzchak Breiter, who introduced Rebbe Nachman's teachings in Poland, recorded the following observation in a letter to his students:

---

[6] See Hitbodedut of the Jewish Sages, page 258.

Forewarned is forearmed. Be aware that since this easy-to-do practice is so potent, the cohorts of evil will not rest. They will use every means at their disposal to prevent and sabotage your practice of hitbodedut. They might try to undermine your faith in hitbodedut, or convince you that you have no time for it or that you have better, more important things—even more important mitzvot—to do in this hour. Their goal is to keep you from this practice. So, dear friend, have pity on yourself!

Some people practice a limited form of hitbodedut—namely, the "accounting" part. They set aside a time to review their Jewish successes and failures vis a vis the outside (i.e., mitzvah observance) and the inside (i.e., their faith, trust and integrity). This is usually done silently.

Some people are aware of hitbodedut and may occasionally practice it. However, they have chosen to take one of the other paths in Judaism. This is certainly valid. Nonetheless, Rebbe Nachman felt that this choice leaves them with a major gap in their devotions. He said:

> "There are certainly many religious people who do not practice hitbodedut. But I call them *fleetis* (drifters), confused and confounded. When the Mashiach suddenly comes and calls them, they will be bewildered and confused. When a man wakes up from a restful sleep, his mind is calm and relaxed. This is how we [who practice hitbodedut] will be when the Mashiach comes, totally without fear or confusion" (*Rabbi Nachman's Wisdom* #228).

Some people do know about hitbodedut, but just don't tell anybody that they practice it! Even though there is certainly great value in helping another person to strengthen his spiritual practice, some people feel that they would place their own practice in jeopardy by reaching out to others. So we don't hear about it from them.

In any event, Rebbe Nachman teaches that it is not a good idea to compare your practices to those of others. In his story,

"The Sophisticate and the Innocent,"[7] the Innocent's wife asks her husband, "Why do all the other shoemakers make three gulden on a pair of shoes and you make only half that?" The Innocent answers, "What do I care about that? This is what I do and that is what they do. Why should we talk of others?"

Lastly, consider that hitbodedut is a solitary activity. Jews have a long history of going it alone, extending all the way back to our first patriarch, Avraham: "Avraham was one" (*Ezekiel* 33:24). Rebbe Nachman teaches that Avraham was unconcerned with the fact that he was the only God-worshiper on the planet. What everyone else did was irrelevant. He didn't even flinch when his father or the police attempted to kill him for his practices. He thought to himself, "I'm the only person in the world who believes in God. I must do what has to be done."

Even if you are the only person in the world who practices hitbodedut, you will be like Avraham, alone in your practice and determination to worship God. ❋

---

[7] *Rabbi Nachman's Stories #9.*

11• IS HITBODEDUT A SUBSTITUTE
├── FOR _____ ? ──┤

Many people ask, "If I do hitbodedut, can I discontinue my therapy?" Or, "Why do I need the formal prayers if I do hitbodedut?" Some push the envelope a little further by asking, "What do I need Judaism for at all, if I do hitbodedut?"

As mentioned earlier, hitbodedut is both a path and a practice. The goal, as Rebbe Nachman envisioned it in his function as teacher, mentor and guide, was for people to take the next step on the journey in Jewishness. The possibilities for what your next step may be constantly change as you experience more of life and make new choices in the context of choices and changes that have already occurred and continue to occur. There is no end in sight—in fact, no end exists—nor is there any particular schedule but your own.

So hitbodedut is either the background against which all your other activities play out, or it is a component, major or minor, of your life. It is not, however, a substitute for anything. Nor is anything a substitute for it. If, for example, you are in therapy, it's probably because you can benefit from therapy. But your hitbodedut can help make the sessions with a trained therapist much more productive. As you re-examine your issues in hitbodedut, the need for therapy may end sooner than expected. Conversely, hitbodedut may extend the need for therapy as new issues arise or current issues are evaluated in greater depth.

Hitbodedut also cannot substitute for the formal prayers, particularly for someone who wants to follow Rebbe Nachman's path in its entirety. "My entire mission is prayer!" Rebbe Nachman stated. The formal prayers were arranged and composed by the Great Assembly, a conclave of 120 spiritual masters that functioned during the early years of the Second Temple in Jerusalem (circa

350 B.C.E.). Each of these 120 masters possessed a high spiritual level; they even had the ability to raise the dead (*Avodah Zarah* 10b). In addition to canonizing the books of the Bible, they invested all their spiritual energies into crafting the prayers that would be recited by Jews for millennia to come. Even in translation, the residue of spiritual power contained in these formalized prayers is enormous and eminently beneficial.

Since hitbodedut is meant to enhance one's belief, enthusiasm and performance of all things Jewish, it cannot possibly substitute for any other practice, and certainly not for Judaism itself. ❋

12 • WILL I EVER FINISH NEEDING HITBODEDUT?

Apparently, Rebbe Nachman thought not. It is one of only two practices that he prescribed to be done universally and daily.[8]

The world is in a constant state of flux. You too are continually changing. As life moves from day to day, certain challenges and situations may be dealt and dispensed with via hitbodedut. Then new ones come along.

The more you live, the more you learn and become aware through study and experience. Take your newly-gained knowledge and awareness and use them to inform your hitbodedut—whether for a day or two, for weeks or for months. Conversely, the practice of hitbodedut itself can increase your knowledge and awareness. Rather than become a creature of habit, doing and thinking the same things every day, you can seize each moment, unafraid to change and grow.

Even if you run out of problems and challenges, you still need hitbodedut. Hitbodedut is not only meant to be an emergency hotline to help you escape from Hell. It is, can and should be a romantic Heaven with your Divine Lover.

> My wife has often told me, "If I didn't know you better, I would swear you were having an affair. You're blah or grouchy, and then you disappear for an hour. When you come back—*voila!* You're grinning from ear to ear!"

Despite—and sometimes because of—everything that I would have preferred not to experience, I know God loves me. I want to love Him back, and continue loving Him. I don't want our daily trysts to end, ever. ❁

---

[8] The other is the study of Jewish law.

ROOM 1
THE REFUGE/ RECOVERY ROOM

A Midrashic parable:

> The dove glided along peacefully. She felt a shadow above and behind her, slowly edging into view. The shadow took form and she recognized it—the falcon.
>
> The dove plunged, aiming for a cleft too small for the falcon. As she made her final descent she saw the snake, coiled and fanged, waiting hungrily.
>
> She pulled up and started to hover, with nowhere to go. She began beating her wings and cooing for all she was worth, hoping her owner would hear and come to the rescue (Shir HaShirim Rabbah 2:14:2).

Have you ever felt hopelessly caught in a lose-lose situation? Take heart. A refuge is available. Its name is hitbodedut. It can even help you recover after you thought you'd already lost. ❊

⊢── 1 • Showing Up ──⊣

As much as you may realize or feel that hitbodedut is a potentially powerful practice, and as much as you may be ready, willing and able to try Rebbe Nachman's advice in general and hitbodedut in particular, you will not benefit from hitbodedut unless you actually do it. As we wrote earlier,[9] Rebbe Nachman said that many people never have the opportunity to meditate and reflect about the purpose of life, much less how they are spending their own lives. Now that you have been introduced to hitbodedut, you have the opportunity.

> Dear Ozer,
>
> I want to do hitbodedut, I really do, but how do I make time for it? It's hard enough getting up on time for the morning minyan. If I want to be a good Jew, a good worker, get a little exercise, be a good dad and a good Jew again in the evening by studying a little, when do I have time for hitbodedut? (I sometimes fall asleep with my head in the siddur, trying to read the Bedtime Shema!)
>
> Sincerely,
> Alex

How do you find time for hitbodedut? How do you justify, to yourself and to others, "doing nothing," retreating from the world, closing the door behind you and disappearing, leaving those who love you unrequited and those who need you to fend for themselves?

How do you find time for hitbodedut? How do you put down the cell phone, your Palm or your beeper? How do you shut off your music, your book and your newspaper? How do you put down your bottle or your personal brand of self-medication? How

---

[9] See page 23.

do you get up and walk away from the computer, the stock quotes, the news, your garden, your Torah study? How do you walk away from your piety? How do you walk away from your impiety?

How do you reduce your commute to work or your hours on the job? Is there someone you can petition for more vacation time, an extra coffee break, a twenty-fifth hour of the day or an eighth day of the week? Help me on this one!

The day starts so, so small. There are so many, many things that can be done; so many things that must, it seems, be done; and some things that *actually* must be done. In contrast to the din of all the material and spiritual "musts," the call of hitbodedut is perhaps the wispiest of whispers. That's enough to get you started.

THE SHOFAR BLAST

Exhale as hard as you can. Pretend you are a true blowhard and blow hard. Your breath didn't make too much noise, certainly. How much noise would you have made if you put a shofar to your lips? What a sound! That same little bit of air, that almost soundless exhalation, would magically amplify into a wake-up call.

One of the miracles of Judaism is that you don't need a lot to get started. You need not become a tzaddik overnight. You don't have to start your hitbodedut career by spending sixty minutes a day on it, just as you didn't have to run marathons or 100-yard dashes when you first began to walk. The trick to getting started is to realize the truth of what Rebbe Nachman often said: "A little bit is also good." Something is better than nothing.

Without your wanting to, you won't be able to even whisper a prayer. But if you begin to weigh the value of another game of solitaire, or another deal brokered, versus five minutes—five minutes!—of talking to God, of admitting to Him your humanness, of expressing to Him your appreciation of His holiness and goodness, you've taken the shofar in hand.

ALONE WITH GOD

The silence of hitbodedut surrounds you. Do you feel the uncomfortableness? Does your computer or Palm really exert so much control over you that you feel strange without them? Are you such a slave to your job, your family or your club that you have *no time at all* to at least groan from the heaviness of your labors? Or are you afraid of what might happen if you begin to develop your own private relationship with God? Are you afraid that He will reject you? Are you afraid to look at yourself? Are you afraid to venture to the edge of your soul and report back to your everyday consciousness what's really "in there" and what's really "out there?"

Can it be that you have time for reporters and actors and athletes and other people whom you would never let set foot into your home if you knew how they really behaved in their personal lives—and let them enter your mind and distract you from thinking about *your* life? Why do you allow their concerns to become your concerns?

These are ugly questions and ones we aren't used to thinking about. Yet your precious time, the most limited stuff of your precious life, is being invested in...*what?* What good do you expect to come of it? What should be more of a priority in a single person's life—watching a movie or meeting a potential marriage partner? What should be more of a priority in your life—treating patients or talking to the Healer Who works through you?

Then there's the claim, "I don't have time for hitbodedut. I'm a busy man. I work sixteen hours a day at my clinic saving people's lives. There's no time." Doctors, for the most part, are intelligent people. Yet this is what one said to me. The rule of thumb for someone who is too busy to do hitbodedut is: The more people depend upon you, the more you need to practice hitbodedut.

The challenges you face each day are new, even—and especially—if they are the "same old, same old." No matter what new wrinkle they contain, you must look forward to the new kindness that God is offering. It is your anticipating His kindness that makes it available to you. This is akin to a shofar. Blowing a breath of fresh air into its narrow opening produces the ripping of a broken heart, a battle whoop and a call of hope.

A simple — though not always easy — way of finding time is to do kindness for other people. Doing kindness itself creates time[10] and has a fortuitous by-product: happiness. The calm state of mind which happiness brings, says Rebbe Nachman, enables you to find time for hitbodedut.[11]

Another way of finding time — if you're tough enough — is by starting anew every day, or every hour if need be. Seriously consider your spiritual situation and think, "If, God forbid, I were to die right now, what would my soul look like? How would I appear to those who greet me Upstairs? How would I explain to them why I look so disheveled and slovenly?" Hopefully, this exercise will make many of the temptations less tempting. Knowing you will be called on the carpet clears many distractions from your mind. As Mark Twain put it, "Nothing focuses a man's mind at night like a hanging in the morning."

> Rebbe Nachman would occasionally recall the times he rowed out to the far side of a lake in order to seclude himself among the reeds and do hitbodedut. Sometimes the waters became rough and choppy. Not being an expert oarsman, he found himself in difficult straits and called out to God to save him. "And so should you," he advised his students. "Realize that your spiritual state — and your material one as well — is extremely precarious. You need God's help — now!" ❋

---

[10] Time was created to allow for the giving of the greatest kindness — namely, feeling the closeness of God. By emulating God and doing kindness, one justifies the continuation of — and creates — time.

[11] *Rabbi Nachman's Wisdom* #20. Of course, a calm state of mind is one of the goals of hitbodedut.

A more gentle way to nudge yourself forward is to consider what you'd like to *add* to your life: blessing, calmness, quiet, well-being. Realize that as old as you may be, compared to the wisdom of the Torah you are still young and green. Set out afresh to explore, examine and discover, "Wow! What a beautiful thing Judaism is."

The simplest way to find time is to ask God to help you find it. Refer to the "One-Minute Hitbodedut" (page 257). Start slowly. If you can't even find a minute to stop, then do it while you're on the go. Don't force the issue, but don't take "no" for an answer, either. When you finally get your first minute, ask to have another and another. Even if they aren't consecutive, take them and use them well.

JOIE DU JUDAISME

Even doing hitbodedut only once in a lifetime would be quite beneficial. A person who does hitbodedut once a week will certainly gain more. One who practices hitbodedut every day will gain still more. Part of what determines how often and for how long you do hitbodedut is how great your desire for Jewishness is. Someone who feels it's sufficient to be a weekend warrior, to actively work on her Jewishness only on Shabbat, is fooling herself. A half-hearted pursuit of spirituality is no pursuit at all. (On the other hand, if someone can only practice hitbodedut once a week, then once a week is more than an acceptable start.)

Hitbodedut is a serious venture, and like all serious ventures, demands a certain intensity. You may not be used to thinking of "Jewishness" and "intensity" in the same breath. In fact, the idea may make you uncomfortable and hesitant to explore how Jewish you can be. Don't let it. Don't be afraid.

Rebbe Nachman wants you to be conscious of the fact that Judaism is enjoyable and immensely rewarding, but not when treated in a haphazard fashion. The true *joie du Judaisme* comes from dealing with life's challenges in a responsible, Jewish way.

You may claim, if only to yourself, that your Jewishness is important to you. You may claim that you want to develop a personal, private, intimate relationship with God, that making and nourishing such a relationship is genuinely one of your life's goals. Showing up for hitbodedut would be proof positive of your claims.

Hitbodedut is a major time commitment, even if your first step is small (like ten minutes a day). You have to dedicate a specific block of time—every day—and show up—every day. Self-discipline is an absolutely indispensable *sine qua non*.

Part of what inhibits our commitment to and scheduling of hitbodedut is the failure to understand that our lifelong struggle with temptations, diversions and personal demons is, as it were, a competitive situation and not a recreational one. The forces and influences that keep us from self-awareness are playing for keeps, not for fun. They want to embarrass you. Don't let them.

One of the benefits of hitbodedut is you get to find out how much you can stretch, how much you can get better. But you've got to push. Do you push enough to get through the day? Do you put more effort into parties or into personal growth?

At some point you have to stand up and be a man about it. You have to decide: "This is how I'm going to do it. This is how I'm going to approach it." When was the last time you did that? Working on yourself is not always fun. Some days it's work. Other days it's hard work. You've got to show up on those days as well.

You succeed by showing up. It's not always a comfortable place to be, admitting to God and yourself how inadequate or weak you are, or how much you're in need of help, or how much pain you're suffering. Stepping outside your comfort zone is instrumental to reaching your potential. That's the path that leads to *joie du Judaisme*.

FEAR AND FAILURE

Even though "winning" and succeeding at Jewishness is wonderful and one of our objectives in life, and even though learning how to sacrifice—and sacrificing—towards that goal is a by-product of hitbodedut, hitbodedut provides something far more important than visible or tangible markers of Jewish success. It provides a means for coping with the two greatest enemies of a well-lived life: fear and failure.

The biggest, most fearsome obstacles are right outside the "Promised Land"—namely, the next step in your journey. Think of the biggest, meanest, nastiest bouncer you ever did see, standing outside the most exclusive club in the world. You're not sure you really belong. That's already two obstacles you've got to overcome. But they are obstacles of your own making, and they exist because you've forgotten two things. You didn't just get deposited on the steps of this club. You worked hard, very hard, to get here. And you're on a mission. You must get in. What you seek may be inside.

This is what the viceroy reminded himself in Rebbe Nachman's story, "The Lost Princess."[12] He had crossed deserts and mountains, sacrificed so much body-based and money-based pleasure in his single-minded search for the princess. He had been sufficiently pained by his king's misery that he volunteered to find the king's most precious child, and had been given the means to find her. Standing outside the palace, standing face to face with the palace guard, did he dare venture inside? How could he not? What if the princess was there and his fear kept him from rescuing her? He mustered up his courage and strode forward, entering unchallenged.

You have to muster up *your* courage. Almost without exception, when a person finds himself backed into a corner, he fights back. This is particularly true when his life is at stake! Rebbe

---

[12] *Rabbi Nachman's Stories* #1.

Nachman attempted to instill in his students the realization that one's spiritual life is always at stake. This is part of the message of the Mishnah, "Until the day you die, don't think you have it made" (Avot 2:5). Challenges, temptations and threats to one's faith, dedication, awareness and observance of Jewishness may be obvious or subtle, unique or common, momentary or chronic — but they are always there.

You can't even win, so it seems. The Talmud teaches that one's penchant for sin has the upper hand and you can't defeat it — on your own. But with God's help, you can conquer your temptations and demons.

In hitbodedut, you are not fighting God — you are trying to convince Him to join your side (which He wants to do). You have to keep your fear of losing and declining in Jewishness from overcoming your fear of talking to God.

Have courage. There are many things that you will be afraid to say. There will be many things that you are afraid to hear. There will be many things that you are afraid to admit. There will be many things that you are afraid to confront. There will be many things that you are afraid to change. Life is a very, very narrow bridge that each of us must pass over. You cannot let fear paralyze you.

> A warrior prepared himself to battle an implacable foe. He strode confidently forward. When he came to his enemy's gate he found it blocked — by a spider's web. Were he to turn around and return home because of this, how foolish he would be!

> There is so much you want — and need — to accomplish. Don't be bashful when you need to be brave.

Failure is very discouraging. You try once, twice, who knows how many times, and there's just no success. The reasonable conclusion is to "give up and move on." This is a reasonable conclusion in most ventures, but not in the venture your destiny depends upon!

Hitbodedut is the practice that allows you a time-out, a breather with all the people in your corner, as it were. Your trainer, manager and coach can restore your confidence. They can point out to you how your opponent is weakening, ease your pain, massage your muscles and cheer you on. The very fact that you practice hitbodedut is already a measure of success and an indication that you can succeed even more—if you keep at it.

However, the subliminal awareness of what's at stake may induce a person to abandon his attempts to push forward. Why? After a certain number of stymied attempts (and each of us has his personal threshold of frustration), one may feel that it is not just outside factors, or circumstances beyond his control, that block his way. One begins to think that he is not cut out for a spiritual life. One begins to question his essential worth.

One may even begin to question his successes. "How holy could I possibly be if, after all my efforts and my progress, I'm still so tempted and overwhelmed by the challenges that I was dealing with years and years ago?!" The response to such a powerful and realistic question is silence. Even though one has no intellectual response, one that can be couched in words, he has the answer of silent faith.[13]

Therefore, the first step to practicing hitbodedut is to make the commitment to do it. Recognizing that hitbodedut is a nice idea is not going to make it happen. The wish and the hope to someday engage in it is somewhat of a start, but far too

---

[13] Silence may seem like an evasion, an admission that the question is too powerful to be adequately answered. However, that misses the point and belies a misunderstanding of the nature of God-awareness. God-awareness is much, much more than that which the intellect can envelop. God-awareness is a combination of whatever the intellect can know, melded with intellect's own awareness of what it can never know, what it is not made to know. For someone who is on the spiritual path, this awareness is wordless. Someone who knows that something must be true, knows that some truths are ineffable.

We must also be aware of Mystery, that ethereal zone between knowing everything we possibly can, and not-knowing the inconceivable, the realm governed by faith, trust and the fearlessness we pray they engender. Awareness of Mystery gives us the daring to walk through Life, that narrowest of bridges which spans the deepest chasms of Hell.

undernourished a desire to actually flower. This seed needs to be watered by a brief prayer or two. Something short and simple, along the lines of: "God! Help me to do hitbodedut today and every day! *Please!*"

The power of such a mini-prayer must not be underestimated. Its importance is crucial. It means that you have made a conscious step towards dealing with Judaism—especially your role in it—not as a hobby, but as a focus. Judaism is rewarding. Judaism is fun. Judaism is not recreational. Once you realize in your heart that you're living Judaism for keeps, your commitment to practicing hitbodedut can begin to become a reality. You'll start to show up. ✻

ADAM

Adam was unique in many ways. He was simultaneously a private individual and the whole of mankind. He prayed as both. Adam surveyed God's creatures and found none suited to him. So he asked God for a partner, and God obliged.

Adam also prayed after God placed him in the Garden of Eden, giving it to him to tend. One might ask, "Why did he need to pray in Paradise? What was he missing?!" On the one hand, nothing, but on the other, the full potential of the Garden of Eden had not yet been realized. That was Adam's responsibility. Specifically, the vegetation that God created on the third day of creation had only sprouted, but not yet blossomed. Adam realized that the vegetation—and the world itself—would not blossom without rain. So he prayed for rain.

Adam, the first human being, was created alone. There were no other people for him to converse with, so why was he given the ability to speak? An answer is hidden in the Hebrew letters of his name.

The name of each Hebrew letter is also a word. The initial letter of the word is that letter itself. For example, the first letter of *ADaM* is *ALePh*, which is spelled *Aleph, Lamed, Peh*. The second letter of *ADaM* is *DaLeT*, which is spelled *Dalet, Lamed, Tav*. The last letter of *ADaM* is *MeM*, which is spelled *Mem, Mem*. Besides the three letters that spell *ADaM*, we are left with the remaining letters, *Lamed, Peh, Lamed, Tav, Mem*, which can be rearranged to spell the word *MiTPaLeL*, "one who prays." A human being is inherently meant to pray (Rabbi Tzvi Cheshin). ❋

┣━━ 2 • Starting a Session ━━┫

You've shown up. Now what? The point of hitbodedut is to talk freely to God,[14] without interruption. So turn off all the distractions and make yourself comfortable. Shut off *all* your phones, beepers and faxes. Shut the computer, the TV, the video, radio and CD player. Close the door and the windows if you need the quiet and will still have enough of an air supply. Do you need to adjust the heating or air-conditioning? Do it before you start. If you're doing hitbodedut during daylight hours and the movement of the sun will bother you, then close the curtains.

Hitbodedut is informal, so wear what you like, as long as you're comfortable and are dressed respectfully enough to be in the presence of the Deity. When I do hitbodedut, I empty my pockets and take off my glasses and shoes. (Sometimes I even take off my socks so I can wiggle my toes.) Having tissues handy is an excellent idea. One never knows when a sneeze or tears will sneak up on him.

This next point is very important: Go to the bathroom before you start. It sounds like a joke, but it's not. If the bladder or bowels are full, it's impossible to concentrate properly. And what happens if you get into the heart of an important issue and have to interrupt? You'll have to rewind your conversation when you come back, but the words and emotions may no longer be there.

> Rebbe Nachman once mentioned that when a person feels a sudden closeness for God, she should stop right where she is and speak some words to God. [He did not mean when crossing the street or while driving!] He explained that the awakening might dissipate if one waits to find a "more suitable" place.

---

[14] Remember, you can talk about whatever you want. It is impossible to bore, surprise or shock God.

Going to the bathroom is symbolic, as well. When we eat, part of the food converts into nutrients that are distributed to the various organs and systems that keep the body alive. The parts of the food that serve as a container or carrier for the nutrients, having served their function, must be disposed of before they poison the body.

Our minds, too, are constantly picking up new knowledge through experience and study. Some of this knowledge is valuable and life-sustaining, but much of it does nothing to enhance our relationship with the Divine. The longer we maintain this excess knowledge in our minds and hearts, the weaker and duller will be our awareness of the Godliness that fills our lives.

In hitbodedut, you use words to attempt to rid yourself of thinking and habits that have no positive effect on your life. Ridding the body of its waste material is a parallel action. Rebbe Nachman teaches that one should take care of this function as quickly as possible, so as not to waste precious time.[15]

Of course, having finished in the bathroom, you will wash your hands. Even if you don't need to relieve yourself, and even though hitbodedut is informal, it's good to wash your hands in preparation. We pour the waters of mitzvah on our hands, the water that symbolizes both the kindness of Creation (can life exist without it?) and the God-awareness that will ultimately encompass the world ("Like the waters that cover the sea" [Isaiah 11:9]). We purify our hands—the archetypal tool with which we make contact with the physical world—so that our interaction with the world, and the world itself, should become filled with kindness and awareness. Born anew as we are each day, washing our hands is a way of thanking God for further opportunities to serve Him. When we wash our hands from a cup, we connect ourselves to the kohen in the Temple, whose service eased the world of its pain and added to its bounty.

---

[15] See Appendix D for more on this subject.

FEELING SLEEPY

What position you assume in hitbodedut—sitting, standing, lying down—is not crucial, as long as you're comfortable, but not so comfortable that you are lulled to sleep. Feel free to get up, cross, un-cross or tuck your legs under you, or pace about.[16] The rule is to be comfortable enough so that you're not thinking about your body, but are able to focus on speaking to God about what concerns you.

As long as we've mentioned sleep, let's discuss it. Many find sleep to be an awfully discouraging hindrance to hitbodedut.[17] More than once I've been asked, "I always fall asleep when I start to do hitbodedut. What can you tell me that will help?"

In his story, "The Lost Princess," Rebbe Nachman tells of a king's loyal viceroy who sets out to find his majesty's lost daughter. After years of intense searching, he locates her. When he asks how he can bring her home, the princess advises him what to do. Above all, she warns him, "You cannot fall asleep."

Yet he does. Twice. After all the yearning and effort he puts into rescuing the princess (who represents his soul), when he's so close to achieving his goal, he fails. The first time, eating an apple puts him to sleep. The second time, drinking wine does him in.

"Sleep" is always a term indicating a shutting off, or lowering, of consciousness and awareness of God. In the simplest terms, it may be something as innocuous and seemingly harmless as "eating an apple"—i.e., having a snack or a drink—as you're on your way to hitbodedut that takes away the sharpness and clarity of your goal of strengthening your connection with the Divine.

---

[16] What if you can't sit still? Rebbe Nachman also had this problem. It was difficult for him to sit still and remain in his room, but in order to practice hitbodedut, he worked hard on overcoming his impatience and fidgetiness (*Rabbi Nachman's Praises* #14). Pacing while you talk may work for you.

[17] On a positive note, in addition to its obvious physical benefits, sleep purges the mind from off-track thinking and confusion, especially regarding matters of faith.

At other times, your curiosity may be the culprit. You just "have to" peruse the headlines, look something up or check your e-mail. Allowing other pursuits to take precedence over connecting to God is what lulls you to "sleep." Even if your curiosity has a spiritual bent, it nonetheless distracts you from your genuine goal.

So, you must *avoid* engaging in "sleep"-inducing behavior in preparation for hitbodedut. What can you do to wake yourself up?

In one of his lessons, Rebbe Nachman poses the following question: Why is it so difficult to fall asleep on Saturday night, after the exit of Shabbat? His answer is based on the Talmudic teaching that the prophet Elijah cannot come on Shabbat or on Shabbat eve (Friday) to herald the coming of the Mashiach. Ergo, Saturday night, Elijah is again on his way. It is the sound of his footsteps that keeps us awake.

The Talmud tells us that this heralding, this wake-up call, involves a two-part process: busting up the lies and delusions from which mankind currently suffers, and bringing together the scattered elements of truth.[18] The fission of falsehood and the fusion of the elements of truth will undoubtedly release a quantity of energy that will be staggering.

What's this got to do with you and your hitbodedut? As you attempt to begin to integrate the practice of hitbodedut into your life, or as you attempt to continue with it, your enthusiasm, if it exists at all, may not always be heartfelt. You may be feeling outside pressure to do (or not do) it, or you may feel it is taking away too much from other practices, or you may be uncertain as to whether it is helping. Perhaps you wonder if it's really for you. (Perish the thought!)

---

[18] This teaching is based on the contiguity of the letters of the Hebrew word for falsehood, and the distance from one another of the letters of the Hebrew word for truth.

When a person gets angry, observes Rebbe Nachman, he gets "all worked up." To prepare for prayer, one must also get "worked up" and pumped up. Get your adrenaline going. Compel your emotions. You may not actually feel excited about hitbodedut, but by getting yourself to realize and feel that this impending rendezvous with God is as special an event as any that you've ever been part of, you won't be able to fall asleep.

Another tip that is effective, but not always practical, is to roar your words. That's right, roar your words. When Nebuchadnezzar, the king of ancient Babylonia, related his dream to Daniel,[19] he said that an angel had come down from Heaven, roaring his words. He described the angel as being "awake."

No matter how many times you've overslept or fallen asleep during hitbodedut, don't be discouraged. Keep trying! Even after the viceroy failed, the princess left him a letter of encouragement — and he began his search anew until he finally found and rescued her.

One more act of preparation must be mentioned: giving tzedakah (charity). It's hard to overestimate the significance and power of giving tzedakah. As a prelude to a practice that can be very much self-focused, it reminds you that your efforts are not merely for your own benefit, but for the benefit of others as well. Before you ask for God's generosity in listening to and granting your prayers, you open His Gates of Charity and show that your own potential for generosity already exists, and is but beginning to flower.[20]

Giving tzedakah before prayer is an exercise of judgment: The person on the receiving end needs to be raised, even at your expense. Similarly, during hitbodedut, you will exercise the faculty of judgment when thoughts arise, determining which

---

[19] *Daniel* 4:10ff.

[20] The actual amount that you give is not as important as your exercise of judgment and honest desire to be generous.

are foreign and need to be ignored, and which are the ones that need to be spoken.[21] Your words of hitbodedut will be truer, more effectively hitting their mark, because you have already exercised your judgment in giving tzedakah.[22]

ICEBREAKERS

OK, this is it. You're alone, face to face, as it were, with the Creator. Now what? Some people never have a problem initiating a conversation, even with a total stranger. Then there are the rest of us. Is there an icebreaker? In fact, there are a few; one is inner-directed, the others, outer-directed. The inner-directed one is a declaration that Rebbe Nachman suggests should precede every prayer: "I am binding myself to all the tzaddikim of our generation."

This declaration is an expression of admiration and love for such people, as well as an expression of willingness to view their guidance and teachings as worthy of being significant, if not decisive, in your life. It also expresses a willingness to adopt their focus and approach to life as a model for your own. It means that you wish to ally yourself with spiritual masters—people who have not merely stumbled upon spiritual wisdom or efficacious spiritual practices, but who have sweated and toiled to open themselves to receive—and relay—God's light. It is a declaration of hope that you can be a partner in their work.

As a pre-hitbodedut (or pre-prayer) declaration, this statement acknowledges that as well as we may pray, a genuine tzaddik prays better. That being the case, we express our hope to live up to the ideals and values that a genuine tzaddik exemplifies. This

---

[21] See Judge Thy Self, page 88.

[22] Since money may not be handled on Shabbat or Jewish holidays, you should not actually put money into a tzedakah box on those days. You may, however, make a mental note to give after Shabbat or the holiday ends. Hosting or otherwise providing meals for others on Shabbat or holidays also constitutes tzedakah.

gives our hitbodedut a bit more *oomph,* because just harboring such an aspiration makes us more tzaddik-like. In addition, this statement invokes the merit of the genuine tzaddikim and gets our hitbodedut a better hearing. Their merit exists, but does not activate automatically. We have to show honest desire to follow in their footsteps to elicit it.

Stating our desire to be more tzaddik-like reminds us that part of what we want to accomplish through hitbodedut is "tzaddikness": self-mastery over even our basest physicality, and generosity towards others.

Now for the outer-directed icebreakers.

OK. You've declared to yourself whom you want to be. Now it's time to tell God. There's nothing wrong or phony in beginning with a simple, "Good morning." If it's Shabbat or a Jewish holiday say, "Shabbat Shalom" or "Chag Samei'ach." Say it like you mean it! After all, if God, as it were, is having a good morning, peaceful Shabbat or happy holiday, everyone benefits.

"It's me, [your name]. Now I begin to cling to you." "Clinging to God"[23] means being tenacious in your effort to maintain God-awareness in all your experiences, whether they be painful, pleasurable or boring. Whatever you are going to talk about in your hitbodedut is something you hope to transform into a clinging experience. Talking it over with God already makes it a clinging experience, but you want to maintain that awareness not just now, but afterwards too, when you're actually living it. Telling God you want to cling to Him makes the bond stronger now, as you talk about it, and later.

Mentioning that you are beginning now, as you start hitbodedut, genuinely constitutes a fresh start. However well you have been doing in your spiritual trek, starting again can only help. A new start brings new energy, new hope and new life to all your holy work. Well begun is half-done.

---

[23] Which is no less a Torah mitzvah than having a mezuzah on your doorpost.

The next icebreaker—and arguably the most important—is thanking God. There are two sides to this: the honey of thanking and the sting of non-thanking. Let's do away with the sting.

Let me tell you a secret: It annoys God when a person is ungrateful. Adam was ungrateful that he was given a wife. The would-be builders of the Tower of Babel were ungrateful for the peace and solidarity they enjoyed. If you don't appreciate what you've been given, don't expect to get more. You have to count your blessings. Do your eyes work? Your ears? Can you go to the bathroom by yourself? Thank Him! They don't work? Did they ever work? Thank Him now for when they did work! Thanking God for the good He's given you in the past gives birth to future good.

Do you know the alef-bet? Have you ever been in the holy Land of Israel? Thank Him! Thank God for the big stuff and thank Him for the little stuff, because He really didn't have to give you anything. For all the good you may have done to "deserve" the pleasantness of your life,[24] there's a lot more that you've done that could have forfeited it. Feel blessed that you have the possessions you do—physical, intellectual, sacred, tangible, intangible! How many people have the privilege of knowing about hitbodedut and the opportunity to do it, to spend quality time alone with the Creator? You're one of them!

The honey side of thanking God is like having money; it's easy to get used to. So try it—you'll like it.

Thanking God is an exquisite pleasure, so much so that Rebbe Nachman tells us it is the major component of the delight granted in the World to Come. He teaches that the more you recognize and are aware of God, the closer a relationship you have with Him. By examining your life, by reviewing your history, you begin to discover the breadth and depth of God's care and concern for you. Events that occurred decades before may become understandable

---

[24] You couldn't have done it without His help, right?

for the first time. Painful memories might only now come to be understood as part of a process that is still continuing or has already ended, while pleasurable memories will become richer as you realize what was involved when you lived them.

The purpose of all this thanking is not to divorce you from the reality of this world by putting you into the Next prematurely, God forbid, but to bring the Next World into this one, where it can already begin to emerge if we but open our eyes and hearts.[25] So start hitbodedut by acknowledging the good in your life and thanking the Giver. Sometimes your hitbodedut may be spent totally on the "thank You's." That's not so bad. After all, we Jews have a whole eight-day-long holiday called Chanukah that's solely dedicated to "thanking and praising Your great Name."

And now, after all the thanking, you can sing the blues. ❁

---

[25] The more you thank God—and other people—the more you become aware of the interconnectedness of all facets of Creation. This Oneness also characterizes the Next World.

NOACH

Noach was a tragic figure. Since childhood, he labored under the yoke of great expectations that he would be the one to save mankind from its suffering. Though he provided great advancements to technology and made people's lives easier, he suffered great abuse from the general public. He did not father children until a relatively advanced age. For hundreds of years, people mocked him for being sterile.

When he received his mission to build the Ark, people scorned and attacked him, accusing him of being a senile religious fanatic.

However, the greatest tragedy was the one that befell him when he exited the Ark after the Deluge. He saw the world was empty—the people, the cities, the civilization, the life the world had contained were all gone. In his pain he cried out to God, "You are the Compassionate One! Where was Your compassion?!" God responded, "Foolish shepherd! *Now* you pray to Me to have pity? Where were you when I told you that I was going to deluge the planet?!"

The media is filled with so much bad news. Are we sensitive enough to hear God's voice behind it, telling us to pray that He exercise His compassion around the globe and on a global scale? Even if the victims are humanity's dregs, they cannot be much worse than the Generation of the Deluge for whom Noach was supposed to have prayed. Pray for the rest of humanity—and for your own humanity. ✸

⊢—— 3 • Singing the Blues ——⊣

What hurts you? What's frustrating you? What mountains seem made of fire? What people look to you like monsters? You don't want to go down the road feeling bad. You don't wanna be treated this-a way. You hurt! You've got things to get off your chest and complain about. "Is there anyone in charge here?" you want to know. "Where's customer service? I'm dissatisfied!"

Relax, you're in hitbodedut. It's your opportunity to sing the blues.

"What? Are you telling me it's OK to sing the blues? Jewish blues? Diaspora blues? My own personal blues?" Absolutely. That's a primary function of hitbodedut.

Rebbe Nachman never suggests (as is commonly misunderstood) that we should deny or avoid our pain. Quite the contrary. Rebbe Nachman tells us that we have to be proactive to confront our difficulties and our hurt[26] in order to transform them into sources of joy. Allow me to introduce you to a person who did just that—he was a Jew who sang the blues, and with good reason.

As a youngster, he was sent out of his home by his father and brothers. When he was a young man, his father-in-law dispatched law enforcement officers to murder him. After he was married with children, one of his sons raped his daughter. Another son fomented a rebellion against him, turning loyal assistants against him. This harried individual was King David.

Throughout the psalms, as throughout his life, King David sang the blues. Who wouldn't have? Rebbe Nachman, too, suffered a number of personal tragedies (he lost several children as well as his first wife) and cried to God many times. As he puts it:

---

[26] This doesn't mean looking for trouble. It means being brave enough to deal with the problems you already have.

The world is full of constant pain and suffering. The natural reaction is to be upset and depressed.

Stuff happens in life. Little things, annoyances. Big things, tragedies. Obstacles. Impediments. It is to be expected that you will want and need to sing the blues at various points in your life. You should ask yourself, however, what's the source of your blues? Not what's *causing* them, like your faucets give nuthin' but muddy water, or your stomach hurt so bad it feel like a lead belly, but from which part of your guts your blues are coming? Are you singing from the spleen or from the heart?

Traditionally, the spleen is seen as the seat of depression. Rebbe Nachman was once asked to explain the difference between a broken heart and depression. "A broken heart comes from the heart; depression comes from the spleen," he replied. "God loves a broken heart because it's holy. He hates depression because it's not."

There's nothing wrong with singing the blues. What you have to be careful about is sinking into the blues and letting them take over. Songs of heartbreak and despair, of viewing life through the bottom of a whiskey glass, from an abandoned shack or a jail cell, too often leave a person at the bottom of the glass, in the shack or in the cell.

Rebbe Nachman often spoke about how music can uplift a person and bring him to a frame of mind in which the possibilities of life seem almost unlimited. Rebbe Nachman also spoke about the potentially detrimental effects of music. Singing the blues or any other type of sad music—which, he noted, attracts most, if not all, people—can draw you in the wrong direction.

Because when you're suffering, when you've got troubles, you're in deep spiritual danger. When King David—King David!—was running for his life, he entertained the notion of abandoning Judaism. If you let yourself be drawn after the sadness, you draw yourself away from the Jewishness that hitbodedut can bring you to. You have to decide. Do you really want to let go of your problems, or do you want to turn them into alibis for failing to reach your potential? Worse, do you want your suffering and problems to be a pretext for abandoning Jewishness altogether?

If you start off in a minor key, don't get stuck there. Make sure to move to a major key. That means if you start out singing:

> Some folks say my blues ain't bad
> Must not have been my blues they had

Make sure to finish:

> Yeah, but that's OK
> Cause I'll be up someday

Now it's time to pull back the curtain and take a good look at yourself. Don't be afraid. You're not that ugly. In fact, you're really not ugly at all. Truth is, you're really pretty good-looking. ✿

AVRAHAM

In a sense, it's much easier to pray for strangers than to pray for someone you know. There's nothing to hold against a stranger, no reason to wish him any harm. But when it comes to someone you've had dealings with, someone who has tried to harm you—that good-for-nothing bum, he can drop... No reason to finish the thought and every reason to change it, as Avraham our first patriarch did.

The holy Zohar teaches that there are two areas of life in which one must excel in order to be a tzaddik. One is sexual morality and the other is the giving of tzedakah. Avraham was a champion of both. God rewarded him with the gift and privilege of brit milah because Avraham understood that without being chaste, one cannot achieve the quietude of mind necessary for experiencing God's presence.

Avraham also understood that in order to experience God, one has to behave like God. So he raised a tent, open to all four directions—north, south, east and west—and invited in any and all comers, providing them with free food, drink and lodging. The Sodomites who lived down the road a stretch behaved in quite the opposite fashion. They were excessive and abusive in their sexuality. Wayfarers who blundered into Sodom did not always leave alive. If they did, they certainly had no desire to return.

Even though the lifestyle and philosophy of the Sodomites was directly opposed to that of Avraham, when God told Avraham that the Sodomites were to be destroyed, Avraham argued strenuously that they should be spared. He tried again and again to have them acquitted. Although his prayers did not save the Sodomites, they provide protection for Avraham's descendants until today.

Later, Avimelekh stole Avraham's wife, Sarah. Yet when the king returned Sarah to her husband, Avraham prayed for Avimelekh and all the members of the royal household. With his prayer, Avraham was able to "untangle the tangle" of confused principles caused by Adam's sin.

For those of us who like to start the day early, Avraham did some of his best praying at the "top o' the mornin'," as night turns into day. ❋

⊢—— 4 • JUDGE THY SELF ——⊣

In hitbodedut, you are judge and jury. You are prosecutor and defense attorney. And, you are the defendant.

The judgment of hitbodedut is somewhat like ordinary judgment in a courtroom: Claims are made, arguments presented, and evidence produced. There is a crucial difference, however. In a courtroom, the verdict is in doubt until it is delivered. In hitbodedut, the verdict is almost beside the point. In hitbodedut, the *process* is the point.

Hitbodedut is an opportunity to settle your mind and take a long, honest look at your deeds, your dealings with your fellow human beings (and others that share your planet), your words, your thoughts and your desires. It is a time when you can sit down and seriously evaluate your motives to see if they live up to the goals or values you subscribe to. You can even give careful thought to why you are alive, and whether you could be doing more with the talents and tools God has given you.

Why do we need to go through this judgment? The answer goes back to two historical events, one pre-Creation, the other at Mount Sinai. Before God created the world, He knew that the crux of Creation, the human being, would most enjoy the eternal good that God wanted to give if he, the human, earned it. Therefore, God created the world with midat hadin, the attribute of judgment (or entitlement). This means you get only what you earn. The flip side is that you get what you deserve.

However, God also knew that mankind could not survive if there was no margin for error. There had to be some wiggle room, some allowance for mistakes. "After all," said the Creator, "it's not for nothing that I'm called 'tender-hearted'" (*Tanchuma, Pikudei* 3). So God also created the world with midat harachamim, the attribute of compassion. Even so, when He was ready to create man, the angels objected. They predicted that the human experiment would be a failure due to man's many innate shortcomings. Objection overruled; God went ahead with Creation.

At Sinai, before God gave the Torah, the angels again pleaded with Him not to favor mankind. "They're just human beings. They won't be able to do justice to such a majestic body of teaching," they protested. "We'll give it the honor and recognition it deserves." God asked Moshe to respond. Moshe pointed out to the angels that the Torah didn't suit them. They could never use the Torah as a vehicle for spiritual advancement because they had never tasted the bitterness or discomfort of being human. God agreed with Moshe and gave the Torah.

As you sit in hitbodedut, you have to ask: "Have I justified God's decision to create the world? To create *me*? Have I proven Moshe right and used the Torah to advance spiritually?"

Before you rush to answer, remember: God *did* create the world; God *did* give the Torah. What that means is that even if you don't measure up—yet—God was aware of that and He decided that despite the risks and the fallout of having you around, He wants you here anyway. So, if you ever finish hitbodedut feeling condemned, doomed or damned, *you've done something wrong! You're not getting it!*

You must find the balance between leniency and stringency. You may not allow yourself to rely solely on God's welfare—that way lies sloth—nor may you be too hard on yourself—that way lies despair and crime (for often when a person feels that he cannot do more good, he does more evil). If, as you scrutinize your life, you see that you are being overwhelmed and coming up short, then pray harder, try to do more hitbodedut, but don't despair! *All of us* come up short in our practice!

BACKGROUND CHECK

Before you can begin to judge and assess what you're doing with your life, you have to know who you are. To paraphrase the Mishnah (*Avot* 3:1): Where are you coming from? This has to be answered in terms of your general background (your gender, age, childhood, health, etc.), as well as in terms of a specific decision (what were you thinking?). For example, no Jew is permitted to eat a cheeseburger, but for some it is a nearly irresistible challenge while for others it is no challenge at all.

By the way, your "background check" is not something you do once and forget about. It stays relevant for years and years. For example, you might have moved clear across the globe and lived more than half your life in the Holy Land, but if your formative years were spent in the decadency of suburbia, that's going to influence a lot of your actions—sometimes blatantly, sometimes subtly. This often works to your advantage: "Not bad for a kid from Long Island." "God, what did you expect from someone who grew up in the San Fernando Valley?"

Equally important, and of course based in large part on where you're coming from, is the other question posed by the above-mentioned Mishnah: Where are you going? A person of your talents, in your situation, will be—should be—aiming at certain levels of Jewish behavior, refinement and awareness. Knowing where you've been and where you're going enables you to determine whether or not your decisions and choices are correct. You're "guilty" only if you don't live up to the Jewishness that you're capable of.

Being "guilty" doesn't automatically mean a harsh sentence, or even any sentence. "Guilt" means that you need to recalibrate your attitudes, preparedness and the like. When you assume the responsibility for judging yourself and keeping yourself focused on improving Jewishness, Heaven doesn't have to intervene to remind you to do it.

"Do I have to judge myself every day? Do I have to walk around 'taking my temperature'?" A good question, answered by a good story (one of my personal favorites):

> One morning after Shacharit, the students of the Baal Shem Tov approached him and asked, "Rebbe, the Talmud teaches us that a person is judged on Rosh HaShanah, yet it also teaches that a person

is judged every day. How can this be?" The Baal Shem Tov smiled and called over the water carrier. "Reb Shia, how are you today?" he asked.

"*Oy*, Rebbe, how can I be? I'm an old man, but I still have to shlep buckets of water up from the river and around the village to make a living. I sit in the back of the synagogue and everyone ignores me. My children and their families live far away and I see them once in a blue moon. How can I be?" The Baal Shem Tov blessed the water carrier that his life should get better and wished him a good day. He told his students to return in a few days.

They came back, again after Shacharit, and again the Baal Shem Tov called over the water carrier. "*Nu*, Reb Shia, how are you today?"

"Thank God, Rebbe, life is wonderful. I'm fit as a fiddle and I can carry buckets of water to everyone in the village till the cows come home. I sit in the back of the synagogue; no one bothers me and I can say psalms to my heart's content. Thank God I have children and grandchildren who are healthy. Who could ask for a better life?!" The Baal Shem Tov blessed him that his life should only get better.

The Baal Shem Tov said to his students, "This is what the Talmud means. On Rosh HaShanah, a person is judged as to what conditions he will be placed in, but every day he is judged as to how he will experience those conditions."

JUDGMENT AND COMPASSION

With self-judgment, you can stay on target despite all the ups and downs that life dishes out. To succeed, you need to know how to balance judgment with compassion.

If you overemphasize and exaggerate the extent and the magnitude of your mistakes, turning compassion into judgment, you will become discouraged. Even the good that you do will lose value in your eyes. Discouragement can cause your good works to become fewer and farther between, and bad works may fill the ensuing vacuum. The calm, trust and faith that you started to cultivate begin to wither and may die, especially if the weeds of cynicism and doubt take root. So make sure to supply enough compassion.

But don't overdo it! Even though you must acknowledge the right choices you've made, perhaps even occasionally toasting yourself with a "job well done," exaggerating the extent and the magnitude of your successes may lead to self-indulgence and laziness. When you turn judgment into compassion, you won't do all that you're capable of. You have to apply enough of each so that you're like a properly wound watch spring—not so unwound that the watch doesn't work, and not so overwound that the spring snaps.

"God, I know I should control myself more, but am I the only one who comes up short in practice? I'm not comparing myself to King David, but didn't even he make a mistake with Bathsheba?"

"God, what I did was mean and rotten, but is what I did as bad as Cain stabbing his brother in the back? Yet, when he pleaded with You, 'Is my sin too great to bear?' You gave him a reprieve. You gave him additional time to set things right."

"God, I have no excuse on this one. After all that You've allowed me to learn and with all the trust You've placed in me, to do what I did was inexcusable. But excuse me anyway and help me to not give up or backslide. Didn't Rebbe Nachman say that even if he were to commit the biggest sin, it would not throw him at all, that he wouldn't backslide, he would simply repent? Me, too."

"God, did You see that?! I haven't had anything to eat since my coffee and doughnut this morning, and I drove right past the takeout place to pray with a minyan. Not bad for a guy who can barely read Hebrew!"

"Lord, can I possibly thank You enough? It's two weeks in a row I've been able to get everything done at work and at home so I can attend this class. It's not enough, though. Please! Let's go for three, four and more."

The common thread underlying these expressions of judgment and compassion is twofold. One is your continued growth in Jewishness. The other is the constant revelation of God's goodness.

By honestly pointing to God's desire to shower mankind with good, you can understand which attribute—judgment or compassion—to emphasize, and to what degree.[27]

THE TRUE YOU

You will always need to be as honest as honest can be. The purpose of hitbodedut-judgment is not to determine guilt or innocence, but to adjust "broken" viewpoints and behavior. You always need to decide in your favor: You are either innocent, winning a reprieve, or getting a second chance. (It may be your second second-chance, or your hundredth second-chance or your millionth second-chance, but you must get another one, no matter what.) The only way to grow is through encouragement, encouragement, encouragement.

> A Breslover once came to Reb Noson, bemoaning his lack of enthusaism for Jewishness. "I have no heart," he cried. Reb Noson replied: "You do, but you have to hearten your heart." ❈

Do you know who you truly are? The true you is not the criminal, the failure, the one who's dropped the ball every time. You are not the Charlie Brown of Judaism. The true you is the one who has said and done all the good things you've ever performed—as few as they may be. The true you is the one who has sometimes—even once, even if fleetingly—thought of living properly.

The treasure that you are may be buried or lost in some distant past, but it certainly exists. How can I be so positive about that? Because Rebbe Nachman says that even the most hopeless

---

[27] Reb Noson offers three tips for improving your self-judgment: Be honest in money matters, judge others favorably and, above all, bear in mind that when God does something or allows something to happen, He's got an excellent reason.

sinner has a good point. And, he says, once you find your first good point, keep looking and you'll find another.

The secret to finding your true self, your goodness, is not just to look for it, but to seek it, to want to find it, and to actually find it. Identify it and claim it! It's yours and it's you. God takes pride in the good you do. You should, too.

Sifting through the past is not always easy or pleasant. It may also be time-consuming—but consider the reward. If your inner cynic is snorting, "Wow! Fifty years and just one good deed. What's *that* worth?" the response is simple: "If I did it once, I can do it again. And besides, Rebbe Nachman says that I have another good point. I've just got to look for it."

"Well, if I have good points, don't I have bad points?" True, you may have missed many opportunities for Jewishness in your life and may even have intentionally done things Jewishly-wrong. Perhaps, with malice aforethought, you caused others to miss opportunities and/or go astray. In a word, you screwed up. That's 100% true. The true truth, however, is, as Rebbe Nachman put it, that the Jewish soul is so refined, dignified and spiritual that it is averse to sin and wrongdoing of any sort. So, is the fact that your life is studded with regrettable and embarrassing choices "proof" of a non-Jewish soul residing within you? No, it's not quite that dramatic. But it shows that you've underestimated the challenges and need to deal with them more intelligently and more determinedly. The future is not yet written. You are not destined to screw up—if you don't want to.

We face so much opposition, from within and without, each and every day. One needs a certain degree of intensity to encourage himself and others (without putting people off).[28] Hitbodedut allows you to express your desire for holiness and improvement, which is an integral part of the encouragement.

---

[28] Don't make others think your intensity is ridiculous. If they do, don't let it discourage you.

Doing hitbodedut also shows that you believe you can change. Even reading about hitbodedut and considering it shows that you believe you can change. Actually doing hitbodedut shows that you believe God will help you change.

> If you believe that you can damage,
> Believe that you can fix!

Use hitbodedut as a shield. Ask to protect yourself, and to be protected from the hooks and snares that are likely to bring you down. Ask for strength to overcome and resist, as much as possible, the challenges and temptations that you must face.

> Rebbe Nachman once remarked, "Common wisdom says that if you're going to give in and eat pork, then let the gravy run down your beard. But I say, if you're going to give in and eat pork, at least *don't* let the gravy run down your beard!"

THE MESSAGE OF TZADDIKIM

Often life is like a roller coaster, both externally and internally. Always remember: The downs are meant to prepare us for the ups, not to smack us down and keep us down. Your personal sanctuary may have been destroyed and your community and family suffered major or minor tragedies. Stubbornness is part of the job description of being a Jew. As a member of a stiff-necked tribe, you have it within you to rally from even the worst setback.

How do you handle a down? An up? How do you tell the difference between them? And how do you use hitbodedut to evaluate them and proceed?

When you know that you were wrong, you may be discouraged by feelings of guilt. You, like many others, may think that according to the logic of the Torah, you have sinned and are guilty. On top of that, relying on God's kindness, you have tried to repent and improve, but nonetheless you failed again and yet again. You might think that you've already tapped into the deepest levels of Divine compassion and still weren't rescued. Therefore, you think, you will remain unredeemed.

At such a point, you need to recall that there are tzaddikim, spiritual adepts, who have accessed a much, much deeper level of Divine compassion. Not only that, but you have to plant in your heart the faith that there are tzaddikim out there who are on such an extraordinary level that they constantly make accessible newer levels of God's love and compassion.

> A group of people dance happily while some miserable individual mopes nearby. Against his will, the dancers shlep him into their circle. Then, again against his will, they shlep him into their happiness.

There is an infinite depth to God's kindness. God Himself prays for our forgiveness (*Rosh HaShanah* 17b). If you ask, you'll certainly be included in His prayers.

> "God, I admit that according to the rules and logic of the Torah, I'm guilty and deserve to suffer being distanced from You. But You know what? I want to be close to You anyway.

> "Because You know that if You really followed the logic of the Torah 100%, swiftly and immediately, no one would be here.

> "So if You're giving me the chance to make a reckoning, the realization that I'm far from You, give me the next bit of closeness. And the next and the next."

One of the drawbacks of overly harsh self-judgment is that you undervalue your influence on the workings of the Godly machine. People whom you know, as well as people you will never know and places and events in which you will not actively participate, are impacted by your interaction with the world. You do them—and us—all a disservice by withdrawing, turtle-like, into your shell.

Instead, open your ears to hear the message of the tzaddikim. Recall all the kindnesses you've ever experienced, and use those kindnesses to build new words that restart your part of the machine.

It's the same when you justify your claim for a stronger, more intimate relationship with the Torah:

> "I've been in plenty of Egypts. I've been slaving my whole life, and for what? So I could ignore and be ignorant of the Torah? Is that what You made me a Jew for—that I *shouldn't* do what You want, that I *shouldn't* know Torah? Is this what the patriarchs and matriarchs had in mind when they pleaded with You to bring a holy nation into being? Where's *my* holiness? Where are Your promises?!"

What makes these types of arguments so successful is that part of the purpose of Creation involves revealing just how great God is. His greatness is shown by the extent of His kindness, which can only be demonstrated by getting you (and the rest of us) out of a jam. This is one of the reasons why those returning to Judaism are in one respect greater than tzadikkim: The latecomer has beaten a trail to Jewishness, a trail whose every turn tells the world of God's amazing kindness.

How Not To Judge

When you look at the defendant, you have to evaluate two separate things. On the one hand, there's her behavior (what she's done, how she actually spends her time). On the other hand, there's her true worth. Just because you're judge and defendant doesn't make being judicious any easier. It may make it harder. Let me tell you how *not* to judge.

Everyone makes mistakes. We make mistakes in ritual observance and in interpersonal dealings. Our faith and trust in God are often weak or altogether missing. We all suffer lapses of judgment, sometimes so severe that we jeopardize both our fortune and our fate. It is quite easy—especially if we have set high standards—to take ourselves to task for failures, real or imagined. "Nothing I do is any good. My mitzvot are meaningless. It doesn't matter what I do, or if I don't do anything at all."

"Don't be too wicked" (*Ecclesiastes* 7:17). King Solomon is telling us not to blow our wickedness out of proportion. What we've done—or not done—may be a failure, yes, a lapse, yes. It may even have been an extremely wicked, bad, evil sin, yes. But is that a reason to give up? NO! Besides the obvious reason for our being so self-critical, the true reason is that we are seeking a way out, an escape from our Jewish responsibilities. If we even slightly accept that way out, our Jewishness suffers until we return to our senses. We will do less good, weaken our faith and diminish our morality. Our individual, physical absence and spiritual distance also weakens our community, no matter how large or small it may be.

Despite the seriousness of what you may have done—even if you have been a repeat offender for years and years, and even if you are blameworthy and deserve to be severely punished—you have to access God's tender-heartedness. (Yes, you can.) You may face a difficult struggle in locating it and turning it on, but it's there. As you search for it, you may find yourself repeating the anguished words of Cain, history's first murderer: "Is my sin too great to bear?" Remember: He was reprieved.

You have to assess your true value—what you're doing, how well you're doing it and what you ought to be doing. When you've finished, you have to "sentence" yourself to rehabilitation. As our Sages say, "If there is judgment below, there is no judgment Above" (*Devarim Rabbah* 5:5). If you are aware of the need for self-correction, God doesn't need to remind you.

Judgment, in order to be accurate and fair, requires that you properly understand who *you* are, what *you* can and cannot do, what *you* ought to be doing with your life in general, and what *you* ought to be doing at this juncture of your life. Some people are daveners, some learners, some good-deed-doers and some tzedakah-givers. Yet each of us needs to perform all these functions at some time or another, to a greater or lesser degree.

Use your hitbodedut to take stock of your talents, to evaluate your physical and financial circumstances, to consider your disposition and health (emotional, physical and other) and to eliminate what is irrelevant to your Jewishness. Focus on the strengths that you have to connect with God. He didn't give you talent so you could lock it up in a safe and make sure nothing happens to it. He gave you talent to use and to shine some more of His light into the world.

Some choices will be black and white, fairly obvious and easy to make. No more non-kosher food. No more white lies. More Jewish education for me and the family. But much of life, if not most of it, is lived in the gray, hazy areas. The need for Divine guidance is more than critical; it can determine the destiny of many. Korach's decision to rebel and the decision of those who joined him (*Numbers* 16) is one example of suffering and loss that came from not seeking sound advice.

> Once the Rebbe was speaking to one of his followers. In the midst of their conversation, they heard someone praying Maariv (the evening prayers). The man was saying the *Hashkiveinu* blessing and he rushed through the words *V'takneinu b'eitzah tovah milfanekha* ("Remedy us with good counsel from before You").
>
> The Rebbe said, "Did you see how that person raced through the words, 'Remedy us with good counsel'? Doesn't he realize that he must say these words with great emotion and feeling, from the very depths of his heart? This is an inestimable prayer. You must always beg that God have mercy and grant you good counsel and advice, that you may be worthy of knowing what is right."
>
> If you truly want to serve God, you must understand this well. Plead before God and ask that you be worthy of His good counsel.

Some of your choices may last a lifetime. There will never be any need to change or even reconsider them. That's fine. However, some choices (even ones you thought *would* be permanent) may need revision or abandonment. Stay flexible. Life changes; what works today may not work tomorrow. But changing horses in midstream, even for what appears to be a sound reason, should be avoided. Rebbe Nachman once said that when he committed to a certain focus in his devotions, he stayed with it even if doubts entered his mind. After giving his choice a chance to stand for a few months, he would review the situation and make the changes that seemed to him necessary.

Another benefit of correctly judging yourself and realizing that you and the Jewish devotions that fit you are legitimate, is increased love for your fellow Jew. By appreciating your uniqueness—your history, temperament, etc.—you can look more generously at the next person. You can appreciate his struggle and his journey, even if he is not consciously involved in the spiritual process. You can understand that others need devotions that are different from yours, or they may need to engage in like devotions in unlike ways. Love yourself and you will be able to love your fellow Jew.

The Rebbe ended by saying, "If people would only hold on to this..." With his gestures, he emphasized its importance. The Rebbe's intent was that there is something to hold on to even if you cannot attain a high level yourself. You can still grasp hold of others and desire that they attain what is beyond your reach.

The Rebbe also said, "Even when I am not worthy of serving God, I am satisfied to let another serve Him." This is a very important concept to internalize. Even though you may not be worthy, you can still long for others to be truly righteous. Wanting all one's friends to be great tzaddikim would be the greatest expression of love and friendship.

People can easily fall away from religion. They can be snared by evil temptations and be trapped in sin. Many such people hate those who are religious. They provoke them, discouraging and degrading them. They do everything in their power to drag others to their low level, proclaiming that every religious Jew will eventually fall away just as they have.

A true Jew must do the exact opposite. He should want others to serve God, even when he himself is unable to do so. ❊

SARAH

Sarah, our first matriarch, was a brave and courageous woman. She was also a tough cookie. She followed her husband Avraham to foreign lands and risked her life and her honor over and over again as a partner in their mission of bringing God-consciousness to mankind.

Why is it, asks the Midrash, that weeds grow strong and healthy without anybody planting or tending them, but before wheat grows a lot of work and sweat must be invested? Why is it that good people are often denied seeing their efforts rewarded? Why were the matriarchs barren? The answer is that God loves prayer. The tzaddik's prayer, in particular, recognizes lack as an opportunity for revealing God's goodness, which lies beneath the surface of pain and frustration.

One of Sarah's prayers serves as a sad but significant lesson in what *not* to pray for. When Avraham was on his way to becoming a parent from Sarah's co-wife, while Sarah remained yet barren, Sarah demanded that Heaven judge Avraham. As a result, she lost thirty-eight years of her life. ❦

┝── 5 • EXCUSES, LEGITIMATE AND OTHERWISE ──┥

Making excuses is an interesting aspect of human nature. We do it to avoid culpability and blame, to assuage hurt feelings and, most importantly, to rationalize and justify what we do, what we've done and what we're going to do.

Excuses also play an important function in hitbodedut. Firstly, they are part of the judgment that we render concerning ourselves. The challenges that God has planned for each of us specifically, along with those that come along with being human, often trip us up. We should certainly try to mitigate our wrongdoings so as to pay as small a penalty as possible. Leaping over extra hurdles and sidestepping debris in the road is just not fun.

Secondly, excuses facilitate the planning aspect of hitbodedut. If you know what and why you flubbed up the first time (and the second time and the third time and…), you are in a better position to think about what goals you can realistically set and devise the steps you can take to achieve them.

It's OK to give excuses, but they must be legitimate. Excuses are not and cannot be spin. Spin only works if you can bluff your audience. In hitbodedut, there are only two members in the audience, and one of them, God, can never be bluffed. That leaves only you. What's the point of fooling yourself? You're practicing hitbodedut in order to improve yourself, and that demands honesty. It also demands a standard.

There is a standard. Each of us knows that, but is unsure what it is. We tend to define it by piecing together different components: the mores of our community and of the Jewish people as a whole (both in its contemporary and historical incarnations), our readings of sacred Jewish texts, and the benchmarks of various facets of Jewishness modeled by tzaddikim (e.g. study, prayer, tzedakah, hospitality, community service, etc.). We accept, modify, reject, re-modify, and continually update and adjust the standard. In hitbodedut, you need to take your standard one step further and check it for veracity: "Will God accept this as a proper standard of Jewishness for *me*?" Intellectual exercises and speculations are one thing, but are you willing to wager your life on them?

If, after an honest appraisal, you feel you are not meeting your standard, most likely you have an excuse as to why.

Beware an excuse that assigns blame to others. Avoiding responsibility is an invitation to trouble. Your next encounter with temptation is likely to be another failure. Being unwilling or unable to accept the responsibility for the wrong you've done is an admission: I wanted to do it the first time, and I'll do it again. As Adam said when God confronted him about eating from the Tree of Knowledge, "The woman You gave me, gave me from the Tree, and I eat!"[29] (*Genesis* 3:12).

This is the hallmark of the illegitimate excuse: It denies responsibility. The falseness of such an attitude makes it repulsive. More importantly for the hitbodedut practitioner, it is dishonest and prevents growth. If there is nothing wrong with me, I need not improve in any way.

Even worse, the subtlety and corrosiveness of such an excuse nag at a person. Deep down he knows it's his fault. Yet since he doesn't want to admit it, he fights it constantly, keeping his pride—and passion—intact. In order to defend his false self—his weak self—wrong becomes right (*Rabbi Nachman's Wisdom* #10).

On the other hand, "God does not rule over His creatures with tyranny" (*Avodah Zarah* 3a). For example, if you stole something, tell God why. Don't be afraid. "God, my father bragged about cheating on his income tax return. My mother boasted how she won a shoplifting contest. I *want* to stop stealing, but it's more deeply entrenched in me than I thought. Help me to stop!" Excuses like these—namely, those based on a realistic appraisal of who you

---

[29] According to the Midrash, Adam said, "I ate, and I will eat again!" (*Bereishit Rabbah* 19:12).

actually are *now* rather than who you wish you were and hope yet to be—are legitimate. They won't absolve you of culpability, but in hitbodedut, not all excuses are meant to. Excuses such as these are also intended to keep your relationship with God honest and open; they will give you hope and strength.

> "OK. My folks were crooks and thieves. It's not going to be easy and it may take a while, but if I'm patient and try hard enough, sooner or later I'll lick this thing, with God's help. In the meantime, I'll be as careful as I can."

In order to avoid more unpleasantness, you also need to avoid complacency. If you meet—or surpass— your standard, make sure you're not stagnating. If you don't raise the bar, it's a sign that you've grown "old." You may already have begun an unnoticed, downward spiral.

Oh, do definitely acknowledge your progress and successes. Not doing so is a denial of God's kindness to you. Also, don't forget to "enjoy the view," the satisfaction that comes with accomplishment and new understanding. Just don't get comfortable. Don't accept this or any plateau as the last stop in your journey. There's a lot more for you to accomplish. If you don't attempt to continue on your own, God will trigger the necessary upheaval in your life to get you to the next level.[30]

As much as Rebbe Nachman pushes and pushes, encourages and encourages, he also provides us with excuses, and very good ones at that. Rebbe Nachman lets us know that relative to God's greatness and infinity, anything we do pales in significance. God is so immense that even the highest angel cannot say that it truly serves God the way He deserves to be served. How could anyone? This excuse can explain away a lot of mistakes and failures on our part. And it also makes every smidgen of Jewishness that we do muster into a very precious gift. Denied perfection, we show yearning. God counts that in our favor.

---

[30] As occurs to the burgher's son in "The Burgher and the Pauper" (*Rabbi Nachman's Stories* #10).

Remember these stories the next time you don't live up to who you can be:

> Rebbe Nachman once commented, "Even if I were to commit the biggest sin, it would not throw me at all. I would not backslide at all. I would simply repent" (*Tzaddik* #453).

> A Breslover chassid once slipped as he was walking, badly bruising himself in the process. He got up slowly, overcoming his pain. Someone who didn't particularly like Breslover chassidim laughed at him: "Ha, ha! You fell because you are a Breslover!" "No, my friend, you are mistaken," the man replied. "Because I'm a Breslover, I got up."

> One morning my friend came late to yeshivah. He looked a bit dejected. "What's the matter?" I asked him. "For the first time in years, I missed praying with the sunrise minyan at the Kotel," he said sadly. "Don't worry," someone else interjected. "You're still Jewish."

The goal is not perfection, since only God is perfect. But here's a secret: You have unlimited longing for God. The goal is to nourish that longing, no matter what obstacles you may face in actualizing it. ✿

ELIEZER

Eliezer was Avraham's servant. He well understood that his role in life was to be subservient to Avraham and Avraham's mission. Thus, when he was sent to find a suitable partner for Yitzchak, his master's son, Eliezer prayed for his master's success. He prayed that the genesis of the Jewish people, which had commenced with Yitzchak's birth, should continue. Right there at the well, Eliezer's prayers were answered. Rivkah, our second matriarch, appeared, and did the kindness of drawing water for Eliezer and for all his camels. ✿

⊢── 6 • MAKING REQUESTS ──⊣

You are a physical being in a material world. You have real needs, such as breathing and eating. You have preferences as to how these needs should be met. For example, if you need to commute to work, you might prefer door-to-door service in a chauffeured limousine to riding the subway. You prefer fresh challah to stale bagels.

At each stage of your spiritual growth, you will have to meet your needs and, to some extent, your preferences. Rebbe Nachman teaches that you *must* ask God to provide your physical needs. He points out that that even though God could (and most often does) provide your needs without your requesting them, living like this puts you into the same category as cattle or fish, which also receive their needs without praying for them.

Not only is this not the type of company you want to keep, but not making requests determines the quality of what you have. For example, if you have a loaf of bread for which you did not pray, it is spiritually equivalent to fodder. The effort you will need to invest in order to transform the physical energy you receive from eating the bread into a well-focused prayer, Torah study or act of kindness may be more than you can give. Fodder-like energy may, God forbid, push you towards the barn. (Don't despair in thinking of your fodder-filled pantry. Even at the eleventh hour, when you've already purchased your vittles, or have them cooked and sitting on the plate in front of you, you can still offer a prayer asking God to provide you with proper food. Even if you've already eaten, the blessing after a meal can retroactively raise the spiritual quality of your food and eating.)

Had you prayed for it, that same loaf of bread would be chock-full of spiritual energy that could help you clarify your faith, awareness and awe of God. (I write "could" because you still need to wage an intense battle to choose and maintain focus on acquiring these traits.) Even though your prayers in general and your hitbodedut in particular should be focused on spiritual concerns, make sure to request what you need in order to function in this world, even if it's "only" a button or a shoelace. It's not beneath your dignity to mention it.

Of course, you also have responsibilities to others that need tending. Junior needs to stop running around with a bad crowd, Missy needs help in school, your spouse needs relief from job-induced stress and your parents need eldercare. Using hitbodedut to help formulate a proper plan for dealing with each situation, as well as for praying for a "happy ending," is a valid way to spend your hitbodedut time.

The primary objective of hitbodedut, however, is your spiritual growth, the nurturing and extending of your connection with God, so that faith fills every nook and cranny of your day. Often as not your motives will be pure, or seem to be, but still you need to be alert to the traps and pitfalls that can damage even the most heartfelt prayers.

THREE TYPES OF REQUESTS

In general, the requests you make in hitbodedut fall into three categories. The first category is asking for something material simply for its own sake. The classic example of this is the thief standing on the threshold of a break-in who mutters, "Please, God, help me get away with it." The chutzpah of asking God for help in acting counter to His hope and desire for mankind is only part of what is wrong with such a petition. The other is that the thief's goal is purely material. He has no real need for God's purpose, only for His power.

While you are not a thief, if you request of God something that you need only for some selfish pleasure, you are "stealing" God's power for your own purposes. This is certainly *not* a desired use of hitbodedut. So a prayer along the lines of, "Lord, won't You buy me a Mercedes-Benz?" is suspect. Yet even a prayer for something that seems spiritual, such as amassing Torah knowledge, can be perverted if one's interest in that goal is only some material benefit (e.g., honor and fame).

The second category, requesting material goods, is more than just legitimate, it's necessary for genuine humanness. Furthermore, if you request the material benefit so you can serve God without headaches or worries, or so you can give tzedakah and do kindness, this type of request reflects what Rebbe Nachman calls "talking to God about what one lacks in service of God."[31] However, because what you're asking for is material, there *is* the ever-present danger that your intentions may be deflected or diverted from the proper goal you initially had, to one that is contrary to your spiritual growth. You may want a car so you can more easily attend Torah classes. Is there any guarantee that you won't end up using it as a getaway vehicle?

The ultimate in requests is the kind which King David used to compose the psalms—prayers pleading with God for His closeness, His kindness, His protection and His help in observing the Torah, its law and its spirit. The requests in this category serve as a crown for the Torah. They don't just make the Torah appear regal, but they acknowledge and accept the Torah's instructions and values as the ruling principles of life.

Rebbe Nachman says that when hitbodedut is used to gain closeness to God, it "rises to an extremely high level." This is especially so, he continues, when a Torah lesson is used as a basis and outline for hitbodedut (see page 176).[32] The delight that Heaven gets from this exercise is extraordinary.

---

[31] Even though the holy Zohar says that one who asks for material concerns is like a barking dog, Reb Noson explains that this refers to one who asks *only* for the material because he is unconcerned about the spiritual.

[32] One who bases a prayer on a Torah lesson is asking *only* for his soul's needs.

THINK BIG

Let me tell you about a problem from which many people, perhaps even you, suffer. They think small, much too small, when they ask God to help them. A person in debt would consider himself fortunate if he could pay his bills on time, so that's what he asks for. *Think big!* Ask for a large fortune so that you can lavish money on worthwhile charities, or so you can honor Shabbat as it should be honored without thinking twice.

Don't just plead to get married or have children. Ask to have a beautiful, intelligent, loving, caring spouse with whom to build a true Jewish home and live happily ever after. Ask for children who will be well-adjusted human beings, who will be Torah scholars and pillars of the community, people who will bring pride and joy not only to you, but to God and the entire Jewish nation.

Pray for a Torah guide who will not only teach you the basics, but who will cure your soul of its pain and diseases. Ask God for a mentor who will draw, ease and tease out of your soul every ray of light and bit of fragrance that it potentially possesses, someone who can teach you to savor each mitzvah and give you legs to walk on even when the journey turns dark and stormy. Don't pray that you will contribute "something" to bettering the world—pray that you will contribute to tikkun haolam to the fullest measure that you possibly can.

> Berel, a chassidic friend of mine, is a big guy. Even by chassidic standards, his yarmulke is big, his tzitzit are big and his mezuzot are jumbo-sized. "Why so big?" I once asked. He answered, "If someone likes steak, does he want a little steak or a big steak? If someone likes ice cream, does he want a little dish or a big dish? I love being Jewish! I want everything about my Jewishness to be BIG!"

Sometimes we stop ourselves from thinking big because we don't want to be beholden to anyone. This desire, a stepchild of ingratitude, prevents us from asking for things that are really beneficial. The price of not asking cannot be measured, for the lost opportunities are legion.

One caveat, however, for thinking big: Pray that you will be able to receive God's goodness without being harmed. Don't be like those rags-to-riches winners of the lottery whose lives are destroyed because they're incapable of managing so much wealth. Don't be like the sage Acher, the master of Kabbalah who entered the highest chambers of mysticism but exited a heretic.[33] Don't be blinded by the light. ❧

YITZCHAK

Twenty years of marriage and still no children. Not only did Yitzchak, our second patriarch, not curtail his efforts, he increased them. He churned out prayers and heaped them upon God, as it were. This was not an easy thing for Yitzchak to do. He was quite the intellectual, basing his entire life on critical thinking: "Is this a good idea or not? Is it going to work or not?" Rivkah, his wife, our second matriarch, was not a silent partner in this prayerful endeavor. In fact, it was her influence on him that allowed Yitzchak to develop his prayerful side.

Their prayers were answered. Rivkah bore children, and the embryo of the Jewish people continued to develop.

For those of us who need encouragement to pause and create an oasis of peace in the tumult of the day's events, Yitzchak did some of his best praying in the afternoon, when the light grows shorter and the shadows longer. ❧

---

[33] See page 236.

⊢— 7 • WHAT ELSE CAN I TALK ABOUT? —⊣

It should not come as a surprise that things and matters Jewish can certainly provide nourishment for your hitbodedut. Shabbat is less than a week away. Besides challah, wine and candles, there's something else you need for Shabbat—Shabbat itself! This was a prayer of Reb Shlomo Karliner: "Dear God! You gave us fish for Shabbat. You gave us meat for Shabbat. Please give us Shabbat for Shabbat!" The calm, the joy, God's quiet embrace—these things don't come automatically. They are "on the shelf." You have to ask for them.

> It was the eve of the Sukkot festival. Reb Noson's student, Reb Nachman Tulchiner, was assigned the mitzvah of building the sukkah. That night, after they had ushered in the festival and were enjoying their meal, Reb Nachman commented, "One appreciates the sukkah much more after he has invested so much time and effort in building it." Reb Noson responded, "One appreciates the mitzvah of sukkah that much more after he has prayed and prayed, 'God! Give me a taste of the mitzvah of sukkah!'"

There are a lot of mitzvot out there. How many of them have you tasted lately? We actually do a lot of mitzvot every day, most of them without even knowing it. We do acts of kindness (called "chessed" in Hebrew) for others throughout the day—domestic functions, lending a pen, giving a ride, telling someone the time and giving directions are some examples. A friendly face and a sympathetic ear are monumental kindnesses that we can and ought to give. The Talmud relates the following story:

> Rabbi Beroka was in the marketplace with the Prophet Elijah. Rabbi Beroka asked, "Are there any people here who are worthy of Olam Haba?"

"Let me see," Elijah answered. "No, not yet. Wait. Those two guys who just showed up."

Rabbi Beroka went over to the two and struck up a conversation. "So, what do you guys do here in the market?"

"We see if there's anyone who looks like he needs cheering up," the men replied. "We start talking to him, tell a few jokes, and don't leave till he's in a better mood. Or, if we see two people arguing, we go over to them and get them to lighten up, so they can resolve their differences peacefully."

Having faith in God and placing your trust in Him are also mitzvot[34] that you can do continuously, literally every second that you are awake, and perhaps even while you are asleep. How many of these mitzvot, or of the mitzvot that you can see and touch, like matzah and mezuzah, do you really *taste*? How often do you ask God to be admitted into a mitzvah and *feel* its simcha?

This is where the study of Torah enters. When it comes to a mitzvah, you're either doing it or not. For example, you either light Chanukah candles or not, wash your hands before eating bread or not, say the Grace After Meals or not. Rebbe Nachman suggests that some of your hitbodedut should be devoted to requesting that you move beyond *wanting* to perform a certain mitzvah (or mitzvot) to actually *doing* it (or them). Sadly, many people think that performance is the end of the story. "I did the mitzvah, I'm OK." They think that there's some "Divine checklist" that has items that need to be checked off, and if they do that, they're sufficiently Jewish. What they don't realize is that doing a mitzvah is just the beginning. A mitzvah is a door; doing a mitzvah opens the door to an incredible wonderland. Behind the door is God.

Recognizing the mitzvah wonderland and finding your way around it requires Torah study. As you study, you become aware of many connections between one mitzvah and another, of the many concepts and ideals embedded in each mitzvah, and of the genius, subtle beauty and love that pervade life, if you know what

---

[34] Having faith in God and Torah may even be among your top priorities. Finding a top-flight spiritual mentor, if you don't have one already, should certainly be a priority!

you're looking at and how to receive.[35] This is what the Midrash means when it says that each mitzvah introduced herself to each and every Jew, asking if she would be accepted. When you said yes, the mitzvah kissed you—on the lips.

When you ponder the meaning and practice of mitzvot during hitbodedut, your Jewishness becomes fresher and more renewed each day. Your yearning, longing and genuine interest for starting and maintaining this process actually feed your hitbodedut.

Chumash, the other sections of the Written Torah, Mishnah, Talmud, Midrash, Zohar, halakhah, Rebbe Nachman's teachings and those of other chassidic masters, as well as of many other tzaddikim, serve both as keys to the doors and maps of the mitzvah wonderland. The sad fact, however, is that many of us lack the necessary skills, time or proper teachers to show us which keys unlock which doors, and how to read the maps.

Thankfully, we live in an era in which many Torah works are available in translation, and in written and audio formats. Most of us have patches and slivers of time, even if we don't have blocks and chunks. There is time on Shabbat, other days off, while commuting and during coffee breaks. If you don't have a teacher, do your best to be your own teacher.

Rebbe Nachman tells us about a person who lived long, long ago. There were no Jews in his community and no yeshivas in any nearby towns or distant villages. This person was all alone in his spiritual quest and had no one from whom to receive instruction about how to live a sacred life. Nonetheless, he was consumed with love for God. God therefore opened for him the primordial Torah so that he would be able to transform his yearning into concrete deeds. This person was our first patriarch, Avraham.

---

[35] Rebbe Nachman teaches that the Ten Utterances with which God created the world (the famous "Let there be's") contain within them the Ten Commandments, which themselves encapsulate the entire Torah. Therefore, any thing, endeavor or enterprise in this world contains Torah. All events, interactions and aspects of your life—past, present and future—are inseparably linked to Torah. Anything can serve as a topic of hitbodedut and as an entree to the Creator, because every facet and grain of Creation manifests some jot of Torah.

Even if you are unable to learn as you would like, this should not prevent you from improving your connection with God. There are other steps and paths[36] that will lead you closer to the Divine. Although Rebbe Nachman advocated extreme diligence in Torah study, he balanced that by saying one should not be anxious if he cannot study as much as he hopes to. One can be a tzaddik even without being a scholar. "Deep perception cannot be attained without Talmudic scholarship, but even the simplest Jew can be a tzaddik. 'You are not obligated to complete the job, but neither are you free to do nothing about it' (*Avot* 2:16)." ✳

RIVKAH

Rivkah, our second matriarch, is the personification of prayer, as alluded to in the Shabbat prayer, Nishmat.

Rivkah grew up in a rough environment. Dad and her domineering older brother were atheists. They weren't above thievery or murder, either. The neighbors were pagans. Yet even as a very young girl, Rivkah found the courage and strength to become a model for kindness to humans and animals. She worked so hard at prayer that she achieved prophecy.

No matter how bleak your situation looks, remember that the light of God's kindness can shine through the darkest clouds. Dig a little deeper into yourself and pray a little more, and a little more on top of that.

Get God to daven for you! The more enthusiastic you are about davening for what you think needs to be prayed for, the sooner God will pray for it, too. ✳

---

[36] The steps include character traits such as patience, kindliness and diligence; the paths are broadly defined as Torah, prayer and acts of kindness.

8 • TALKING TO THE BODY

This is a type of hitbodedut that is certainly not for everybody. If this mode of hitbodedut seems too extreme, then most likely it is not for you. Please feel free to skip this chapter and go on to the next one. If you are brave, however, you will gain some helpful advice.

> Rebbe Nachman advised one of his students to use his hitbodedut to speak to each part of his body. He was to tell each limb, in its turn, that physical pleasure was futile because ultimately the body would die. Then it would be taken to be buried in a grave where it would decompose and rot.
>
> The student duly followed Rebbe Nachman's advice. Some time later, he reported to the Rebbe that his body was not responding. Rebbe Nachman told him not to be discouraged and to continue his efforts. Ultimately, he would see results.
>
> Eventually, he did. The student was so successful at convincing his external limbs and internal organs that there was no point in enjoying physical pleasure that they became almost totally deadened, so much so that the student required great determination to hold on to his life.

(Well, I told you it was extreme!)

While this particular mode of hitbodedut is reserved for a very special few, there are nonetheless some lessons that we can glean from it.

First of all, we see that our hitbodedut doesn't have to be exclusively directed to God. Our words can be directed to "others" who are able to "hear" what we say. In fact, Rebbe Nachman teaches that words can even be effective when addressed to a gun, preventing it from firing!

Secondly, although Rebbe Nachman's advice to that long-ago student was extreme, you and I can use it effectively in a lesser degree. For example, if someone is prone to violence, he can talk to his hands and tell them not to hit, explaining to them why it's wrong to hurt people. If one suffers from kleptomania, she can tell her hands about the evil of stealing. A person can lecture his eyes about avoiding immorality and viewing other people kindly, and tell his mouth to speak encouragingly and not harshly.

Admittedly, this path in hitbodedut is not for everybody, but it is a good tool to have at your disposal. Keep it handy. ❋

YAAKOV

Yaakov, our third patriarch, spent fourteen years as a yeshivah student. To squeeze the most out of his time, he said psalms. When the next phase of his life commenced and his circumstances changed, he changed the focus of his prayers accordingly. He prayed for food, clothing and God's overall protection.

Yaakov faced many dismal situations. His only brother wanted to kill him. His nephew stole everything he had. He came penniless and empty-handed to a foreign land seeking his bride. His father-in-law tried to cheat him dozens of times, and his brothers-in-law slandered him. So for those of us who think that the sun has set on our life and will never rise again, take heart. Yaakov did his best praying at night. ❋

⊢ 9 • Daydreaming My Hitbodedut Away ⊣

A very big obstacle in the practice of hitbodedut is one of the very obstacles that hitbodedut is meant to get rid of—daydreaming. You've made the time, you've found the place, you want to talk and you know what you want to talk about. You're not sleepy, you're feeling fearless and you're ready to get into the nitty-gritty, yet...instead of focusing and getting down to business, your mind starts to wander.

Every sort of nonsense and irrelevant topic keeps rising up in your mind. You keep swatting at them, but they just don't seem to go away. *Oy!* Lots of folks just give up after a few minutes. "Darn! I was so psyched and it just wouldn't go." The disappointment and frustration are often palpable. They don't have to be. There are ways to succeed. In order to access them, though, you've first got to have the will. *Don't quit—sit!*

Rebbe Nachman teaches:

Thought is under a person's control; he can direct it wherever he chooses, for it is impossible to entertain two thoughts simultaneously.

Even if one's thoughts occasionally fly off into the fantastic and the bizarre, it is still within his power to redirect his thoughts—against their will—to the straight path, to think what is fitting.

This is analogous to a horse that turns off the trail and heads down the wrong path. You grab him by the reins and guide him back to the trail.

Thought is exactly the same. It can be grabbed against its will and forced back to the proper path.

There are two general categories of thought. One is what Rebbe Nachman calls seikhel (intellect or reason), the other is imagination. Here, as in all his analogies, Rebbe Nachman chooses his comparisons carefully. He draws on the Zohar's teaching: The rider is not subordinate to the horse; the horse is subordinate to the rider.

You are the rider. You are in charge of the horse, not the other way around. No matter how confused, damaged and weak your seikhel may be, it is strong enough to overcome your imagination. You have to grab the reins.

The main battleground of life is in the mind. Your ability to perceive clearly, versus your tendency to fantasize, is the hardest, most enduring, subtlest and fiercest test. You must wrest the reins from imagination's hands!

Confusion and distractions disturb not only you. They disturb everybody. The human condition in general is one of struggle, the incessant toil with internal and external conditions that are uncomfortable and contrary to our desire. The most pervasive struggle is the battle against the unwanted thoughts that bombard us. The struggle for control in order to maintain proper, focused thinking is never-ending. It will continue to your final moment. Before death there is no ultimate victory (and so the battle continues), but neither is there permanent defeat (and so there's no reason to give up).

You are fortunate that your struggle involves ridding your mind of unwanted thoughts. Your struggle itself is your precious gift to God. Your struggle is a win-win situation, because even if you *just can't* get rid of a particular ugly or dire thought, the struggle is a victory. Why? Because it indicates that you consider your mind *yours*, not someone else's, and that you want it to be a welcome home for God.

If you do get rid of that ugly thought, whether permanently or even just temporarily, you've certainly won a significant victory. The fact that you purged the ugly thought was not accidental. It represented a successful choice as well as a struggle on your part. It serves as proof that you *can* control your thinking.

Your thoughts may be used to running to the absurd and perverse. You may have never realized that you can tell them, "No!" Just grab hold of the bridle and drag them back to where *you choose* them to be. Whatever you do, *don't look back!* That gives legs to the thoughts you want to escape! Stealth is your *modus operandi* here. Think about Torah or your business, comedy (highbrow or low-brow), but don't look over your shoulder—those dire thoughts may be gaining on you![37]

THE HEART OF THE STRUGGLE

Struggling is, well, a struggle. It's hard—it may even hurt—to keep your mind free of wrong-thinking and keep it focused on right-thinking, but it's part of the medicine the soul needs to take. The brit (covenant) which we Jews made with God includes the attitude, state of mind and dedication that is necessary for and characterized by tzaddik-like self-control in the face of temptation and distraction. The struggle takes serious effort and often drains us of happiness, a counterproductive by-product if ever there was one. So be smart enough, while you're struggling, to take joy and smile: Despite my setbacks and failures, I'm fortunate to be allied with a teacher such as Rebbe Nachman.

Many an individual finds it disconcerting and discouraging that he has to battle his thoughts so long and so hard. Wouldn't it be better, he thinks, if he could spend his time and energy discovering the cure for cancer? Wouldn't it be better to spend his time on the obviously holy, like Torah study and prayer? Not necessarily. This kind of conclusion betrays our limited perspective. Do you think that while we're busy doing our tikkun haolam, God is just sitting back, watching us and letting us make all the decisions about what to do next? Not at all. He intervenes, pointing each of us towards his next job. Often that "next job" is the "Battle of the Thoughts," the score of which is not tallied by how many unwanted thoughts you cast out, but by your beads of sweat.

---

[37] See Appendix E for more about quieting the mind.

The fact that you invest so much time and effort in struggling against wrong-thinking and are prevented from coming up with a cure for cancer is not your concern. That's Heaven's affair. What you are thinking (i.e., your need to struggle) may be wrong for the goals you had hoped to achieve, but they are right for what God hopes from His creation. Just follow your teacher's instructions.

Kola b'machashavah itberiru ("Everything is purified through thought" [*Zohar* 2:254b]). *All* tikkun haolam has its genesis in *your* thinking. *All* tikkun haolam begins in *your* mind. As thoughts come into your head, you have to select which ones to keep and which ones to reject.

The Midrash tells us that when Pharaoh set out to capture the Israelites by the Red Sea, he and his army came on horses of different colors—red, black, white and spotted. Each horse in Pharaoh's cavalry had its own gait. Red horses ran to anger and to violence, and to passion for food, sex, money and power. Black horses galloped to the quicksand of depression and despair. White horses had the zealous gait of mistaken religious fervor for seeming mitzvot which are sanctioned by Rabbi Pharaoh, but which are not really mitzvot at all. Spotted horses had a drunken gait—thinking that is inconsistent at best and unstable at worst.

When the Egyptian army appeared on the horizon, the Israelites were rightfully terrified. They were so many of them! Moshe told the Jewish people to remain silent; God would fight their battle. We shouldn't be frightened when encountering the unruly thoughts represented by Pharaoh's horses. Moshe, the clear thinker, taught us to not respond directly to the wrong thought.

Surprising, counter-intuitive, but true: Direct combat with such thoughts only makes them stronger. Much too strong for us. The silent response (a la "don't look over your shoulder") is your strongest response. If one of Pharaoh's horses canters into your mind, wait with patient silence. God will send one of *His* horses to take its place, and you'll be back on track.

Pharaoh's horses, the products of fantasy and imagination, are there only because *God put them there.* He put them there to get you to see through the illusion and choose God rather than the illusion.

Put your hand in His. Cry out for His help. If you cannot actually cry out, at least raise your eyes to seek His help.

BACK ON TRACK

We've said it before and we'll say it again: The first and most primary battleground in your life is your mind. The clearer it is, the clearer will be your thinking and the more successful you will be in your Jewishness. That's because clearing the mind of foolishness, and keeping it clear of bad thinking of every sort, forestalls the blurring of your faith.

You can keep your thoughts on track by making use of two features of the mind. One is that thinking never stops, even when you're asleep. The other is that the mind cannot entertain more than one thought at a time.

The fact that thinking never stops is quite to your advantage. If your thinking always came to a stop at a wrong thought, you would be a loser (somewhat akin to a roulette wheel coming up on a number other than the one you played). Since, however, the mind will continue on to another thought, the wrong one can be dislodged and replaced by a proper one.

The less obvious advantage is that you are forced to continuously work at feeding your mind right-thinking. There is no "magic trick" or "knockout punch" at your disposal. It's a lifelong struggle that you must accept and learn to deal with. Seeking right-thinking demands devotion and forbearance, because a pursuit of right-thinking that is not persistent is no pursuit at all.

So whenever you sense your thoughts spinning out of control, it won't work to just slam on the brakes ("I will not think about cheeseburgers! I will not think about cheeseburgers!"). Instead, interject a series of quick, short thoughts to replace them. Think of things that are easy and brief, like the alef-bet or the Shema. If it isn't distressing, you can think of your bank balance or of errands you need to do. Above all, remain calm. Even though your guard might have been down and your thoughts veered off your chosen road, or even if your thoughts spin 180 degrees into the opposite direction, you can always steer yourself back on track with different thoughts.

A second feature of thinking is that at any instant, the mind can hold only one thought and no more. A quart jar can contain only one quart. Add another and the first one is displaced. The human mind can contain only one thought. Add another and the first one is displaced.

So as soon as you notice that you're thinking something that you'd rather not, just substitute something kosher and wholesome. Notice what you're thinking and refocus. All you need to do is gently nudge a kosher thought—even a small, weak one—into your mind. The ugly, non-kosher thought will automatically be displaced, no matter how big and powerful it was. Even a fleeting thought of good leaves a permanent trace. So does each one that follows. All of them combine again and again to help you face the next challenge.

The appearance of not being able to control your thoughts— the seeming inability to keep at bay the fantasies, delusions, mistaken perceptions, naughty thoughts, confusion, sadness[38] and contemplations of sin that vie for space in our minds—is just an illusion, another lie to keep you away from Jewishness. The constant, exceedingly rapid, perpetual motion of thought creates this illusion.

---

[38] Even though Rebbe Nachman teaches that joy resides essentially in the heart, he also teaches that the mind has to be joyful, as well.

As powerful an illusion as it may be—and it is often overwhelming—it is still only an illusion. You can step in and take control. Reb Noson writes that anything a person wants to say or do starts with a thought. That initial thought arises imperceptibly, without conscious awareness. The thought evolves and unfolds, moving into the conscious mind. At that point, the person begins to consider whether he should say or do something, or refrain from saying and doing; how and when he should say or do something, or refrain from it. He then makes his decision and acts.

This sequence takes place with even the most insignificant word that one utters. It happens so very rapidly, however, that one is not at all aware of the process or any of its stages. It is only when considering a matter of import that one can follow the stages of development and watch the thought develop.

However, this sequence does not take place at all if you have rejected the incipient thought for being spurious, the kind of thought you don't want to entertain. For example, the time to decide not to eat a cheeseburger is not when you're unwrapping it at the local drive-through (although if you think of it then, wrap the burger back up and toss it in the trash). The time to decide not to eat a cheeseburger is the moment you realize that you're thinking, "Gee, I'd really like to eat a cheeseburger."

> The millionaire was interviewing candidates for the position of chauffeur. "If you were driving on a mountain road, how close to the edge of the cliff would you go?" he asked his applicants.
>
> "One inch," answered the first candidate.
>
> "Half an inch," replied the second.
>
> The third said, "A quarter-inch."
>
> The fourth responded, "I would stay as far away as possible."
>
> "You're hired," said the millionaire.

Admittedly, ignoring unwanted thoughts is easier said than done, because these thoughts are so persistent. Many of these thoughts are, in and of themselves, innocuous nudniks and pestering bores. But they do get in the way of progress and consume valuable time. What's particularly annoying is that they seem to show up when you specifically want to practice your hitbodedut!

Like all good nudniks, they thrive on attention. Therefore, the best defense is a good offense. Just pay attention to what you are saying. Even if you have to repeat a phrase or a sentence over and over, keep at it. You can also be a nudnik. And don't look over your shoulder to see if those bothersome thoughts are gone.

THE SECRET WEAPON

Some of the thoughts that try to hijack your mind (remember, it is yours) do constitute a present and immediate danger. You may feel that your mind is swarming with them and has been teeming with them since forever. Sometimes the workings of your mind may get so bad, so palpably dark, that you feel you can't go on for another hour, let alone another day. You may feel as Emily Dickinson did, that there is a funeral in your brain, with mourners treading to and fro. Or perhaps Samuel Johnson's black dog is constantly at your side, barking from breakfast to supper. The details of depressive thinking are definitely different for each individual, but many have suffered this phenomenon to a greater or lesser degree.

Relax, there is hope. The happier a person is, the better will be his thinking and the more control he can exert over his thinking. The more unhappy a person is, the worse will be his thinking and the more his thinking will control him. Simcha is the key to banishing those black demons.

Why simcha? Simcha means joy, optimism and enthusiasm. The flip side of simcha is pessimism, negativity and despair. Pessimism breeds cynicism, destructive criticism and a "can't do" attitude. Negativity creates its own failure—the excuses are built-in. Despair is usually measured broadly. If it is not writ large, it goes unrecognized, which can be a serious—and potentially fatal—mistake.

The ultimate of despair is suicide. The pain and frustration of failure, of being ignored or actively rejected, combined with the nausea of a futile existence and the never-ending disappointment of fleeting pleasures, make suicide not only seem like a genuine option, but like the best one. This is wrong-thinking at its ugliest. It presumes to see a void where there is a future; it pretends to see that which is not there. "There is no such thing as despair!" Rebbe Nachman exclaimed. "Don't give up!"

Don't give up—on any of your goals or aspirations. To think that you've reached a plateau in your understanding or awareness is despair. To think that you've already prayed from the bottom of your heart, or that your heart contains not a drop more of love for others, is despair. To think that a cigarette or alcohol or a cookie or a website is stronger than you, that you cannot overcome an addiction, is despair.

Nu, so what's wrong with a little despair? Firstly, since it doesn't exist, it is a fiction. Making fiction-based decisions is not a wise way to live. More crucially, despair is anti-Divine. Rebbe Nachman points out many a time that despair precipitates the abuse of sexuality. The abuse and misuse of sexuality can take place in many, many ways at all levels of behavior, speech, thought and desire. The commonality of all misused sexuality is that it produces nothing good and too often produces bad.

The Zohar teaches that the main challenge a person faces in life is the challenge of sexuality. Our desire to connect with another and become part of something greater, to give up our self and give of our self to create life, becomes so twisted that our giving becomes taking, our connecting begets distance and anonymity, and the only life we want is our own, convenient one. Despair is what causes this.

God hates despair. (Don't despair because of this! You can change your attitude.) Despair pushes us out of His presence, as it were. Despair denies God's care and concern, His wisdom and His goals. Despair kicks God out of creation and prevents Him, as it were, from providing good. No wonder He hates it!

Human failure is built-in to life. You are human, therefore you will make mistakes. Big ones. Little ones. Often. At the worst possible moments. Colossal, cruel and stupid ones. Accidental and malicious ones. Unavoidably, every one of us is forced from the throne of right-behavior. How do we respond to losing the crown so that we may regain it? By maintaining—or re-creating—an attitude of simcha.

To rule over your self (and, by extension, the corner of the universe with which God has entrusted you), you must be b'simcha, in a state of joy. It is one of the indispensable qualities that a monarch must have.

The rewards of simcha are many. Simcha makes you smarter and more perceptive; it brings peace and healing; and it gives you greater self-control, enabling you to do what you need to improve your Jewishness.

Here are some suggestions that Rebbe Nachman gives for cheering up:

1. Give tzedakah or do favors for people (or volunteer work).

2. Dance or do some healthy physical activity.

3. Sing.

4. Put some more trust in God.

5. Read Talmudic stories. ❧

So be patient. Ask for the resolve to keep on keeping on. Distract yourself from what needs to be forgotten and do nothing. Perhaps you will be able to do something good. Even if not, at least you will have done nothing bad.

If necessary, *scream the screams you need to scream.* Play the games you need to play. Pray the prayers you need to pray, even if your brain and heart are uninvolved and far, far from where you are. If you cannot do even that, then just look to Heaven for help. You are in the throes of the harshest, most unforgiving struggle. Even if you were caught off-guard, even if you have already been brought to your knees, it is not too late to ready yourself for the struggle that remains.

Attempting to fight off the mourners and the black dog is *already* victory. Another weapon at your disposal is the toughness of the tzaddik, the spiritual master who serves as your guide, mentor and teacher. He has been down this way too, and cleared a path so that you may arrive where you must. The worse life appears, the more you have to thank God: At least I know of such a tzaddik and want to follow in his footsteps.

Even if you have stumbled badly many, many times, and you feel like you cannot control your thinking, you know that this is not true. The proof is that here and there, you have succeeded in exercising such self-control. If you believe that you can mis-think, believe that you can right-think. In the interim, do no evil.

KEEP TRYING

Rebbe Nachman is well known for his motto, "It is a great mitzvah to always be cheerful and optimistic." Yet Rebbe Nachman knew that this mitzvah was all too elusive, often slipping between our fingers before we even grasp it. So he revealed a most important tool for sowing joy: *Pretend* to be happy.

Some people have difficulty with the idea of pretending because it's false, an act. "I'm not happy. Pretending that I am is dishonest, a lie that keeps me from dealing with the harsh truths of my life." To this I say, "Don't pretend to be happy. *Practice* being happy."

This is not some verbal sleight-of-hand to trick you into pretending. Imagine that you have the goal of becoming a concert pianist. It's not enough to take lessons; you must practice. At first—and for a long time—you will play poorly. The more you practice, though, the better you will play. The more you practice simcha, the more you'll get the hang of it.

Reb Noson reports that Rebbe Nachman spoke many times of the impossibility to fathom God's kindness. The future does not yet exist; don't project any negative thoughts onto it. The small wheel—your life—may be on fire, turning and turning, so that you feel you can't hold on. It's impossible to go back or to stand still. You feel that if the thunder didn't get you, the lightning will. Don't think like this. The big wheel—of Life—turns by the grace of God. Each time it does, you cover a little more ground.

And so Rebbe Nachman indicated that you need to maintain your composure. Don't crumble, no matter what. Try just a little bit harder. Try just a little bit more. Not only will this pass; it will become good.

> The prisoner had already spent twelve years in jail. He wasn't given a sentence. He was just placed in jail on a trumped-up charge. No judge, no jury, no witnesses. He was a stranger in a strange land, with no friends "on the outside."
>
> The prisoner awoke that morning just as he had the previous thousands of mornings—a prisoner of the state. Nothing indicated that he wouldn't go to sleep just as he had for thousands of nights— a prisoner of the state. Then the king's guards entered.
>
> The prisoner was given a shave, a haircut and presentable clothes. Then he was brought to Pharaoh. Yosef interpreted Pharaoh's dream and instructed the monarch how to prepare for the impending famine. Pharaoh appointed Yosef as the new viceroy.
>
> Wake up serving life, go to sleep viceroy of the world's biggest superpower.
>
> One never knows. ❁

LEAH

"Leah's eyes were soft." Rashi comments: Her eyes were soft
from weeping, because people kept saying, "Rivkah has two
sons and Lavan [Rivkah's brother] has two daughters. The older
son should marry the older daughter [Esav to Leah] and the
younger son, the younger daughter [Yaakov to Rachel]" (Rashi
on *Genesis* 29:17).

Leah was curious: Who was this Esav that was being suggested
for her? She did some investigating, and what she found out
distressed her no end. Was this to be her lot, to be the partner
of one whose life revolved around murder, adultery and self-
worship? Who covered himself with a veneer of respectability,
so that he appeared to be virtuous and civic-minded? Was she
supposed to live a lie?

She cried to God. She cried and cried until her eyes were "soft"
from tears. She cried until God heard her prayers and changed
her intended husband. Not only did Leah not marry Esav,
but she was the first to marry Yaakov. She was privileged to
give birth to half of the Twelve Tribes, the progenitors of the
Jewish people. She is the grandmother of King David, author of
Psalms. She is the grandmother of the Mashiach, whose coming
we await every day. All this as a result of her tears, the tears
that made her eyes beautiful.

What's this got to do with you? You—your soul—are Leah.
People want to marry you to a lifestyle of dishonesty, adultery
and self-worship. Do you want to live that lie? Any lie? It is all
too possible. Can you avoid it?

Yes. You—your soul—are Leah. You can pray, beg, beseech
and cry to God to be saved from such a "marriage." You
can plead to be worthy of Yaakov-like truthfulness, honesty,
respectability and closeness to God. The more you pray, the
more you'll be divorced from Esav and married to Yaakov. ✽

⊢── 10 • MEASURING YOUR OWN WORTH ──⊣

Some people are trapped by a different feeling, a feeling of worthlessness. Nothing will change even if outside circumstances and events do. They feel like a little *i*.

Do you know what *i* is? *i* is the square root of -1. In case you've forgotten, the square root of a number is a number that, when multiplied by itself, yields that number. For example, the square root of 4 is 2. When 2 is multiplied by itself, 2 x 2 equals 4.

When we multiply two negative numbers, the result is always positive (e.g., -1 x -1 = 1). The only way to get a negative answer is to multiply a positive number by a negative one. However, since a square root is a number multiplied by itself, it seems that *i* does not exist. In mathematical jargon, *i* is called an imaginary number.

Many people feel this way about themselves. They feel like an *i*. "Even if you had me multiplied by myself, I would be nothing but a negative. I'm not even real! I'm just imaginary. I don't exist!" For the record, imaginary numbers do exist. In fact, they even have practical applications in electrical engineering, mechanical engineering and other fields. So, even if you are an *i*, you are not nothing.

Not only are you not nothing, you are something rather important, even essential. You are a crucial component of the solution to the world's problems. War, injustice, crime and pornography all obscure and contradict God's presence and goodness. Each of these starts small, with a thought that is bellicose or unjust, lawless or lewd. Such thoughts may once have been part of your mental repertoire, and perhaps still are. It's painful, disheartening and at least a tad distressing to discover that you are part of the problem rather than part of the solution.

Devote yourself a bit more to nurturing your own Jewishness by opening a Torah book and reading the words with your heart. The Torah was given to make the world more peaceful, harmonious, just and chaste. Such a world corroborates God's existence and presence. And...

> This is why you were created. Every Jew, even the least of us, has a necessary role in bringing God-awareness to the world.

We mentioned earlier that Rabbi Pharaoh often sanctions mitzvot that are really not mitzvot at all. One of the most troubling strategies that he uses to propagate and perpetuate his "mitzvot" is the Tzaddik Myth. This is the well-intentioned but severely misguided idea that one must be a super tzaddik—a perfect davener, consummate Torah scholar *and* exemplar of interpersonal behavior. Perhaps in some alternate universe people like this exist. In our world, however, one rarely, if ever, meets them.

> I often point out to people that if a baseball player has a lifetime batting average of .360, he would be inducted into the Hall of Fame. If just one year a player hit .350, he would get quite a hefty raise in pay or a bonus. Even someone who hits .290 is considered a good hitter. But think for a moment: Even if someone bats .400, that means he is striking out, hitting into double plays or otherwise failing at least sixty percent of the time!

No baseball player thinks his career is a failure because he isn't perfect. He's still contributing to his team's success. Immediate or automatic Jewish perfection is an artificial goal. Don't berate yourself for not attaining something that doesn't exist. Don't aim for it, because it's not there. Even your small triumphs contribute to those of every Jew.

CONNECTING TO THE DIVINE

Perhaps you feel estranged from any form of Judaism or Jewishness, even after a long period of connectedness. Even if not in its entirety, some of its parts, or people, or the next level of intimacy seem remote, in exile. This estrangement is too strong and has been going on too long for you to overpower unwanted thoughts. If so, how can you ever form a closer connection to God? Your best hope is to send those thoughts away by turning your back on them again and again, as often as need be. Stubbornness is part of the job description.

What makes disturbing thoughts so difficult to overcome is that we don't know how to be helpless. If we were genuinely helpless—which we are not—the thoughts that we want to get rid of would quickly flood our minds. Knowing that we are not helpless, we engage these alien thoughts in face-to-face combat, which gives them an automatic victory. We need to adopt a posture of helplessness—pretending to concede defeat and moving on to think of something else.

Once you've succeeded in banishing the confusion by letting it dissipate on its own, and taken possession of the words you wanted to speak in hitbodedut, speak those words with an honest heart. Even if the confusion returns in yet another incarnation, don't worry. The honest words that you have already spoken are yours. However well or poorly you continue to speak, their truth remains.

Another means of banishing the aliens is Torah. The Torah you carry, carries you. This is true of all Torah, and particularly of the teachings of a tzaddik whose primary goal is to serve as a guide for those who hunger for the Divine. Studying the words of such a tzaddik can bring a Shabbat-like peace to your thinking.

Rebbe Nachman teaches that when one who is truly interested in the Divine enters the garden of spirituality and attempts to partake of its fruits, he is relentlessly pursued by unseen demons that drive him out, terror-stricken. The only safe way to be nourished from the garden's fruits is to stand with the tzaddik, to let the Shabbat-mind of his teachings and the straightforward practice of his advice push out the devilish thoughts from one's mind.

Your study of the tzaddik's teachings, in order to put them into practice, improves your mind's ability to sift through the thoughts with which you will have to contend. As you carry the Torah in your mind and heart, it will carry you safely through the battleground of wrong-thinking. ❊

RACHEL

Our matriarch Rachel is "the beautiful girl who has no eyes" (*Zohar* 2:95a)—so faithful that she is blind to anything that may erode her faith, but not blind to reality.

Beautiful, intelligent Rachel learned early on that being gifted did not guarantee success. Her self-seeking father treated her as a captive. Yet her spirit remained at liberty. When her father cheated her out of gifts and groom, Rachel prayed out of the box—to rescue her sister from disgrace, even as she herself stared at the face of spinsterhood.

Somehow her daddy's self-seeking aims backfired and she, too, married Yaakov. Yet the gift of marriage nearly killed her. Broken and unfulfilled as she felt, Rachel did not languish in her barrenness. She would not accept a bad situation. She had nerve and determination, faith in God and in herself. Rachel was unafraid to speak up or to seek a creative solution. Her willingness to do what was necessary to get her prayers answered resulted in motherhood. Her motherly prayers acknowledged both her shortcomings and her gratitude for having them overlooked.

When the Jewish people erected an idol in the Temple's MostHoly, God spurned the defenses offered by the patriarchs and matriarchs. Even now, when it entailed out-debating God, Rachel refused to accept a negative outcome. She stepped up to the bench.

"God, am I more compassionate than You? When forced out of my bridal chamber in favor of my sister, did I shame her by revealing the truth? No, I rescued her from disgrace and allowed her to marry my intended even though I faced spinsterhood. So if Your children have allowed rival beliefs into their hearts and minds, don't reject them. Forgive them; let them be."

God responded, "Hush your crying, dry your tears. Your kindness will be rewarded."

So if *your* talents and circumstances don't add up positively, don't be afraid to pray out of the box. God is up to the challenge. ❈

⊢—— 11 • Coming Back ——⊣

Time's up! Your hour, your twenty minutes—whatever amount of time your hitbodedut lasted—has come to an end. How do you sign off and transition back into the world?

You finish hitbodedut the same way you started it—with a prayer! In regard to the Shemoneh Esrei, the standard model of prayer, our Sages teach that one should finish by saying: "May the words of my mouth and the prayers of my heart be acceptable to You, God, my Rock and my Redeemer" (*Psalms* 19:15). Reb Noson often used this verse to conclude his hitbodedut.[39]

The idea of asking that your words and thoughts should be pleasing doesn't only mean that God should be satisfied by them. It is also a prayer that God will help you convert those words and thoughts into deeds, creating a life that both you and God will be proud of. After all, what was the whole point of this exercise of hitbodedut, if not to reach a state and position from which you can best continue the work of becoming the best possible you, to becoming who God meant you to be? Some of His light that He wants to shine into the world is supposed to come through you. Your hitbodedut has removed some of the obstruction.

Now you have to live those words, to build a base and provide a home for the longing for the Divine that you claim to have. How can closing with a prayer help you prove your longing and show it to be genuine?

Closing your hitbodedut with a prayer is not unlike saying "amen." "Amen" itself is an expression of faith that God hears our prayers, even if they are too brief and too lacking in proper

---

[39] Many of Reb Noson's prayers are collected in his work, *Likutey Tefilot*, which contains many examples of his hitbodedut based on Rebbe Nachman's teachings in *Likutey Moharan*.

motivation and sincerity. By closing hitbodedut with a prayer, you admit that all your fine words and best intentions don't adequately acknowledge God's kindness and correctness. This "one final attempt" in which you try to pack an hour's worth of honesty into a last few words retroactively fills your entire hitbodedut.

"Dear God,

"May the words of my hitbodedut never be far from my mind. May they come to remind me of what my goals are, and of my self's true desire. May they keep me going forward and reduce, eliminate and prevent my backsliding, my straying and betraying of my self and my goals. I don't want to let go of You.

"Thanks for listening."

When God helps, the whole world looks new (Tzaddik #4 [107]). When our Patriarch Isaac finished his hitbodedut, he saw kindness already on its way.[40] Coming back from hitbodedut means putting your best face forward for the balance of the day. This means doing business honestly, living all aspects of your life with faith, and mingling and getting along with people so that God gains respect and honor thanks to you.[41]

When you're finished and ready to move on to the rest of the day, you can try to capture your hitbodedut in some holy words of Torah, letting the sparkle of its wisdom shine more clearly on some new corner of your life. ❊

---

[40] Based on Genesis 24:63, reading gemalim as gomel chassadim (doing kindness).

[41] Inspiring others Jewishly is always by example, never by proselytizing or preaching.

MOSHE

There are many lessons in hitbodedut taught by Moshe's example. Here are a handful:

- He prayed for his fellow Jews to be healed and saved — even after they insulted and berated him.

- When his sister Miriam was seriously ill, he prayed for her in five short words: "Please, God, please heal her."*

- After one difficult incident in the early years of the Jews' travels in the desert, God told Moshe that nothing happens without a reason. If something goes wrong, "Pray to Me to make the bitter, sweet." Moshe learned from that experience. Later, after the sin of the golden calf, Moshe turned to God in prayer and said, "You taught me to make the bitter, sweet, so now I ask You: Please, turn our bitter inclination to sin into sweetness" (Shemot Rabbah 43:3). ✽

---

* When Rebbe Nachman was sick, he asked his grandson Yisrael to pray for him. The child asked for a gift. Upon receiving it, he offered the following: "God, God! Please make Grandpa well!"

⊢——12 • WHAT IF I'VE BEEN DOING IT WRONG?——⊣

Not likely.

Of course, when you've had a session of hitbodedut in which you cried and cried and felt a catharsis, or sang and danced and felt a catharsis, or walked out of a session and literally saw your prayer answered, you feel you're doing something right because you can see it's effective.

But hitbodedut is always effective, even when you can't see it working. We all know the famous Midrash in which Rabbi Akiva suddenly realizes that he, an unschooled, forty-year-old man, could begin a successful career of Torah study. He came to a well and saw a stone upon which drop after drop of water had fallen, boring a hole in the solid surface. Rabbi Akiva understood the hint that God was giving him: "If each drop of water can contribute to piercing the stone, each word of Torah can lead to my having a Jewish heart."

Rebbe Nachman teaches that this Midrash applies to prayer as well. Each groan, each sigh, every "*oy*," all wear away at the stoniness that seals your heart. Even your breathing, as you yearn and hope for a better Jewish future, chips away a piece of rock-heartedness. So, no, you haven't been doing it wrong.

Could you have been doing it better? There's always room for improvement. Perhaps more time, more effort or more preparation can or need be inserted? Maybe some topics should be more defined and others eliminated (at least for the time being). Certainly, a prayer—short: "God, help me to improve my hitbodedut" or long: "God, please show me how to improve my hitbodedut, to drop what needs to be dropped, to listen more closely to what I'm saying…"—will make it better. Beating yourself up for "failing" to do it right is not going to improve past sessions or future ones, so don't do it.

"But what if I've been focusing on the wrong topics?" you ask.

There's a secret about life. Every one of us has a certain place, as it were, that he needs to reach, a destiny to achieve. We call it his tikkun, his rectification and perfection of his soul. Does that dictate or predetermine in any way what he chooses to do? Not at all. It only indicates that each one of us has a role in the "big picture," and however long it takes, each one of us will get there.

Getting there, as they say, is half the fun. Since each of us must get to a unique destiny, each of us must walk a unique path. Your path is made up of countless variables, some of which are given—such as your gender, your age and your era (Baby Boomer, Gen X'er, Gen Y'er). Other variables include who you know and who you don't know, where you've been and where you haven't been, what you're capable of doing and what you're a total klutz at.

Your path includes, surprisingly and perhaps frighteningly, what you choose to think, say and do. Part of the paradox of free will and foreknowledge[42] is that as we choose what to think about, God is also feeding us ideas. Much of life's struggle is to purge our mind of wrong-thinking and direct it to right-thinking.

This attempt to direct the mind is a constant process, one that started when you were born and ends only with death. The road to your destiny includes thinking certain thoughts at certain times and experiencing particular events at specific moments of your life. For example, had you been introduced to Rebbe Nachman's path of meditation at too young an age, you might not have appreciated it. At a later stage of life, you may have despaired of ever practicing it. It was presented to you when you were ripe for it.

The same applies to other thoughts, including the ones that need purging. Certain temptations at too young an age are

---

[42] Meaning, we get to freely choose and decide our actions, even though God knows precisely what we will choose before we do.

irresistible for the vast majority of people; at too advanced an age, they are no longer temptations. When you find yourself in a challenging situation, whether the contest between right- and wrong-thinking is produced by external stimuli or internal, you are ripe for the challenge.

The topics and problems upon which you have been focusing in hitbodedut may have been real or illusory. They may have been symptoms rather than root causes. That's OK. If they were genuine, then you were dealing with issues that needed your attention. If they were illusory, then you weren't ready to deal with the real issues. You needed to be distracted until you were ready, and given more time to practice (that is, sharpen and hone) your hitbodedut skills. What needed to be done was done.

> A musician was playing a Mozart sonata for a private audience. When he finished, he apologized, "I'm sorry it didn't come out right. I made a mistake in the second movement."
>
> "That's quite alright," replied one of his listeners. "You played something else perfectly." ❊

KING DAVID

King David had a rich and varied life. At different times he was a shepherd, a soldier, a king, a yeshivah student, a practicing rabbi. He was married more than once, lost a child in infancy, lost an adult child, and had a child attempt to usurp his throne. His political enemies were many. Some even suggested that King David was not Jewish!

Through it all, King David prayed. He did hitbodedut whenever he tended his flocks, wandered in exile, or ruled his nation. What became of King David's hitbodedut? It became our Tehillim (*Psalms*).

Rebbe Nachman recommends you write down the hitbodedut that you feel was truly inspired. Why? So you can say it again in the future. It may not become a world-famous classic, but, Rebbe Nachman teaches, its effect and impact are no less psalms-like. ❋

13 • HELP! SIXTY MINUTES IS ⊢—— TOO MUCH TIME! ——⊣

What if you feel that sixty—count 'em, sixty—minutes is too much? After all, who can sit still for so long? How much of a monologue can a person give, especially day after day? "It gets so boring and monotonous to listen to myself. And it's not like I'm getting any feedback or seeing any miracles as I live the other parts of my life. Really. Sixty minutes? It's too much. And besides, I've got other things to do. Unless you can make this doable, I'm going to look for my Jewish spiritual salvation elsewhere. What do you say about that, Ozer?"

The first rule of growing Jewishly is: *Thou shalt not bite off more than thou canst chew.* This applies not only to Jewishness in general, but to specific practices as well. Different people have different strengths and different capabilities. Even you can do things now that you couldn't do when you were three months old, like read, write and play cello. And even if you still can't play cello, you can read and write.

It's the same with hitbodedut. Just because you have a genuine, abiding interest in cultivating your Jewishness, it doesn't mean that you're ready to sit for a whole sixty minutes of hitbodedut every day, right away. So take baby steps.

If having two thirty-minute sessions a day works better for you, then by all means, do it that way. In the Holy Temple in Jerusalem, the kohen gadol brought a flour offering every day, half in the morning and half in the afternoon. Thirty plus thirty also equals sixty. Does that sound like too much for you? Then do less! Is fifty minutes OK? How about forty? Even if you do only *five minutes* a day, it's a noteworthy accomplishment. It's five minutes more than a billion other people do.

More importantly (because it's *never* a good idea to compare your practices to anyone else's), it's a noteworthy accomplishment because it's "baby's first step." It makes little sense, if any, just to sit and feel as if you're being punished. The most central concept of hitbodedut is creating your own direct, self-defined relationship with God. If you're sitting there tapping your fingers and becoming annoyed and frustrated, you will not soon develop a healthy, fertile relationship with the Creator. The world already has too many fruitless ones. You don't want yours to be one of them.

So before getting started, think about how much zitsfleish you have. Be flexible. Maybe you overestimated, maybe you underestimated, maybe your evaluation is right only eighty percent of the time. As you begin a particular session, don't look at the clock, either literally or figuratively. Just keep in the back of your mind the amount of time you want to sit. And begin to talk. If you feel you've gone over your time limit but still have more to say, keep talking. Going overtime today doesn't obligate you to spend the same amount of time, or even the tiniest bit of extra time, in hitbodedut tomorrow.

On the flip side, if you feel you're talked out before the time you set is up, you have some options, all of them excellent. You can get up and walk out (or whatever your equivalent of "signing off" is). You can just sit and let your mind wander for the remaining time. Often this quiet time serves as a period of absorption in which your mind and heart assimilate more deeply the bond that you've just spent time creating and enhancing. Many times this silent period enables you to imbibe the calm and strength you've only a moment ago worked to achieve.

Many times, as you sit quietly and patiently, other subjects—which may or may not be related to what you've spoken about—will come to mind. You may have something to say immediately about some or all of them. You may merely desire to note them and consider them as future topics. Or—lo and behold!—they may actually be insights or solutions to matters that you discussed minutes ago.

Whatever choice you make, it makes sense to allow for extra time beyond what you think you're capable of. If you end up needing it, you won't feel pressured about taking time from some other activity that needs doing. If you don't use it for hitbodedut, you'll use it for something else good.

Having said this, remember that the five or ten minutes you designate as your "first step" in hitbodedut are just that—a first step. Don't fall into the "good enough" trap. You may find those five or ten minutes satisfying, fulfilling and productive—and then think that you don't need more, or that you are incapable of more. You may be afraid to tamper with a good thing. "If it ain't broke, why fix it?"

ROADBLOCK UP AHEAD

At times you may find that waning interest, boredom, frustration and plain old weariness keep you from getting the most out of hitbodedut. To counter these expected obstacles, Rebbe Nachman offered a number of suggestions:

- Use your Torah study as a springboard for new ideas and goal-setting that you could apply to hitbodedut.

- Pretend you're really passionate about hitbodedut.

- Ride out the boredom and just keep "showing up" for your sessions.

- Remember that hitbodedut is the practice of champions. Rebbe Nachman himself and many other great tzaddikim achieved their spiritual success by regularly engaging in hitbodedut.

Other times it seems that "life," "they" or "someone" is conspiring to prevent you from succeeding in your goal to come closer to God. This is a product of what is called, in Yiddish, "karma." OK, karma isn't really a Yiddish word, but it is a basic Torah teaching.

The obstacles that might block your path are really challenges to make you think about what you're doing. Are you really sincere about your commitment to achieving the next level of Jewishness that awaits you? Are you perspicacious enough to see through various notions and temptations that, if you don't resist them, will prevent you from realizing accomplishments that can be yours for the price of but an hour a day?

Life *will* get in the way. You need to be extremely patient with events, with others in your life (for example, spouse, children and parents) and perhaps most of all, with yourself. As Rebbe Nachman said, "When you want to do something holy, at first you are confused and unsure. Barriers seem to spring up on every side. When you want to improve your Jewishness, you are almost overwhelmed by confusion and frustration. There are great barriers in your path. The more you want God-awareness, the more difficulty you encounter. But I believe and know the following to be true: No thought or movement involved in striving for a holy objective is ever lost."

AVOID COMPLACENCY

"As one measures, so is it measured to him" (*Sotah* 1:7). "If you squander the time you have to study Torah, others will squander your time for you" (*Avot* 4:12).

You can't get away with anything in life. Sooner or later, it all catches up to you. That's not only good; that's excellent. Firstly, if you know that you reap what you sow, you'll be more careful about what—and how—you sow. Secondly, as you reap the bitter fruits of your previous mistakes, you can more easily recognize them for what they are—namely, the weeds, thistles and thorns that have to be cleared from the path you have yet to walk. They are not rejection notices from Heaven (or Hell).

Rebbe Nachman always warned against complacency, even good and pious complacency. "It's not good to be old. Even to be an old tzaddik is not good," he said (*Rabbi Nachman's Wisdom* #51). As we mentioned above, in his story, "The Burgher and the Pauper," the burgher's son finds spiritual comfort at quite advanced stages of spiritual growth. Yet since he chooses to remain where he is rather than grow further, he is buffeted by the winds of change.

Being complacent and resisting voluntary change may invite forced change. If someone doesn't happily choose to spend more time deepening his relationship with God, God may need to do something to get his attention. A proper reaction to that — admitting God is right — will ensure a happy result, but can you guarantee a proper reaction? Even if you can, why not be courageous and initiate change? The increment of time that you add to your hitbodedut is time *for you*. It is time that enables you to probe your soul more deeply.

Don't pressure yourself unduly to make progress. You're on no one's schedule but your own. There is no benchmark by which you will be measured, except the one Heaven expects you to meet. But don't refuse to set any standards, either. There's no reason for you to be complacent and settle for mediocrity.

Say a little prayer and ask God for guidance: "What's my next step?" ❋

CHANAH

Chanah was the mother of the prophet Shmuel who, in his own "league," was as great as Moshe and Aharon combined. It was Shmuel who anointed King David, who was prayer personified. Whence did Shmuel gain this ability to bestow kingship on such a person? From his mother.

Chanah had been barren for many years. Constantly she prayed to have a child. She prayed so well that she aroused not only the ordinary level of Divine compassion, but the extraordinary level, as well. (The holy Zohar teaches that in relation to His compassion, God is not only perfect, but also "more perfect." Levels of infinity, as it were.) In fact, her prayer was so special that it was almost as if God Himself was praying!

It's difficult, if not impossible, to describe the enormity of the pain of being infertile. Our Sages tell us that it is like being dead, though it may be worse. One sees that others are fruitful while she herself is like a stick of dry wood.

Chanah had to be persuaded to share her husband's spiritual gifts, his offerings to God, but they did not satisfy her. A vicarious connection to the Deity is insufficient. When a person truly feels that way, she tries harder and prays with extra focus. She cries as Chanah did—copiously—and seeks to "strike a deal" with God.

These are keys that can open the "womb" of Divine compassion and allow one to bring into the world a "Shmuel"—a source of fairness, foresight and stability. ❧

14 • HELP! SIXTY MINUTES IS
⊢—— TOO LITTLE TIME! ——⊣

"WOW! Hitbodedut is amazing!

"I never realized how much can be accomplished in life, so quickly and so easily. I never knew that so much of my life is right there within my grasp to observe, evaluate and, most of all, change. Even on those days or weeks when it's hard for me to find the words or the calmness to speak what I *just know* needs to be said, words which are at the tip of my tongue, it's just so incredible a feeling and sensation to know that I'm alone with God. He's patiently waiting for me, even if I'm the one who's to 'blame' for the temporary lack of communication. I need more than sixty minutes! What do I do?"

If that's how you feel, make sure you increase your minutes *safely*. There are many factors to check before you start to put in overtime. The first is to make sure that if you will have to *decrease* your time at some future point, you won't abandon hitbodedut altogether, God forbid.

It's good that you want to do more, but is it really you? Are you sure it's not a trap, that you're not being set up for a fall? Because if you reach too high and don't make it, you may fall lower than you ever thought possible and never get up again. As the Kabbalah texts warn us, "Too much oil douses the flame."

Rebbe Nachman teaches that one of the most difficult traps to avoid in the pursuit of the Divine is going too quickly, too soon. Care must be taken not to fall into the trap of believing, "If a little is good, a lot is better." And our Sages have warned, "If you grab too much, you'll end up empty-handed" (*Sukkah* 5b).

Your task now is to enlarge and add to your spiritual vessels. This is best accomplished by steadily continuing with your other practices—Torah study, "ritual" mitzvot, kindness and tzedakah—with extra doses of patience and sincerity. As always, a little prayer asking God for some guidance is never out of place: "What's my next step?"

If you decide to try for more, here are some things to be careful about:

- Don't watch the clock—if you do, you're not ready for more.

- Allow yourself enough time so that if you end up doing more than an hour, you won't feel or rushed or harried afterwards.

- If you feel you didn't "do the job" because you didn't "do enough extra time," then most likely you're on the wrong track.

- Don't think you're better than the next person because you do more hitbodedut. If you really think that, you're totally missing the point. You need to start again. ❀

THE ANCHOR

Of course you're trying. I'm sure you're really giving it all you've got. But—are you?

Rebbe Nachman once told his followers: "You put as much effort into your prayer as I did in raising anchor. The crew was short-handed and they told us to raise anchor. I had no choice but to grab hold of the rope and pull. I went through the motions and made the appropriate faces, but I wasn't really exerting myself at all.

"That's the effort you're putting into your prayers." ❀

┝── 15 • SPECIAL OCCASIONS ──┥

A s we wrote earlier,[43] it's best to schedule your hitbodedut. But what about Shabbat and holidays, when the whole face of the day is different and you may not be able to find a good time for hitbodedut?

What about special occasions? What happens if it's your bar mitzvah or your wedding day? What if, God forbid, there has been a tragedy and your physical presence is required to take care of other people and immediate concerns?

What if you're traveling? What if you're sick? What if you just wake up late?

For most of these questions, the answer is: Expect to have an abbreviated hitbodedut. In most cases, the bulk of your abbreviated session will be focused on the cause of the brevity!

SHABBAT AND HOLIDAYS

Let's take the easy ones first. Shabbat and holidays are already on the calendar, so they're not going to surprise you. You've experienced a certain number of Shabbats. You know more or less what the pattern and rhythm will be—the prayers and meals will be *approximately* at certain times, and will take a certain amount of time. You can reasonably predict when some chunks of time may be available, so you should be able to schedule time for hitbodedut. Of course, you may have to forgo some of that delicious Shabbat nap, but it's a worthwhile trade-off.

It's not only worthwhile because doing hitbodedut is better than sleeping. It's also worthwhile because Shabbat and holidays were made expressly to give us a "day of rest," a day when making

---

[43] See page 48.

and taking the time to settle our minds would be easier. The extra sanctity of these days adds something to hitbodedut, even if you can't always taste it. And it's also worthwhile because when those you live with see how important hitbodedut is to you, they will come to expect it from you and allow you the time and space for it.

CELEBRATIONS

You certainly want your big day to go just right. The caterer, band and photographer should all show up on time and do a great job. Family and friends should be in good spirits and on their best behavior. Don't forget that personal milestones are days that have a special holiness for you. Take care to have quiet hitbodedut that day so that your heart will absorb and store away all the joy and holiness it can. Say some words of thanks and blessing as you watch people dance around you.

Since it is your special day, you have some prerogatives. You can tell people that you have something that you need to take care of—in private.

TIMES OF TRAGEDY

Now for the harder ones. You can't plan for a tragedy.[44] The sadness and pain of tragedy clouds our thinking and makes us forget: God is here even now.

In times of tragedy, hitbodedut needs to be whispered: "May this person get through this." "Help me to feel the pain and to properly offer my care and genuine concern." "God, You do so much kindness; help me to partner with You at this difficult juncture." Such words could be said silently as you hug someone,

---

[44] This is a good reason why you should try to have your hitbodedut as early in the day as possible. If something unexpected comes up later on, you'll have already had your private time alone with God.

murmured as you make tea in the kitchen, or whispered as you merely sit with the person suffering.

Rebbe Nachman taught: As the day begins, I surrender it to God. Whatever may be in store, I accept it as God's will, and know that what I was able to do or not able to do was part of His plan.

ON THE ROAD AGAIN

Traveling is time-consuming and stressful. Most people find it hard to concentrate. So start off your hitbodedut with exactly those things that concern you and that you need to have a more pleasant journey—a comfortable seat with good neighbors, no mechanical or human failure in the course of the trip and no delays, your kosher meal served properly warmed, and, of course, your luggage arriving on the same flight as you do.

If your flight (or train) is scheduled so that your only free time will be on board, try to get a window seat. You can use an airline blanket to cover your head, tallit-like, or simply turn your head to the window with your eyes closed to whisper your hitbodedut. If the only time you have is at the terminal, you can almost always find an unused gate not too far away. You may not have all the privacy or time you would like, but take what you can get. You could even flip open your cell phone and pretend to have a very long, one-sided conversation without attracting any notice. It's a good idea to set a timer, unless you really don't care if you miss your connection.

UNDER THE WEATHER

If you're sick, your mood and energy level will be lower than usual. Take it easy. Do what you can, even if it's just a minute or two. You want to get well soon so you can start going full steam ahead, so for now, let your body recuperate.

Work on your *desire* for hitbodedut. Instead of feeling bad ("This is terrible; I can't do hitbodedut the way I'd like to"), think of hitbodedut as someone you love, whose return and re-embrace you look forward to. And if you're not too groggy, try some silent hitbodedut.[45]

WAKING UP LATE

If you wake up late, Rule #1 is: *Don't panic!* Part of what you're aiming for is yishuv hadaat, the opposite of panic and stress. By all means, move quickly so you won't be any later than you are, but accept the fact that today's hitbodedut is going to be a little shorter—and then just do it! What should you leave out? It's your hitbodedut. You decide.[46] ✻

LATE AFTERNOON

It was late in the afternoon. Rebbe Nachman stood at the window, gazing outside with tremendous longing. He sighed and said to Reb Noson, "I have so much to accomplish, and the day passes so quickly." ✻

---

[45] See Room 4, pages 230 and 232.

[46] Think about why you woke up late. Is God trying to point out that a particular area of your lifestyle or attitude needs fixing?

16 • I'VE BEEN DOING HITBODEDUT FOR SO LONG, ⊢— WHY AM I STILL GOING BACKWARDS? —⊣

Lean a little closer to the book. I'm going to tell you a secret and I don't want anybody to hear what you're reading.

There comes a time in the life of every good hitbodedut practitioner when she feels like skipping a day or two. Or more. Or even giving up altogether, God forbid. Days, weeks, even months and years may have been invested in achieving a goal, but she still feels as far away from it as ever. She feels hopelessly ignored. "What's the point of continuing? Some progress has been made, yes, but not enough to warrant this daily commitment. I need a break."

The more "religious" among us may be thinking, "Heavens! Such blasphemy!" Well, it's not. It's more human than blasphemous. For many, it's part of the growth process. In fact, Rebbe Nachman himself entertained such feelings a number of times in his youth. He recounted that he would get discouraged and think God was ignoring him, so he wouldn't speak to God for a few days. After all, if no one is listening, what's the point in talking?

Yet after a few days, Rebbe Nachman would remind himself that God is truly kind and caring. Part of His kindness is that He seems to push you away right when you're trying to get closer. In truth, God's push is an invitation for you to come even closer. God is compassionate and favoring. There are many reasons why you may feel that He is ignoring you, but whatever the reason actually is, He's testing your resolve. God wants to see if you can see through the smokescreen, if you're strong enough to walk a few steps on your own. In the hollow of Creation that you feel you have entered, God wants to see if you will call to Him and invite Him in.

This is part of the koan that Rebbe Nachman taught later in his life: *All rejection is really invitation.* Any time you feel rebuffed by the Divine, when any of your forays or attempts to turn body into soul or moment into eternity are scorned, talk your way in. Even when God says, "Goodbye," He means, "Please don't let Me go."

Let's go back to your question, "Why am I going backwards?" There are two answers: *Who said you are?* And: *Why shouldn't you be?* Let's analyze each of these answers in turn.

WHO SAID YOU ARE?

Rebbe Nachman said that chassidim make a mistake: They think up is down. What did he mean? From the moment that you realized life is a serious endeavor, with stakes greater than your own vanity and pleasure, you made efforts of various sorts to improve your self, your inner workings and your outer behavior. Undoubtedly, you made real, tangible progress. Then, BOOM! A mis-thought, a poor choice of word or deed, and progress seems to collapse like a house of cards. You may feel like someone in Alcoholics Anonymous who has been sober for years and then goes on a bender and blacks out—you've fallen off the wagon. It's not so. You didn't fall down; you fell *up*.

In formal education, graduation from a lower school to a higher one is usually marked by a fine ceremony, with grand speeches, marches and music. You're handed a piece of paper proving or certifying that you are competent in certain academic venues. You have time till the next semester to prepare for the next set of academic challenges. Not so on the Spiritual Success Highway.

As you lay brick after brick of advancement in front of you, you finally reach the zenith of your spiritual talent at a particular level. No applause. No "thank you." No clap on the back. Instead, a fresh can of spiritual worms, genetically engineered to challenge your power of sacred determination and ingenuity, is opened in your honor. The lush, fertile Garden of Eden you inhabited and enjoyed just moments ago has been replaced by a desert teeming with vipers, scorpions and unnamed monsters.

You're frightened, scared, frustrated and flustered. "All my hard work—*for naught?!*" No, says Rebbe Nachman. You are misunderstanding and mis-feeling. You should be saying, "I *succeeded!* I did such a good job that I'm capable of handling *more!*" The initial setback(s) and distress at your failure, coupled with the feeling that your spiritual legs have been cut out from under you, are *not* of your own making. It is God handing you your next assignment. This is a subtle point which you must deal with carefully. It's not your fault. You are not a failure—yet. If you make no attempt to start again, *then* you have failed.

Part of the difficulty of recognizing that you've graduated is the similarity of new challenges to old. The subtlety or intensity may be the difference. In Kabbalah-speak, the test may now be taking place in a different sub-sefirah than the previous ones. Whatever the case, you've arrived. Congratulations. You're still going to have to wait for your eternal reward. And good luck.

WHY SHOULDN'T YOU BE?

Sometimes you find yourself going backwards because you underestimated the opposition—namely, how much you're really attached to the things and traits that you now realize you want to give up. In part, this means that your regret has become subverted and your attachment to wrong-living has become stronger. You need to dig in and fight harder—and smarter.

Let's face it, why shouldn't you be going backwards? It's not as if you've been a saint all your life. It's not as if your practice of hitbodedut has made your soul as pure as the driven snow. There's a lot of asymmetry in the universe that you're responsible for and that you must correct. In order to move forward, you may have to go back and revisit situations in which you didn't do too well. Whether you need to pick up something you dropped, or leave a message for others who will pass that way, part of your future progress may require reliving the past again and again.

Still, you must believe that despite what you see, you don't see the whole picture. For it is not only you who is doing or acting on the world and on your soul. God also is actively involved. He, more than anyone else (even you!), wants you to have the greatest success of which you are capable. In order for you to plumb the depths of your power and truly accomplish, God knows what you must experience.

Sometimes you need His warm smile, other times a frightening frown, and yet other times the chilling, withering feeling of being ignored. You may even need to pass through dark nights when your soul is set adrift, friendless, alone and unable to communicate with anyone because you feel there is no one who can possibly understand you, let alone sympathize with you. The darkness may be so thick, so penetrating, that it fills your guts and comes rushing out your throat. You may believe that God isn't there; you may feel that there is no "you."

This is God's doing. The shame and filthiness you may feel, the discomfort of your mis-lived past and the dread of mis-living the future, are His *invitations* to you, His way of goading you on to the greatness you can achieve. Why does it have to be *this* way? Because it is *your* way.

But, why does this have to be your way?

Inscrutable. Wrong question to be asking. The appropriate question is how to survive such experiences, how to weather them, how to alchemize their leadenness into twenty-four-carat gold. Rebbe Nachman recommends that you ask, "Where am I?" The response you get may be nothing more than your voice fading away in the distant corridors of your mind.

Should you not have the strength for words, scream. Scream from your heart, from your brain, from your stomach, from wherever it hurts, from the greatest pain or the greatest emptiness you feel.

If your lungs and throat fail you, scream in your mind. Let the sound of your silent scream fill the valleys and the canyons. Let your roar fill the gap between the ocean and the sky; let it pass through the clouds and pass the sun and the stars.

Keep knock, knock, knocking on Heaven's door. It may take a while, but they'll eventually open it for you. In the meantime, they're preparing your palace. ❄

ROOM 2
THE CONFERENCE ROOM

The worst aspect of any problem is not knowing the solution. Should I buy or sell? Should I take this job or wait for a better offer? Should we do the surgery or not? The feeling of helplessness, the futility of grasping at straws, the uncertainty of which competing option to choose, complicates the matter.

It's worse when the dilemma involves your eternal future. What do I need to start doing to get out of my rut? Which practices am I ready to take on?

Hitbodedut won't help you predict the future, but it will help you gain clarity. Then you can make your choices with more confidence and hope. ❧

—— 1 • EYE ON ETERNITY ——

Sometimes hitbodedut ends at hitbodedut. You want and need to express your pain, your appreciation or your love for God. Sometimes, things being the way they are, that's all you can do.

Sometimes hitbodedut is not the final stop, however, because prayer is not enough. God created the world incomplete, assigning mankind the mission of finishing His work through our own actions. Whenever we are faced by a decision, we can go ahead and just act, or we can plan out what we think is the best course of action. Either way, something will happen. But Rebbe Nachman teaches that for the world at large—and for your personal world—to come to its fullest potential, you must think first, pray second, and then act.

> Considering the centrality of prayer in Rebbe Nachman's path, you might be surprised to learn that Rebbe Nachman teaches that in certain circumstances, prayer is not the primary course. In common, run-of-the-mill situations and endeavors, like running a business or studying Torah, although you need to pray for success, it's not enough to rely on prayer. You must also engage in whatever activities are considered normal for that endeavor. In certain situations, one could theoretically pray to God for help, but it's much simpler and more effective to go ahead and do the job yourself!
>
> If you can save yourself or someone else by spending money, that is what you should do. When you no longer have enough money, then pray (*The Aleph-Bet Book*, Sweetening Judgments, A:67). If, God forbid, you find yourself in a war zone, though you must certainly pray, you also must prepare your armor. Miracles may happen—and they do—but you cannot count on them (ibid., Strife, A:5, 101). ✿

Hitbodedut can function as a Conference Room in which both everyday and big decisions are discussed, picked apart, and prayed over. For some of the most important functions you will attend to, such as the big decisions and milestones in your life, your hitbodedut will include a lot of time thinking and planning how to achieve your goals. You will think, consider and weigh alternatives; re-think, re-weigh, deliberate and decide; and then do what needs to be done.

There is something that's even more important to think about and plan for: your eternal future. The most effective use of hitbodedut (as well as the most effective way of living one's life) is in preparing for the really long haul, for eternity.

Simply leaving it all up to fate or chance won't work here. God put each of us into this world to earn his own eternal reward by using the talents and opportunities given him, to succeed in areas that are reasonable for someone with those gifts. It is your responsibility to recognize what you can and cannot do, and act accordingly. In addition, you have to recognize the cues to exercise your abilities. Your trust in God and your prayers, including hitbodedut, have to accompany your efforts, not replace them.

The local river had flooded and the man climbed up to the roof of his house. The water was lapping at his feet when some people came by in a rowboat. "Get in!" they called to him.

"No, thanks," he called back. "I trust in God."

The water continued to rise and was up to his waist when a motorboat came along. "Climb up!" the crew called.

"No, thanks. I trust in God."

The water continued to rise and was up to his neck when a helicopter hovered above him. They rolled down a rope ladder and yelled, "Climb up!"

"No, thanks. I trust in God."

The water continued to rise and the man drowned. When he got to Heaven, he asked God, "I trusted in You. Why didn't You save me?"

God answered, "I sent you a rowboat, a motorboat and a helicopter. What more did you want?" ❦

We know, yet find it frightening to admit, that our time in this world is limited. We are mortal. We will leave this world. Our dreams of temporal, material success are like seed mixed with chaff; they contain good but are muddled with confusion and misinterpretation. If we select the wrong focus, our time and energy are in jeopardy of being wasted on ventures which will be swallowed up, and of which nothing will remain.

What do you really want? Before you answer, do what King David did — do hitbodedut. "I have considered my ways and set my feet to Your testimonies" (*Psalms* 119:59). He got where he wanted to go by reflecting about what he wanted his ultimate fate to be. You say, and perhaps even sincerely believe, that you genuinely want to live a particular lifestyle. Are you living it? Or are you ending up going to places, or doing and thinking things, that contradict your stated objective? The sage Hillel said: "Where do I go? The place I love, my feet take me" (*Sukkah* 53a).

The Talmudic sage Mar Ukva knew where he was going. In addition to Torah study, he devoted his life to tzedakah. Nonetheless, shortly before his passing, he sighed, "So few provisions for such a long road" (*Ketubot* 67b). The reward waiting for each of us in the Next World is potentially so great that it defies description. However, each and every aspect of that reward is rooted in some good deed, some moral decision, that we made in this world. We need to prepare and act now if we want to access all the reward that we can possibly enjoy. It is for your eventual journey on this long road that you need hitbodedut to begin to prepare.

So Many Choices

Every now and then, use your hitbodedut as the first stage of defining and refining the values by which you want to live. Use it also as the venue in which you begin to formulate the goals and the plans that, stage by stage and step by step, will reflect your chosen values.

What exactly are those chosen values? Until you choose what you want out of life, you cannot formulate or pray for a plan to live by those values. As every good novelist knows, you always write the ending of your book first. Why? Because how the book ends will determine everything else that will be written in the story. Similarly, the ending which you choose for your life's story will impact every decision you make. There is no more important choice you will ever make.

> Alice asked the cat, "Would you tell me, please, which way I ought to go from here?"
>
> "That depends a good deal on where you want to get to," said the cat.

To make the right choices in life, you must turn your ear—and your heart—to listen closely and carefully, to hear through all the reverberating sounds and calls, the cacophony of wild beasts and wild claims. Your goal is to detect the genuine voice of Creation and reject its echoes. The genuine voice is a quiet, subtle, barely detectable whisper—until you hear it. Then it roars. You'll never be able to hear it, though, unless you want it. If you don't hear it, it's either because you don't want it at all or you don't want it enough.

> Rebbe Nachman once said to Reb Noson: "Everything you see in the world, everything that exists, is for the sake of free will, in order to challenge people."

There are so many choices and oh so many voices—some yelling, some whispering, some in your face, some tugging at your sleeve. Some are so seductive, some so compelling. It can be maddening. A person may feel so overwhelmed that he makes a blind decision just to silence the noise.

Even if you have a fairly clear idea of what you want, some voices can mimic yours so well that you may believe that what they are saying is really you speaking. Is the choice you are making really yours? Is that really where you want to go? Are you fooling yourself or being fooled? Even if you're sure that the choice is yours, are you certain that it leads to safe harbor?

> Rebbe Nachman once remarked to Reb Noson, "You speak to people. Ask them, 'What?' Ask them to cut through all their excuses and rationalizations and honestly consider: *What legacy will you leave for yourself? What will be your destiny?*"

There's an interesting experience one has almost immediately upon dying, an experience that is forced upon him: he gets to see that this world is vanity. He finally takes note that many of his "important concerns" were nonsense. This insight results from the great yishuv hadaat, the calm reflection, that comes when a person finally stops running and starts observing life from an unbiased perspective. Sadly, it is then too late to make use of this all-important piece of wisdom.

> Lying there dead, one realizes that he wasted his days in vain. He will know that his most overwhelming desires were nonsense and confusion. Who really forced him! But a person must die before he fully perceives this truth.

> Most things that people fear cannot harm them at all. The only time a person can think clearly is when he is dead. When he is lying on the ground, with his feet to the door,[47] he will finally see the truth. Then he will realize that all his fears and worries were foolish and for nothing. What could anybody have done to him?!

While your fullest and most complete realization of this truth will hopefully wait for a good long while, Rebbe Nachman offers a valuable tip in the meantime: Use hitbodedut to reflect well on what you are doing. There is no need to wait till you're absolutely dead and no longer able to busy yourself in the world to take a good, hard look at what's truly important—and what is not.

Dedicating some of your hitbodedut to "comparison shopping" can be of inestimable value. An honest appraisal of the success

---

[47] It is customary for the burial society to position the deceased in this manner before preparing the body for interment.

that this world offers reveals that such pleasures are as permanent as passing shadows. They are, as Rebbe Nachman pointed out, as real as sunbeams in a dark room. It looks as if something is there, but if you try to grab it, you come up empty-handed.

Understand that this world is transient. From the day you're born you begin to die. You're never again going to live this day, this hour or this minute, ever. You need to remind yourself of this fact often because part of God's genius was to hide it from us. Nothing is going to remain of all your fame, fortune, steak dinners or sexual pleasures. It may be necessary to occasionally make use of any or all of these for some nobler goal, but in and of themselves they have no value.

With hitbodedut you can detach from the furious and spurious pace and gauge accurately where your current path is leading. It usually takes more than an hour or two of hitbodedut to come to the intellectual realization and deep-rooted acceptance that this world has no enduring value. However long it takes, the hitbodedut invested is well worth it. Those sessions are your first steps and the crucial keys to easily divest yourself of your phobias and desires. From there, you can make hitbodedut the forum in which you determine, affirm and create your desire for living a life that is Jewish inside and out, from the inside out.

HOLY DESIRE

Choosing to live a Jewish life means more than just knowing how to do mitzvot and successfully following rules that can deceive you into thinking that you're living a "religious" life. A Jewish life is not only about what you know and what you do; it's about what you *want* from your knowledge and from your doing. This holy desire can be gained from your planning sessions during hitbodedut. With this kind of desire, you can more readily maintain focus on your goal, how you want your life's story to end. This makes the choice of what to think, say and do clearer, if not more immediately obtainable.

Rebbe Nachman said, "Don't let a word of wickedness leave your mouth." Don't say that you will commit a sin or be wicked, even though you're joking and have no intention of carrying out your words. The words themselves can do great damage and later compel you to fulfill them. This is true even if they are uttered only as a joke. ✿

Even when you decide that "improving my Jewishness" is your goal, that's too undefined, and most likely too big, to be accomplished without further definition. Again, because hitbodedut is yours—written, directed by and starring you—you'll be able to define what exactly is the Jewishness you seek, and what are your next steps to achieve it.

Although hitbodedut is basically talking to God, that doesn't mean you can't actually think and plan, maybe even with pen and paper, what to talk about. To start defining your goals, you need to ask your self some questions. What are your greatest strengths? (Yes, you have some—two or three at least.) Thank God for giving you these strengths, talents or whatever you would like to call them. Looking at your life to date, name your life's purpose, and thank God as well for giving you the purpose that He did. (If you need to, apologize for misusing or abusing your talents and failing to do all you could have towards filling your purpose.)

What aspects of Jewishness excite you now? Which of these are you looking forward to making a part of you? Are these wishful impulses or genuine "I'm willing to work for it till I get it" goals?[48]

To build an honest, holy desire for Jewishness, put it into words. This will give you a better chance to organize your thoughts and structure your Torah knowledge so that it comes out right.

What generates proper holy desire? Study of Torah is crucial. The Torah is the blueprint of Creation and its function is both to instruct and to inspire. The Torah does her job best when you're

---

[48] See Appendix A for more questions.

best prepared to understand it. That happens when your mind is not preoccupied by carnal desire.

Your desire and yearning for Jewishness is weakened and undermined any time your mind is unduly absorbed by this primal urge. You need to protect yourself by being cautious without being nervous or anxious, and without being prudish or "holier than thou." Keep your mind cheerfully occupied with something gainful.

Your desire, now resting on a stronger foundation, makes your mouth more powerful. Your words and hitbodedut will be more effective. Rebbe Nachman teaches that many new words will be born from the purity of your heart, as it becomes more enthusiastic about being Jewish. ❊

Even just being in a room in which someone has longed and yearned to be a better Jew is beneficial because you can inhale the holy desire. ❊

⊢—— 2 • GETTING HELP FROM A TZADDIK ——⊣

We all know that the road to Hell is paved with good intentions. Wanting to live right is not the same as actually doing so. There are simply too many unexpected and difficult roadblocks that can crop up and steer you off course. The only way to make sure your desire for Jewishness results in proper planning is by fortifying yourself with proper instruction and guidance ("eitzah" in Hebrew). The people who succeed in life are the ones who possess the right eitzah when they need it. Where do you get it? From whom do you get it? And what does it have to do with your hitbodedut?

When you need legal advice, you don't go to a mechanic. You don't rub a rabbit's foot if your brakes need fixing, and you don't go to a 7-Eleven for medical advice. You turn to someone who is an expert in his field, someone who can see beyond the immediate concerns and envision the ramifications of your decision. The planning that takes place in your hitbodedut has to be based on eitzah that will help you now and in the long run. You need to find a tzaddik.

We've already mentioned the tzaddik, the spiritual master who serves as guide, mentor and teacher. The teachings of the tzaddik are not theoretical or abstract concepts. They are tried and true practices that have been forged not only in his experience and struggles, but in those of many, many other people as well. What's more, these practices are verified by something greater than common experience: They are practices that flow from the very wellsprings of God's Creation-wisdom.

In order to start receiving these life-giving eitzot,[49] you have to find the tzaddik. Rebbe Nachman considers this so critical to

---

[49] The plural of "eitzah," which also translates as suggestion, advice, counsel, recommendation, proposal, etc.

your Jewish well-being that he says that you have to beg, plead and implore God a great deal to find such a teacher. This is so fundamental a Rebbe Nachman teaching that a motto for Breslov could be: *Find a tzaddik.*

As with anything else that is valuable, finding a tzaddik has its price. Be patient. Your hitbodedut will have to see you through wrong turns, mistaken impressions, legitimate candidates and charlatans. You may have to detect and deflect false reports about various candidates, sift through obnoxious words and questionable behavior of those who claim the mantle of "student," as well as analyze many other types of barriers that can keep you from getting the advice you need.

As always, honest hitbodedut will keep your motives honest. Are you looking for the tzaddik because you want to fit in, need a father surrogate, or want to have influence with someone important? These may be important psychological needs, but they are not going to help you find genuine eitzot. Your motives will draw you to a leader that matches them, but he won't necessarily be a tzaddik.

On the other hand, you may discover a number of genuine candidates and find yourself in a predicament: Which tzaddik? Reb Noson answers this question by comparing it to one of the laws of Shabbat.

> A person is lost in the wilderness and has lost track of time. Which day should he keep as Shabbat? The answer is all of them, since each day *could be* Shabbat. This applies until he finds out which day is really Shabbat.
>
> Similarly, one should treat each legitimate candidate as if he were the tzaddik. Keep pressing forward in your hitbodedut, beseeching God that He send you a Moshe to take you through and out of the desert.

If you're expecting me to endorse Rebbe Nachman's candidacy, I won't disappoint you. My endorsement is not based on "it's my opinion and it's very true." Rebbe Nachman has a number of things going for him which make him a font of long-lasting wisdom and personal guidance. Firstly, he was the great-grandson of the holy Baal Shem Tov and descended from a long line of tzaddikim dating back to King David. This means that he was blessed with a "genetic" predisposition to saintliness and leadership (which by definition includes bravery and sagacity).

Secondly, Rebbe Nachman himself was a hard worker. Not only did he push himself to master the texts of Judaism, but from a young age he devoted himself to do more than simply "talk the talk and walk the walk." With tremendous self-discipline, he exerted himself until he had total control over the body's passions. Thirdly, in his own lifetime, Rebbe Nachman was widely recognized as a master by his peers. Many who have studied his works over the intervening two centuries are startled by his perception and have the uncanny feeling that "Rebbe Nachman is talking to *me*." And even those who don't experience this personal connection from his works, do recognize and acknowledge the Torah and psychological genius contained in them.

You may be wondering, "Gee, isn't Rebbe Nachman long buried? How can a tzaddik who is dead be my spiritual mentor? How will he answer my questions? How can I even *ask* him my questions?"

Paradoxical as it may sound, a tzaddik who has passed away is more accessible than one who is alive. You do not need to travel to his home or office, you do not have to make an appointment, and you do not have to feel pressured that someone else is waiting or that "the great one" is in a hurry to take care of some other matter. Nor is his ability to offer advice limited by his inability to speak. His writings do the talking for him.

Rebbe Nachman teaches that the written word reveals a person's thoughts. Therefore, a spiritual master can commit his teachings and advice to writing, and an individual seeker can glean what he needs for his personal growth. This is not as far-fetched as it may seem. Each of us constantly bases many decisions on material written by experts (as well as quacks), including which diet to follow, which stocks and bonds to buy and which horses to bet on. Professionals refer to published formulas and algorithms to program computers, build bridges and develop new vaccines.

However, spiritual decision-making differs markedly from other types of decision-making in this respect: We can evaluate the aptness of non-spiritual decisions within a short amount of time. We will soon see whether or not we lose weight, our horse wins or the bridge stands. In addition, our bias to make the right choice and succeed is so strong that we usually try to read and understand the instructions to the best of our ability.

In contrast, the "rightness" of spiritual decisions is not always evident in any immediate result. Nor is it always apparent during the decision-making process, nor in how we feel before or after making the decision. And our bias to make the right decision in a spiritual context is greatly compromised by our emotions, desires and lack of spiritual wisdom, all of which we think we have enough of. What a person needs is honesty. If you think you cannot be honest enough on your own, talking it over with a trusted friend, or with someone wiser or more experienced, can help provide the honesty necessary for a true decision. (Genuine honesty is also necessary when receiving oral advice directly from a living tzaddik.)

It is certainly possible to have a viable spiritual master who is no longer physically present. Thousands and thousands of people have, and so can you.

UNDERSTANDING THE EITZAH

While finding a tzaddik is critical, it is by no means the end of the journey. In many ways it is just the beginning. Rebbe Nachman teaches that mere affiliation with a tzaddik is beneficial, even if you can't see any progress in your Jewishness.

Of course, you want actual growth, true fulfillment of your spiritual potential. That means that once you've found a tzaddik, you need to be prepared to accept his advice. This calls for not a little humility. "I need help—his help.[50] He knows the score better than I do." Part of humility means acknowledging that you don't always know how an eitzah works. Many times, the eitzah of a tzaddik is part of a package deal: One eitzah does not work fully or effectively unless it is practiced in conjunction with other eitzot.

> When considering candidates, bear in mind that the tower of genuine Torah, a tzaddik's Torah teachings, widens upwards and outwards from a few initial axioms. A few wisely-distilled words encompass and unify an ever greater range of Creation. ❋

Yet this point, as well as others, escapes us. We don't understand why or how something will or could possibly work. One eitzah seems so difficult, another too easy. Oftentimes your own Torah knowledge, or teachings heard from another tzaddik, seem to contradict what is being suggested to you now. It is imperative that you put your ego and mind on the shelf!

This can be very difficult, even painful. It requires a tremendous amount of trust, a letting-go to which you may be unaccustomed.[51] Deferring to the tzaddik, however, is vital for proper practice of the eitzot that will bring you closer to your goal. Think of yourself as a brain surgeon who needs brain surgery. Even if you've written the book on brain surgery, you are now in the position of having to rely on someone else. There is simply no other choice.

Being willing to accept advice and being able to understand it are two different things. Even at this point, even if you have been given all the pieces of the puzzle, it is still possible to arrange them in an ineffective or harmful way, God forbid.

---

[50] Technically speaking, a female can serve the role of eitzah-giving tzaddik (tzaddeket) publicly. Historically, however, this is rare.

[51] A fully honest letting-go may itself require years of dedicated hitbodedut.

One tool you can use to properly understand the eitzot of a tzaddik is our old friend, simcha. By now you know that no matter how bleak life looks, opening a hitbodedut session by thanking the caring Creator makes it look better. Reminding yourself that you've already enjoyed some happiness and good as a beneficiary of God's kindness (including the kindness of being able to thank God) can already bring a curl of a smile to your lips. Reflecting on the tikkun haolam that will ultimately be mankind's—and yours—shines a beautiful light, a truth-light, on all the thoughts that enter your mind. You will be able to see inside to the truth of an eitzah (even if you won't be able to put it into words).

Being b'simcha also allows you to keep a firmer rein on the wild horses of wrong-thinking, especially the stallions.[52] A mind astorm with passion is incapable of right-thinking. Every word, even if twice removed from suggestiveness, will be immediately cast into the boiling muck and soiled, to the point that it is not only covered with filth and unrecognizable as Torah, but becomes cast as pornography, God forbid.

Another tool which will help you understand a tzaddik's eitzot is the tool of right-thinking. As discussed earlier,[53] you can control your thoughts. To begin to properly understand the eitzot of the tzaddik, you need to begin to police your mind. The effort may be slow and tedious, but it is immediately effective. You become more proficient, despite occasional mistakes, at detecting which ideas need to be polished in order to light your way, and which are masquerading as good. You become more adept at recognizing which thoughts are beacons and which are false fires. The curtain begins to drop on the charade. Even if you continue to be bullied by undesired thoughts, don't enfranchise them.

By mastering your thinking, even by taking baby steps, even by running away from "them," you also maintain and strengthen the honesty of your focus. Even subliminal urges begin to be permanently stilled.

---

[52] See page 120.

[53] See page 117.

Mastering your thinking doesn't just mean "getting rid of the bad guys." It also means populating your mind with "the good guys"—namely, thoughts that are inherently able to produce kindness, faith, cheer and every other aspect of desirable Jewish living (including, ultimately, moments of intense longing and clinging to God[54]). The best source for finding these new citizens of your mind is the Torah.

You have an excellent precedent for using Torah as a guide for rebuilding your life. When God created the universe, He didn't create it "off the top of His head." First He carefully studied the blueprint—He delved into the Torah. Then He created the world by praying it into existence (*Chakhmah U'Tevunah* 14:10).

The blueprint is there to both inspire and instruct, but can do neither until it is perused. This is where you come in. When you approach Torah with proper appreciation for what it is, and with an open mind, you are already preparing yourself to consider what must be done and to deliberate how it must be done—hitbodedut! If you need more encouragement to study, think about where the tzaddik quarries his eitzot—yes, the Torah.

> Don't despair if you can't learn Torah as much as you would like, whatever the reason. It's impossible for any human being to study Torah 24/7. Rebbe Nachman reassures us that one who is not an accomplished Torah scholar can still be a perfectly fine Jew.
>
> If you're genuinely interested in finding God, you can find Him wherever you look. All the world can serve as a Torah text: the fury of the moment, a trembling leaf, a grain of sand. There is nothing in which you cannot see the Master's Hand, if you but wish to see It. Words, encouragement and true eitzot are all around you. ❈

Often, you may feel a sense of familiarity when studying the teachings of a tzaddik. A particular eitzah rings so true that you wonder why you never realized it before. Now that you do grasp

---

[54] "Deveikut" in Hebrew.

it, you think, "OK, I'll take the ball and run with it." Even in those instances when instant action may work, the eitzah will always produce better results if you first "turn it into tefilah"—i.e., use this Torah-based idea as a springboard for your hitbodedut.

The temptation to rush to act on a particular teaching partly stems from believing that an eitzah from a tzaddik is complete unto itself, a finished product. The eitzah of a tzaddik is not a fruit—it is a seed. The tzaddik plants it in your mind (if you let him); then it must blossom in your heart and bear fruit in your aspirations, actions and behavior. It is nurtured with your words and watered by your tears.

To make it grow, you have to use your hitbodedut to turn Torah into tefilah.

Turning Torah into Tefilah

Turning Torah into tefilah isn't particularly mysterious. It's a two-step process that combines two of the primary goals of Jewishness. First you study a teaching of a tzaddik, note the teaching's suggestions, and ask God to help you properly integrate those suggestions into your life. In fact, this is one of the primary goals of Jewishness.

At the same time, you constantly strive to improve your faith, observance and enjoyment of Jewishness. The Torah (the lesson of the tzaddik) becomes the springboard for your hitbodedut, and your desire to move from theory into practice helps you integrate your conclusions into your own life. The tzaddik's lessons help you plan your route, avoid closed roads and dead ends, and determine which exits you should take in order to bypass "accidents up ahead." Step by step, you can become more of the holy, integrated human being Creation is meant to house.

The first step in the process is to determine what the lesson is trying to emphasize. For example, one of Rebbe Nachman's lessons (*Likutey Moharan* I, 2) discusses generosity, morality and staying more focused during prayer. Is the lesson indicating a logical connection between its themes and goals, or perhaps a practical order for pursuing them? Acknowledge which of the points in the lesson most excite and intrigue you.

When you've determined how the various pieces of the lesson relate to one another, decide which piece is the easiest for you to integrate into your life right now. Following the topics we mentioned, perhaps it's easier for you, for whatever reasons, to be a little more generous than to curtail your flirting. At some point in your next session of hitbodedut, you could simply say something along these lines:

"God, You know I just learned that [tzaddik's name/book] recommends generosity as a way of improving concentration during prayer. You know how much my mind wanders when I pray. I barely realize what I'm saying—that I'm even saying anything!—till I'm almost done. So I've got to make some headway there.

"But You know generosity doesn't come easy to me. I've got plenty of money, thanks to Your being generous with me and giving me the great job that I have, but I'm always afraid that I might be fired tomorrow. I know it's ridiculous, but I do. And also, I don't like when people ask me for money. Why are they so lazy? Why don't they work harder? Sure, they might not become millionaires, but at least they won't have to take my hard-earned money from me!

"I know it's really not right to judge people like that. After all, what have I done that was so great that You give me so much? I need to move myself down a half-notch and look at the person asking as if it were me asking from You.

"Maybe I could start small by having a tzedakah box in my living room—a tzedakah box for an orphanage in Israel, let's say. Putting in dimes and quarters won't be painful. And they're just poor kids who need a break. I can handle giving to them.

"And You know what else, God? Since when I pray I want You to be generous with me, maybe *before* I pray I'll practice some generosity of my own and give some tzedakah then. Yeah, that's a good idea.

"I've got another good idea, Lord. If I'm willing to give up some of my money—even if it's just small change—maybe I can also give up some of my naughty daydreams about my co-workers, and think some more about the assignments I'm responsible for. We both know it won't be easy. I've been daydreaming since I was in seventh grade. But maybe I can apply the brakes at least sometimes. After all, I am a grandchild of Avraham, who was both openhanded and moral.

"And if I can think more about my work when I'm working, I'll be able to think more about my prayers when I'm praying. Please, God, let's give it a try. Help me start putting some money aside for an orphanage.

"God, thanks for listening, and thanks for putting these good ideas into my head. Please send me more."

That's it! No deep Talmudic reasoning necessary, nor any knowledge of Kabbalah or how the sefirot are aligned. All you need is a truly honest desire to live a more Jewish life, and you'll be able to understand the Torah well enough to figure out *your* next set of goals and the steps *you* need to achieve them.

Turning yourself around to follow the tzaddik's guidance— itself a step of the plan to meet your goals—and putting into words the desire and steps you need to take to follow the recommendations, is the master plan that will give birth to the major and minor parts of your short- and long-term goals.

As you speak of your new desire and anticipated changes in the Conference Room of hitbodedut, you will simultaneously confront past mistakes that may stymie forward efforts. By planning to overcome these mistakes for the sake of your future, your past becomes unbroken.

Looking for a common denominator for Shabbat and all the other holy days on the Jewish calendar? They are all days of teshuvah, of turning your life around so that you don't lose sight of your most important goals. A pity not to have hitbodedut on those days. ❊

In making your plans for Jewish progress and maintaining and cultivating your enthusiasm for same, let me warn you: It's not going to be a smooth ride. There will be plenty of ups and downs. Why is that? Well, one reason is that they've got your number. ("They" being your own propensity and desire for anti-Jewish living.) They've suckered you before into all sorts of things that would not do a tzaddik proud.

It may seem that they won't let you go, but with sufficient hitbodedut, the sprouting of the seeds that the tzaddik has planted within you will surely crack the walls of the prison, allowing for your eventual escape.

As you learn more Torah, formally and informally, the inter-connectedness of her teachings and messages also becomes clearer to you. This new perception allows to you to expand and deepen your hitbodedut. You come to know, for example, how the mitzvah of mezuzah can help you overcome greed and be more generous; how it can fill the rooms of your home with the holiness of the Land of Israel and potentially imbue you with more determination to stay moral. In this way, your hitbodedut becomes the "mother" of more and more of the good that you do.

Since it's your life that you're living and your life that you need to fix, you need to take what *you've* learned and turn it into a handmade, homemade prayer. Hitbodedut-planning is unlimited; you can touch any mitzvah, practice or trait that concerns you.

Sometimes simple is best: "May it be Your will that I not sin."

Sometimes simple is all you can manage: "May it be Your will that I not lose my temper—or my mind."

Sometimes you can shoot one arrow in two directions and hit both targets: "God, please let me know You forgive me for all the slander I've spoken, by helping me to speak no more slander." ❧

Why Pray?

At some point you may be struck by the question, "I have the Torah's wisdom to guide me. Why do I need to 'turn it' into hitbodedut? Why don't I just do it?"

Because all by its lonesome, Torah doesn't always work! This was Moshe's realization and desperate plaint after the sin of the golden calf: "If after the thunderous revelation we had at Sinai, when everything was made so clear and God Himself spoke to us, we still had it within us to go to the other extreme of belief and behavior, what hope is there to live by the Torah?!" God answered Moshe: Get to the core of the Torah by coaxing out of it the Divine mercy upon which it is based. In other words, turn Torah into tefilah.

> The Rebbe saw one of his lessons in writing. "The religious encouragement in my lessons is deep and wondrous. If it would be delivered as a sermon, it would inspire you and break your heart, because it is a great piece of ethical teaching.
>
> "Do as I suggested and turn my lessons into prayers. When you bring a lesson into words of inspiration and prayer, it will greatly inspire you and break your heart." ❧

Torah and tefilah share one crown. They have the same *raison d'etre*—namely, to bring us to live right. Torah is a necessary first step towards that goal because the road to Hell is also paved with good intentions. One must know what God defines as good. Yet even a Sinaitic revelation may not permanently change you. You may come to see the eitzah as old and stale, or the authority of its voice no longer impresses.

Prayer—particularly hitbodedut, which comes from the heart—takes the Torah's message from your mind and returns it more deeply to your heart, so that you become Torah, degree by degree. The outer manifestations of the Torah—its invaluable mitzvot—take on a multidimensional quality as the Torah's values become more and more a part of you. Your hitbodedut gives the body of the mitzvah its heart.

This is what is meant by the teaching, "Prayer is greater than Torah." It is this kind of prayer—and only this kind—that leads to genuine fulfillment of Torah in its outer observance, inner values and promotion of God-yearning. This is also the meaning of our Sages' statement, "Everything is in the hands of Heaven, except fear of Heaven" *(Berakhot 33b)*. Everything is under the purview of the Torah except for awareness of God; yet with prayer one can achieve that too.

> Three tzaddikim passed away on Shabbat afternoon: Moshe our teacher, who received the Torah on our behalf; King David, author of Psalms, who personifies prayer; and Yosef, the only one titled "Tzaddik." The tzaddik, by virtue of his morality and generosity, connects the brain and the heart, Torah and prayer.
>
> Shabbat afternoon is an *et ratzon*, a time of extra Divine favor. It is a time when all that we know (Torah/Moshe) and all that we feel (prayer/David) is meant to be awash with the desire to meld into giving to creation, receiving from the Creator, and giving to His creation (the function of the tzaddik/Yosef).
>
> It is a time to rise and realize what Creation can be before stepping back down into your body, ready to live that promise. It is the time God commits to creating the universe for another week. ❦

LEAVING THE PAST

The act of transforming Torah into tefilah can also help you overcome the shame of your past and approach your Jewishness afresh. If you are like most people, you don't have the inclination to look back on your mistakes. You must. The weeds of yesterday will continue to choke you for as long as you continue to avoid breaking the chain of events that led to them. The Torah you learn will open your eyes to your mistakes and motivate you to acknowledge them for what they are—mistakes. "Gee, God, I didn't know that sharing a juicy piece of gossip was such a big deal. I'm sorry I did that. I'll do my best not to let it happen again." Seeing things clearly for what they are will help you advance your own goals and tap into the essence of Creation, the reason God put you here on earth in the first place.

> Having our eyes suddenly opened to the immensity of what we have done may leave us close to speechless. Sincerity trumps brevity. Even the following can be effective: "I'm sorry. May it be Your will that I not sin again." ❋

In light of your horrific past, you may be too embarrassed to approach God for any kind of help. But you should go ahead and ask for His assistance to start living a more Jewish life. Our whole return is a plea to God: "Please take me back! Save me and help me from here on in to live by the Torah! I know I've failed and that's exactly why, and exactly what, I'm asking of You: Give me Your help to fix myself."

What gets in the way for many people, and what may be nagging at you, is that they have already tried, honestly and sincerely, many, many times—and failed. They saw no progress, or negative progress. The repeated efforts that resulted in repeated failure took the wind out of their sails. They weakened in their efforts and then despaired. The prophet Jeremiah addressed this lack of hope when he observed, "How long will you waver, rebellious daughter?" (Jeremiah 31:21).

What? You're too embarrassed to come back to God because you constantly repeat the same mistake? So what? That's no reason to be discouraged! It's not a reason for a person to be discouraged if he practices hitbodedut, transforming Torah into prayer. This is so because hitbodedut is the Future Path, which contains the

Spring of Salvation that never runs dry of God's compassion. If you call Him from there, there is no need for you to be ashamed or embarrassed.[55]

In your struggle to take the next step, to maintain your practice of hitbodedut and to continue the journey, remember: The Torah and mitzvot are all love.

Some fool once had the temerity to describe God as a mean old man with a stick. Nothing could be further from the truth. At Sinai we saw God as He is seen by a kosher eye: as a wise, compassionate elder. One expression of God's compassion is that He is not at all unreasonable. God knows better than you how difficult it is to be a human being. You can deal with Him, talk to Him and explain what you think is not working, and why.

When you point out why you think His current demands on you are too difficult to handle, or note that He is not supplying you with sufficient assistance to overcome the challenges you are facing, you aren't guilty of chutzpah. You can't be a nudnik with God; in fact, just the opposite is true. God *rejoices* when you "conquer" Him with your prayer (and song), when you convince Him to let you come another step closer. ❋

---

[55] Whether your focus is on sins of omission, or sins of commission.

⊢── 3 • ALL ABOUT FREE WILL ──⊣

At any stage of Jewishness, taking the next step seems overwhelming. This is true even for someone who has grown up in Judaism, who is long familiar with its challenges and its methods, and who has been dialoguing with God since way back when. All the more so for those who are taking their first tentative steps. Judaism appears so overwhelming: Familiar activities and foods often have to be jettisoned; new friends and acquaintances, with new social mores, join or replace old ones; one wonders if he or she will ever be able to actually observe Shabbat properly, say the prayers and blessings accurately, or even learn Hebrew. There's so much to do in Judaism—how can I ever do it all?!

> When Rebbe Nachman began his studies as a child, he found it quite difficult. He cried and cried to God: "Please help me to understand what I'm studying!" Even when he was older and began to learn the mysteries of the Kabbalah, Rebbe Nachman cried to God to help him properly understand the Torah's secrets. ❦

Rebbe Nachman reassures us, "Take it easy. Don't panic. Just go step by step." As discussed earlier,[56] hitbodedut is part self-judgment. You need to reflect on and evaluate what tools and vessels you have *today*. What can you do with them? What are the situations you face *today*? Do you have to defend your Jewish turf from internal or external heathenism, or is it your responsibility to cast sacred light onto some heretofore pagan portion of your life?

As you weigh the factors and ask God for His necessary help so that you may make the best choices for the path ahead, don't be

---

[56] See page 88.

a copycat. God doesn't want two of that other guy, no matter how big and impressive his Jewishness is. If God wants another of that other guy, He'll have him cloned. What God wants is that you be the best Jew *you* can be.

Rebbe Nachman teaches that the ideal place for hitbodedut is a derekh yechidi—literally, a solitary road. In a deeper sense, he is saying that you must take a path in life that is solely and uniquely yours.[57] That takes guts. You must walk, talk and perhaps even look like everyone else in your community, but at the same time think like the individual you are. Walking your path is a fine balancing act on the high wire of the narrow bridge called Life. On the one hand, you must submit your ego to the Jewish community's needs for compliance to external standards (law and order, if you will); on the other hand, you need to express your self so that the community's Jewishness will be richer. This also may take some holding back of the ego. Playing second violin—or second fiddle—does not have the cachet you seek, but it does add depth, luster and harmony to the first violin and the orchestra as a whole. It's a job that God wants done cheerfully and well.

> You may not like your job, or some of your associates. Draw some inspiration from Yosef the Tzaddik and the Grim Reaper. The Midrash relates that even though he was imprisoned for ten years, Yosef the Tzaddik kept himself cheerful and danced every day.
>
> In the holy Zohar it is told to Rabbi Shimon bar Yochai, "Do you think the Angel of Death is happy that he has to go around all day killing people? No! But he pretends he's happy because killing people is the job God assigned him. He even dances at funerals to give the impression that he's happy to do whatever God wants."
>
> How bad did you say your job is? ❋

---

[57] Everyone's mezuzah has the same text and is affixed to the same side of the doorpost, but no two people kiss it the same way as they enter or exit the room.

Do you have any idea of the greatness you can achieve? Do you have any conception of the power of the Torah and mitzvot at your disposal, the level of refinement to which they can bring you, the intimacy with God for which they can prepare you? Without the tzaddik to teach you what you can be, without your weaving the threads of his wisdom into the fabric of your life, your choices will be copycat, non-human choices. You will ape the spirituality of others, but never have your own.

Decide For Yourself

The tool that will give you the most strength to assert your self, choose your direction and achieve your goals is free will.

Free will—the ability to change your direction at any time, for the good or the bad—is one of the biggest mysteries in life, if not the biggest. It is what drives Creation. The whole of Creation was brought into existence just so that you and every member of mankind would be allowed to decide what to make of Life. It is the element of "why" and "what for" that underlies every thing, activity, concept and event that God has brought or will bring into existence. Angels don't have it. Animals don't have it. Only human beings have it. It's all to present you with the challenge: What do you really want?

Free will means that no matter how much physical or intellectual strength you have at any given moment, you have the ability to freely decide among the options given you. In other words, no matter how low you have sunk in your Jewishness, or even in your basic humanity, you can always decide—right now!—to turn it around and start living the way you ought.

The flip side of this is, of course, that one can always make a U-turn and start heading in the wrong direction, God forbid. Your lifelong job is to seek His will and give in to it. The struggle to master your will ends when life ends.

The hard part of anything a person has to do for God is the part left to his own free will—the things he has to decide for himself without being explicitly told or asked to do. In all acts of devotion, an element is left for the individual to grapple with and decide by himself. He must decide and choose for himself. Free will is where the essential spiritual work lies. There is always room for doubt about what God really wants, since He has given no instructions.

You can literally choose to become a sinner or a saint. Your desire can be so strong that you can even force God to allow you to fulfill your every wanton desire! "What?" you exclaim. "Is this guy telling me that if I want to become a jet-setting, international playboy, I can? If I want to be a dean of a yeshivah, I can?" Yes and yes—if your desire is strong enough and you truly believe that you can achieve your goal. Hopefully, after studying Torah and imbibing a tzaddik's eitzot, your desire will lean more towards the latter than the former. There are no guarantees, though. This is why your practice of hitbodedut is so necessary. You have to keep your hitbodedut going to maintain your positive desire.

"Me, holy? A spiritual beacon? Not in a million years. It can't be done!"

What you think you know, and what you accept as incontrovertible about who you are, can be your worst enemies. Such intellectual, material, emotional and spiritual "facts" bar your entry into the Jewishness you cherish and for which you are beginning to yearn. Your prayer to be saved from such "enemies" is psalms-like.

"As a matter of fact, I do want to follow the tzaddik's advice, but..." I know, I know. You're not the only one who complains, "If only I had more money, more time, more health, lived there, didn't have to deal with..., etc." We all fall victim to this false self-pity. Reb Noson shares with us some of his faith:

Anyone who wants to have mercy on himself must know and believe that his free will depends specifically on these exact conditions—poverty, illness, confusion, troubles, aggravation and stress, as well as life's happier aspects—that God has arranged, and that they are for his eternal benefit.

Always remember: Your free will would no longer be free, and your ability to choose between right and wrong would completely collapse, if the immediate circumstances of your life were different.[58]

The fact is, God is always behind the scenes, trying to nudge your hand so that you'll select the "winning" ticket. In everything that happens (even that which seems counter-productive) and in everything you say and do (even that which is wrong by every standard), God attempts to make you feel His presence. The events in your life and your decisions do not take place in a vacuum. God's moves are weighed in response to yours, so that they prepare you and hold the door open for you, until you bestir yourself to choose to enter.

One of the greatest challenges of free will is to hone it to such a degree that you are able to anticipate and intuit what God truly wants from you before you actually know it. To be more attuned and sensitive to what God wants, you have to seek His will. You might want to follow the proactive lead of Rebbe Nachman's eldest daughter, Udel, who would often be heard asking herself, "What can I do for God now?"

You choose the direction. You program the response. "One who comes to purify himself is helped; he is told to wait. One who comes to corrupt himself is given opportunities to do so" (Yoma 38b). The kind and quality of good that God provides—including Torah, mitzvot and guidance—is unformed. You determine how it gets molded and actualized. You need to pray a lot that you "get it" and that you not be led astray, because the direction you choose is the direction you will be shown!

In Rebbe Nachman's writings, choosing wrongly is directly connected to the galut HaShekhinah (exile of the Divine presence). She is caught and trapped, imprisoned in people's mis-wanting, mis-thinking and mis-doing. Yet to spring the Shekhinah from

---

[58] This does not preclude requesting a bettering of your state. But be aware that the "new and improved" situation demands abilities you may not possess in sufficient strength, if at all.

prison, intuiting the Divine will, seems like a lot of Jewishness to ask from someone who can perhaps barely read a word of Hebrew! It seems so for one reason only: You don't know your own strength.

How hard is it for an elephant to put a mouse permanently out of commission? Not hard at all; just one soft press of its pachydermic pedal. We have the same relative strength in battling our temptations. The problem is we are like Dumbo—we think the mouse is mighty.

Sometimes a false inner-voice tells you: This thing has beaten you so many times, you ain't never going to beat it! Behold a mystery of free will: Even after you've failed and failed and failed, and find yourself in the position and frame of mind to totally resign from Jewishness and Judaism, you still have the ability to choose otherwise. You can regain all you've lost, and then some.

Rebbe Nachman puts it this way:

> Your mind can withstand any temptation. It is written, "God gives wisdom to the wise" (Daniel 2:21). Every person has potential wisdom. This potential must be used. This potential alone can overcome all temptations. …This can give you greater strength.
>
> You may have succumbed to desire and sinned in many ways. Your intellect may be confused and weak. Yet you still have some intelligence. With one grain of intelligence, you can overcome the world and all its temptations.

The wisdom to which Rebbe Nachman refers includes the awareness that you can defeat temptation, if you want to. You are no match for your evil inclination—you are much stronger, as strong as an elephant in comparison to a mouse! To succeed, you must first believe in your strength and potential. Don't ever sell yourself short! The next step is to follow our Sages' advice and use hitbodedut to ask God for His help to resist temptation.

The only way to defeat the negativity of temptations, emotions and influences—past or present—is to ask God for His help. The necessities of human life, which God in His kindness has made so pleasant for us to enjoy, are highly susceptible to corruptive influences. Sights and sounds of advertisements, of other people's enjoyment, tease our less-than-perfect characters into jealousy, selfishness and excess. By targeting a trait that is particularly irksome and detrimental and aiming at it heartfelt words, you can free your will to choose what you want, not what someone else wants you to want.

The effects of your decisions not only impact your life, nor are they only for the here and now. Any time you are faced with temptation, the Talmud enjoins you to consider that you—and all of mankind—may be equally balanced between merit and demerit. Your choice, made in the dark of night, in the privacy of your own home, in the innermost chambers of your heart and mind, is of great consequence. What you decide makes a big difference.

The story and career of the prophet Balaam, the wicked and perverse, is a cautionary tale. He was able to achieve a degree of Divine revelation that rivaled Moshe's! He did so by sheer dint of his free will.

Balaam had such tremendous determination and drive for money and fame that he was able to engineer a situation that endangered the lives of the entire Jewish people. When God told Balaam not to go near the Jews' encampment in the desert, Balaam countered God with words. When God told Balaam that he would be permitted to speak only the words God chose, Balaam countered God with words. Even when the donkey spoke to Balaam and Balaam saw the angel barring his way, Balaam again countered God with words, so determined was he to gain his fortune and vent his anti-Semitism.

Balaam didn't want to submit to God! Each time he was told "no," he bluffed his way along with a high-sounding, well-worded excuse. So although the Divine will was clearly that he stay home, Balaam arrived at the mountaintop, ready to perpetuate genocide, God forbid. Why was he able to get that far? A person is led on the path he wants to go! If one can go so far, acting contrary to God's will, using the wrong words, imagine what a person can achieve using the right words. ❧

You can achieve anything you want—if you want it badly enough. You need to be determined, for the process may take years. You can quit at any time. There will be obstacles and hindrances enough to dissuade you from your objective. But you can refuse to weaken your will and keep pushing forward till you succeed. Your success, made up of your determined exercise of your free will in choice after choice, will have immeasurable bearing on what you, your family, your community and the world will look like.

THE GREAT VOID

There exists a stage in life where your free will be tested like never before. This is the Great Void, a "place" or stage in which you have to believe that God is there even when everything indicates that He is not. In a concentration camp, a war zone, or the darkest recesses of your own heart, no amount of knowledge or intelligence can save you—only faith.

> The primary example of the Great Void is Akeidat Yitzchak, the Binding of Yitzchak. God said to Avraham, "Bring Yitzchak as an olah (a wholly-burnt offering)…" (*Genesis* 22:2).

> This commandment contradicted everything that Avraham stood for. At the time of Akeidat Yitzchak, Avraham was 137 years old. For over 100 years he had been teaching about the one true God, a God of kindness and mercy. He imitated God's quality of kindness and opened his home to travelers. Slaughtering his son would undermine his entire credibility.

> It could also seriously damage his relationship with God. He could very well ask, "Where is the God Who promised me descendants? Where is the God Who promised my descendants the Land? Where is the God Who promised that my teachings about Him would be perpetuated?" Where, indeed?

In order to survive the Great Void, you have to acknowledge the testimony of your senses and experience—emptiness, complete, total and absolute—and override that testimony with faith—God's presence. For however long you may have to endure the Great Void, you must be able to live with both elements of the paradox simultaneously.

Despite the many questions and doubts he could have raised about this inscrutable command, Avraham knew one thing: He had heard it directly from God. For him, God was manifestly present in this torturous test. Avraham practiced the simple rule for success in Jewishness that Rebbe Nachman later put into words: *Make sure that God is in everything you do. Don't consider whether it will bring you prestige or not. If it brings prestige to God, do it! And if not, don't do it!*

Yitzchak also came to this realization, albeit in a different way. As father and son climbed the mountain, Yitzchak said to Avraham, "Here is the fire and the wood, but where is the lamb for the olah?" Avraham replied, "God will choose for Himself a lamb for the olah—my son" (*Genesis* 22:7-8).

"Where is the place of His [God's] glory?" (Shabbat Mussaf Liturgy).

In contrast to Avraham, Yitzchak did have a question. And he posed a question that turned out to be not only an answer, but a revelation. His father told him that God had commanded an olah to be brought. Yitzchak bore the firewood on his back. His father carried the fire and the knife. The only thing missing was a lamb, unless...unless *he* was the lamb. How could the God of kindness be present? How could God be responsible for such a command? He turned to his father, the man who had championed God across the globe, and asked, "*Where* is the place of God's glory?" It doesn't seem to include my situation. God is not manifest here.

But, Rebbe Nachman teaches, the situation in which "Where?" is asked, *is* the place of God's glory. Asking, "Where?" *is* the lamb for the olah. It contains the belief that, no matter what, He is here. Even in a situation in which you do not see God—when, for all intents and purposes, God is absent, and you want to scream, "GOD! WHERE ARE YOU?!"—realize that you have just revealed His presence.

If you find yourself in the Great Void, soul survival demands your practicing hitbodedut every single day. Free will—the decision to choose God or not—is tested as in no other situation because it's winner take all. The honesty and sincerity, if not the outright desperation, of pleading for your soul, of begging to be granted life, to be privileged to be invited closer, and to honestly live God's work with your every breath, is the only coin of value.

It's impossible to survive the Great Void without hitbodedut. The onslaught of questions, the persistence of pain and the sense of total meaninglessness cannot be withstood without continuous knocking on the doors of a markedly abandoned, empty castle. This is why Rebbe Nachman told us many times that all the great, genuine tzaddikim, himself included, said they achieved what they did only through hitbodedut.

Hitbodedut, then, is the foundation of all your Jewish practice, study and attitudes—indeed, of your entire Jewishness. ❋

⊢— 4 • STRENGTHENING YOUR RESOLVE —⊣

You know what you want. You've silenced the noise in your mind and heard the only voice that has a right to cast a vote—yours. You've made the choice for how you want to live; now, how do you maintain it?

I must let you in on a well-known secret, one that is spoken in words unclear, mumbled, whispered and hurried: You're still torn. You haven't yet admitted it—maybe you haven't yet sensed or recognized it—but you're still torn. Part of you wants so very, very much that which connects you to God (a.k.a. mitzvah), but part of you still licks his lips for the desire.

What did you expect? Did you think that after decades of pursuing physical pleasure, comfort and honor—actively, passively and subliminally—your body and mind would now acquiesce to the soul without a struggle? Nah. That happens so rarely, it's statistically insignificant.

This is a lot of what hitbodedut is about and what a lot of your hitbodedut has to be about—namely, strengthening your positive soul-will, drumming it into yourself: "I want that next good objective, and if I don't want it, I want to want it."

The essential purpose of your hitbodedut is to capture the sacred focus of your mind and aim it at your heart in order to heal your soul.

Yet pain and spiritual confusion can leave you wordless, emptied of prayer. No matter what your spiritual history predicts for your soul's future, use your free will to keep speaking sacred words, including Torah. Why? Because as long as you're still breathing, there's hope. How? By declaring your faith, loud and clear, that God will take you back because you mean that much to Him. By uttering the High Holiday prayer, "God, please grant eloquence to those who yearn for You."

Keep speaking with the sincere hope that maybe, maybe you'll find your way to reclaiming your Jewishness. This is the essential exercise of your free will: your words of prayer and hitbodedut.

MOSHE

Moshe erred but slightly. Instead of speaking to the rock, as God instructed him, he struck it. God immediately informed Moshe of the awful punishment: Moshe would not be permitted entry into the Holy Land.

Moshe was distraught. Being in the Holy Land was so special, so precious, so crucial to being a Jew. He acknowledged his mistake and regretted it mightily. He pleaded and begged God again and again, in so many different ways, to rescind the decree. He didn't voice the same prayer over and over, but continually changed tacks and even negotiated: "Perhaps as a deer, perhaps as a bird, just to fly through the holy air of the Holy Land—*something!*"

Nor did he beg God once, twice, a dozen or a hundred times. Moshe prayed *515 times* for permission to enter the Holy Land until finally God told him, "No more! Do not ask Me again." And Moshe never asked for it again.

The Midrash tells us that had Moshe prayed *one more time*, his request would have been granted.

The moral of the story? Everything has its price in prayer. You never know when one more will bring you the Jewishness you crave. ❀

DON'T GIVE UP

"The cat says: 'I will pursue my enemies and overtake them; I will not return until I have destroyed them'" (*Psalms* 18:38).

The Midrash puts these words of King David into the cat's mouth to teach us that one of the lessons we can learn from feline behavior is persistence. Whether your enemy is envy, meanness, overeating or depression, keep going after it. Don't give up.

Rebbe Nachman was annoyed when others said that his success was due to the gift of his especially lofty soul. "NO! I achieved what I did only through *hard work. Only through hard work!*"

Whatever your job is and whatever plan you have, Rebbe Nachman regularly stressed that in order to succeed you have to work hard. Don't take too many coffee breaks (or play solitaire!), because the job won't get done. Too many breaks and self-interruptions mean you are confused, that your mind and heart are in exile. They also indicate that your desire is not strong enough. ❉

Doubts of a practical nature are also part of the path you can expect to tread. You are challenged by a situation in which you see no option or can't decide between competing options. No option seems good and you feel that you're in a lose-lose situation. It may be impossible to know which option you should choose.[59] Your frustration is palpable. Silence is just not possible; it would close your heart more, making you like a deer caught in the headlights. The remedy for such a situation is to scream!

There definitely is a way out. It's just that you need an immense amount of hitbodedut—perhaps even screaming yourself hoarse—

---

[59] Rebbe Nachman taught that even super-tzaddikim don't automatically know what to do.

to find the escape hatch.[60] If you don't find it, at least you did what you were supposed to do. Nothing more is required of you. God chose for you.

> What if a spiritual or material plan backfires despite your best hitbodedut efforts?
>
> On the last Yom Kippur eve of his life, Rebbe Nachman was visited by two of his followers, one of whom was ill. The other said, "His illness has gotten worse because he immersed in the mikveh." Rebbe Nachman responded, "Why do you blame his suffering on a mitzvah? Better to blame it on a sin."
>
> Don't lay the blame of your failure at the feet of your good desire or deed. Blame it on bad karma from previous mis-doings! ❋

BE KIND TO YOURSELF

Sooner or later, gentle reader, even the most slowly chewed session of hitbodedut ends. You must step back into the ring to face many—or all—of the challenges for which you have been preparing. You may ask yourself, "How will I fare? How well have I wielded the gentle sword of hitbodedut?" You will know by how charitable you are with yourself.

"God is judge, lowering one and raising the other" (*Psalms* 75:8). Rebbe Nachman says that this verse applies to you. You have to "lower" yourself by taking away time and interest from activities that once commanded your attention. You need to "raise the other" activity, the one that will lead to your chosen goal.

This is an act of charity—charity to your self. Although we usually think of charity as being a gift given out of tenderness

---

[60] Words may not exist when you are in spiritual stalemate or when your heart is dizzy. Screaming helps at such times as well. This is what King David would do (see *Psalms* 38:9-11).

or weakness, Rebbe Nachman teaches that genuine charity calls for a certain toughness to weigh where (and how) to place your resources so that they will be the most effective. In order to get things to their rightful places, you've got to make some tough decisions. Something is going to have to give. Something is going to have to suffer a loss.

"Fortunate is the person who gives charity to the poor, and conducts his affairs judiciously" (ibid., 112:5). When you realize how impoverished your soul is compared to what she should have, you will give her—your self—the "charity" of living life in a more humane way.

> "God, there's this class in Rebbe Nachman's teachings that I know I should go to. I want to go. But there's a special TV show/movie/ concert at the same time. Rebbe Nachman said that he succeeded only because of his hard work. I need to do this, to go to this class, even though—because!—it's so hard for me. Help me to do it! Let me go.

> "Rebbe Nachman said that that the greatest thing I can do for You is that which is the hardest for me to do. Help me tear myself away from that other stuff and do what I need to—for You, if not for me! For me, if not for You!"

There are many levels of desire, even in one person. At every moment your desire can change. The main thing is to yearn for God. To do this you must remain young. Renew yourself and make a fresh start each day. This way you can improve in any area of Jewishness you choose. ❊

Room 3

The Bedroom

Love songs. Looking for love, being in love and losing one's love have captured people's imaginations from time immemorial. King David's love for God is the source of our most precious book of prayer, *Psalms*. King Solomon says that our love for God can be filial, spousal, fraternal, affectionate and ecstatic, all rolled into one.

Hitbodedut is the rendezvous for planting and nurturing that love, for meeting and sharing it with absolute intimacy. ❈

—— 1 • FINDING YOUR PARTNER ——

"Our bed is lusty" (*Song of Songs* 1:16).

Earlier we wrote[61] that you might not be used to hearing "intense" and "Jewish" in the same sentence. You might not be used to hearing yourself string together the words "I," "love" and "God" in the same sentence, either. But loving God is, in fact, a mitzvah, and an integral part of the Shema. And "love songs" defines King David's *Psalms*, the quintessential book of prayer.

Rebbe Nachman points out that lovingly daydreaming about God is a way of connecting with Him, no less than wearing tzitzit or tefilin or doing other mitzvot (*Rabbi Nachman's Wisdom* #24).

The types of love for God are many—they include all the loves we have for people like parents, siblings, spouses, children, lovers and best friends. They also include different kinds of love, from the ecstatic "drunk with love" to the "staying up all night to take care of the baby" kind. The love of our patriarch Yaakov for our matriarch Rachel (the Kabbalistic paradigm of God's love for the Jewish people) provides a model of love that covers the entire spectrum.

When they first met, Yaakov recognized the spectacular beauty of Rachel's wisdom and faith, as well as their innate relationship and that they were intended for one another. Ecstatic at his find, he immediately sealed their connection with a kiss.

Yaakov didn't give mere lip service to being in love. His thrill at having met Rachel was not satisfied by their brief initial encounter. He was undaunted by the prospect of having to work for seven years to win her hand, and his desire for her was not dampened when he was duped into working an additional seven

---

[61] See page 67.

years after that. The bitter cold of long winter nights and the broiling heat of long summer days were all a price worth paying to realize his union with Rachel.

Even the presence of other wives and the welcome addition of children to his life failed to detract from his love for her. Rachel was Yaakov's *numero uno*, the mistress of his home. As soon as they became "one flesh" with the birth of their first child, Yaakov and Rachel headed for the Promised Land.

You can build and nurture a love relationship with God that has the same intensity and commitment as that of Yaakov for Rachel. You can experience the thrill of an "embrace," a "kiss,"[62] "courtship" and union with God that exceeds any earthly pleasure. How? Through hitbodedut. Each time you use hitbodedut to bring God-awareness to your heart, "marrying" various spiritual energies of Creation to one another in an appropriate way, you feed new and stronger God-awareness into the world. Each time you use hitbodedut to turn your heart from fulfilling your own desires to fulfilling God's, Creation—God's "child"—is born anew.

Your Partner longs for you. God is, as it were, unsatisfied. His unfathomable powers mean nothing to Him without you. Prior to creating mankind, God exercised His wisdom and sculpted a planet and a universe whose depths of wisdom and grandeur have yet to be adequately described. To give it meaning, He then created mankind, breathing into the first human being the ability to speak and to unite with Him. Being your Partner is His overriding desire.

God trusts you. He knows that you can run His "house" and do a masterful job of it, at that. He trusts you so much that He gives you the ability to pray to Him, to ask for whatever you want so you can better express your love for Him. Prayer—hitbodedut—

---

[62] Please bear in mind that terms like "embrace" and "kiss," as they are used here, allude to stages or degrees of closeness, and not to the physical actions these words ordinarily refer. This is true for all study of Kabbalah.

becomes the vibrant, dynamic force that can bring the two of you together in a passionate embrace.

Too often, though, we misunderstand prayer as request, as a submissive, dependent, classically feminine practice. Rebbe Nachman teaches that our prayers are also husbandly, providing God, as it were, with "livelihood, clothing and intimacy" (*Exodus* 21:10). Your hitbodedut, sung in honesty, will simultaneously provide all three.

Are we a match? you're wondering.

When Eliezer told our matriarch Rivkah's family how he had found her and recognized that she was Yitzchak's intended, they responded, "This match is from God" (*Genesis* 24:50). The Midrash interprets the exchange this way: Where did the match originate? From Mount Moriah, the site of the Temple. The Hebrew Name of God used in this verse is the holiest one, the Tetragrammaton. Rebbe Nachman relates this name to matrimonial prospects (*Likutey Moharan* II, 2:4).

It was with this same Name of compassion and unity that God took us, the Jewish people, as His bride at Mount Sinai. Later He told us to construct the Mishkan, the portable sanctuary in the desert. There, as in the Holy Temple in Jerusalem, His Divine presence, the Shekhinah, dwelt among us. For over 400 years, the Jewish people demonstrated their affection and devotion to God, and He to us, in the Holy Temple. Today, that same union can be achieved in hitbodedut.

In a very real sense, your hitbodedut can be a Holy Temple, a place where Earth kisses Heaven. The Holy Temple served a number of functions. It was the place where God was able to "stretch out" — that is to say, to fully allow Himself to reach out to embrace His people and make His presence more strongly and widely felt. It was the place where the Shekhinah could rest and could call "home." And it was the place that brought the blessing of children to the Jewish people.

Hitbodedut is where you can offer God a place to "stretch out," to allow Him to fully reach into the depths of your being as you curl up and nestle into His arms. Here you can lie down comfortably and securely. Here you can feel that you're "home"—you have no more need to wander elsewhere for satisfaction or meaning. And here is where you and God can multiply your offspring—your good deeds born of your interaction in the Bedroom.

> The Midrash asks why the site of the Holy Temple is named Mount Moriah (*moRiYah* in Hebrew)? To allude to *heiRaYon*, pregnancy and fecundity, which it facilitates. ❀

The Holy Temple served other bedroom-like functions as well. There people offered thanks, sought forgiveness and expressed appreciation. In short, the Holy Temple was a place of love, a home for God and both the Jew and the Jewish people. Any Jew, even one who had made serious mistakes, could always "come home," make amends and make up, and start again. This was true even for the people as a whole; their communal infractions could be washed away.

Your hitbodedut is a place of such love. It too is a place of rapprochement, a place you can—and are invited to—go if you've lost your mindfulness and left the fires of passion untended. So many things can go wrong between a couple, yet they turn and return to one another, to forgive one another, wipe the slate clean and embrace anew. That's why you need to know that hitbodedut is your Bedroom, where you meet God in total privacy. ❀

> Rebbe Nachman strongly recommended having a hideaway for hitbodedut. Some things just need to be private. Just to spend time in such a room is beneficial (*Rabbi Nachman's Wisdom* #275). ❀

⊢— 2 • PREPARING YOURSELF —⊣

Coming into the Bedroom requires a certain attitude. You've got something on your mind and you want your Partner to be as interested and excited as you are. You want your Partner to enjoy what's on the way, so you'll get yourself primed to perform as best as you can. So start things off by primping yourself.

> When you say the psalms, Rebbe Nachman told him, read it in the "first person," that you're the hero. But, asked the chassid, how can I apply to myself a verse like, "Protect me because I am devout" (*Psalms* 86:2)? There are times, Rebbe Nachman responded, that you've got to make your heart swell with pride in your Jewishness. This is the meaning of, "He elevated his heart in the ways of God" (II *Chronicles* 17:6) (*Likutey Moharan* II, 125).

The practice of recounting your good points, the things that are right about you, is not always meant to be a last-ditch effort to maintain or establish dignity or worth. Instead, it's meant to "wake up" something that exists but has not yet developed. In the Bedroom, it is specifically meant to stir the passion that expresses the love of you and your Partner for one another, so that you can be united in your "children" — the good that can yet be born from your relationship. You want to make yourself and your Partner aware that you are not only alive, but interested and interesting. You are a fertile source of potential new life, and you want that potential to be used to further *His* interests.

"Children" can mean flesh-and-blood offspring,[63] but one's most authentic "children" are his good deeds (*Bereishit Rabbah* 30:6; *Rabbi Nachman's Wisdom* #253). We, the Jewish people, are God's children (*Deuteronomy* 14:1). Through "uniting" with Him and having "children," we bring Divine goodness and positiveness into the world.

---

[63] See below, page 213.

Coming Clean

Sometimes, however, you may come into the Bedroom feeling "back to back," not ready to be with your Lover. You may feel that God doesn't really love you. "I'm not so lovable. I feel and look so yucky."

Alas, if you're feeling yucky and think that you're not so beloved, that may in fact be the case. It's hard to be intimate with someone who feels he has nothing to share. So you have to show yourself that you're attractive, that you've got something that your Partner wants and can't get anywhere else. Look in the mirror and wash yourself off.

In the Holy Temple, before the kohen could approach and begin his service, he had to wash his hands and feet at the kiyor (sink). The original kiyor in the Mishkan was made from the mirrors that the Jewish women used in Egypt to beautify themselves in order to arouse their husbands.

To improve on those feelings of being unloved, come clean and admit your mistakes, even your worst indiscretions. Don't be scared—God already *knows* what you've done. That's not the point of confession. The point is to remove the barriers that perpetuate the distance and the distrust that inhibit Him from giving you more of His closeness. Rebbe Nachman teaches that speaking words of confession casts the wrongdoing out of your bones, and instead bonds you to God with wholeness.

Any sort of guilt or deceit that lingers because you whitewashed—instead of cleansed away—your wrong-living is going to make your hitbodedut-bedroom a cold, cold place. You will avoid it to the best of your ability.

Since it takes two to tango, you need to let God know that you're honest about who you are, what you've been, that you know He loves you, and that you want to love Him in return and be with Him. Expressing your desire for His help in this increases your love for Him and creates the space in your heart to receive His love for you.

> In praising the Jewish people, God says, "My bride, you loved Me with one of your eyes" (*Song of Songs* 4:9). Why with only one eye? asks the Talmud. Because the other eye was already on the golden calf (*Shabbat* 88b). Even if your sincere love of God is all too brief, God still loves you for it (*Rabbi Nachman's Wisdom* #123). ❧

> Need more proof that God loves you? He had it written into this book and had you read it! ❧

As crucial as it is to admit past mistakes, it can be just as crucial to confess concerning the future: "I don't know where to go from here." As you proceed along your spiritual path you will come to many crossroads. Should you turn right? Left? Keep going straight? Expressing your love for God by showing your trust, showing that you can "confess" to Him, speak of your mistakes, failures and successes, and make yourself vulnerable by asking for direction in spite of—and because of—your shortcomings, extends to Him a powerful invitation to express His love for you in return.

Rebbe Nachman points out that these first words of reconciliation, bitter as they may be, are the parts of hitbodedut that make peace.

> If you feel that God is angry at you, sing your hitbodedut. When the King sees you presenting the Queen—your prayer—in such radiant clothing, His anger disappears (*Likutey Moharan* I, 42:1). ❧

LOVING YOURSELF

Whenever you enter the Bedroom of hitbodedut, keep in mind the distinction between the emotion of love and the partnership of love. Before you can start working together as partners, you must first elicit and then feel the emotion of love. Eliciting the love (and more and more of the love) entails looking for it, *wanting* the emotion and *trusting* the emotion, *on both sides* of the equation—yours and, as it were, God's. This is because in hitbodedut you're doing both parts of the work, carrying both sides of the conversation (but not the load!). When you speak out your pain, the Shekhinah speaks out Hers (*Likutey Moharan* I, 259).

Before you can love someone else, you have to be in love with yourself. If one party in a relationship feels down on himself, he makes himself a rather unlovable partner indeed. In addition to recalling your good points and confessing your mistakes, another way to be in love with yourself is to interpret the events of your life positively. Accept and realize that all of God's interactions with you stem from His immense love towards you.

You must also be at peace with yourself. Such peace is had by acknowledging your shortcomings and failures and accepting the responsibility to set things aright for as many mistakes as possible. Two important teachers are available to help guide your hitbodedut in this effort: the Torah and the tzaddik. The Torah can teach you not only *what* your mistakes may have been, but what prognosis your mistakes can offer.[64] The Torah's guidance, properly understood and followed, will impart information and clues to help you better understand your Partner and your life.

The personalized touch and example of a tzaddik goes a long way towards generating peace in the world and in every human heart. A tzaddik, by definition, has pacified the storm of sexual lust, maintaining the integrity of the covenant between Jew and

---

[64] For example, if passionate curiosity has led one to peruse other people's personal matters, he might, after proper preparation, devote himself to the mysteries of the Torah.

God. Rebbe Nachman teaches that we have a promise that such a person will know inner peace (see *Numbers* 25:12). Rebbe Nachman often equates the function of the tzaddik with that of the kohen in the Holy Temple, as both serve to bridge the gap between Jew and God, and forge peace and harmony between both parties.

As the high priest/ess of your hitbodedut, your function is to forge a true peace with your Partner so that love can flow in its wake. Many times during hitbodedut, particularly in the Bedroom, you will have to speak your Partner's piece. What your Partner has to say—couched in the letters of the Torah you study—has to be turned into a *Shalom Aleikhem*[65]—a peace song and a love song.

Song draws a couple closer together (*Likutey Moharan* I, 226, 237). ✤

Just like a pie is too big to be swallowed whole, so is the love the Torah contains too big to be swallowed whole. Therefore, it is encased in letters, words, verses and chapters. Just as a child begins to recognize the letters one by one, and then learns to combine them into words and read them in sentences, so too your appreciation for your Partner's love—and your ability to express your love for Him—grows slowly,[66] but with dedication and determination, surely.

The Torah is not only a repository of information, facts, do's and don'ts. It is a love letter. However, the message of love it contains has to be revealed. You have to read and heed the messages your Beloved, the One you seek, has concealed. One way of doing this is by holding it up to the light of kindness, viewing it as a guidebook of how to be kind to God, to others and to yourself. ✤

---

[65] The song traditionally sung Friday night upon returning home from Shabbat services.

[66] If it grows too slowly, remember that this too is an expression of love. Be patient. If you "stay in the game," the pace will pick up and you may be able to cover lost ground. Not so for those who quit before they see the finish line.

Your ability—in fact, your desire—to sense and express the love your Partner and you have for one another hinges on your acceptance of the tzaddik as a role model. Recognizing that the tzaddik is a human being—like you—who has managed to achieve angel-like behavior vis a vis the body, affords other human beings—like you—some "angelic" insight into reading life and Torah. As a result, his interpretations—and yours—will be life-giving, rather than thwarting and choking. Then not only will the Torah be a life-giving text, but so will life itself.

As with any endeavor, the more you do it, the better you do it. As you read the letters of life and Torah with more fluency, your ability to transpose the letters into a love song increases. The more hitbodedut becomes a setting for singing your love songs, the more your love will grow. Don't be afraid to be assertive. Be the initiator in expressing your love towards God, to sing Him new songs, to try new avenues of expression in hitbodedut. Don't hesitate to surpass the old love with a greater, new love. There is no end to the depths of God's love for you in return.

SELF-CONTROL

The tzaddik also teaches the importance of self-control for creating a loving partnership with the Divine. Metaphorically speaking, your heart is quite fraternal. She sits together with all your limbs and is easily persuaded by them to enjoy their pleasures. Yet she is connected to the brain as well, and attuned to what the brain has to tell her. Your mind is naturally "above" the petty desires of the rest of the body. Its love is for something higher, the Divine. The heart struggles to persuade her more immediate neighbors to give up their desired pleasures so that Divine love can be communicated in action.

The Midrash teaches that a person who lives wrongly is controlled by his heart. If he controls his heart, however, he will live rightly (*Bereishit Rabbah* 34:10). A person who knows that God exists may still succumb to his emotions and passions and follow his base desires every now and then. Only one who thoroughly loves God in his heart will not do anything that defies His will.

When you point your heart towards God, all your attributes (which are rooted in the heart) will be focused upon Him as well. This is why the Talmud teaches that it is not the quantity of mitzvot you perform that counts, as much as the degree of your heart that is focused on your Beloved (*Berakhot* 5b).

Since your soul is higher than your personality and emotions, evil can have no real effect on her. This means that when you "return to your senses" after a single, solitary mistake—or a lifetime of mistakes—you can still access your love for God and His for you.

You *know* that God exists and that "His glory fills the whole world." However, the wickedness within you may have overcome you and taken control of your heart. The bad days—moments when you were overwhelmed and undermined by an untamed heart—prevent you from responding to the light of your soul and feeling its influence. You need hitbodedut to bind your heart to that glimmer from afar in order to accept its truth, so that you can control your heart. The hitbodedut patter of unadorned trust and affection is the Bedroom chatter that creates tranquility (*Likutey Moharan* I, 239:2 on *Amos* 4:13). ❊

—— 3 • COURTSHIP ——

It's the little things you do for your Beloved that indicate your desire for closeness, your willingness to connect. The mitzvot you do out of love open a new channel of prayer, of revelation, of willingness on the part of your Partner to tell you more about Himself. There's always deeper. For instance, you know that wanton cruelty to animals is forbidden, but you don't have an obligation to open an animal shelter. Then you learn about the Talmudic sage who suffered for years and years because when a calf ran to him for protection, he sent it on its way (*Bava Metzia* 85a). Then you realize: His compassion extends to all His creatures (*Psalms* 145:9). Yours should, too.

You've known for a long time that God gives you better than you deserve. Then it dawns on you that you should act the same way towards others (*Tomer Devorah*, Chapter 1). This opening of Himself to you is God's returning His love to you. It may be in small ways, but it is in all ways.

And in all these small ways—even the littlest of the little—He can smile at you His infinite smile, or wink at you His infinite wink. And you can wink and smile back.

> One aspect of the kindness of His love, and of being in love, is that you can complain to God of your hurt and your feelings of rejection. Your Lover is always there to hear you; He won't shy away from it. It's you and about you, and He's in love with you. Tell Him how you feel. ✱

As close as you want to be with God, you may still feel unworthy and unable to approach Him. "How can I sing a love song? How can I even open my mouth? I have no gifts to bring, no presents to offer. There's no one poorer than I!" You may think that way, but

God doesn't. Read what the holy Zohar (3:195a) has to say about a pauper's prayer:

> God tells the angels, "Put all other prayers on hold. I don't want any members of the Heavenly court here with us now. It's just Me and him [the pauper]." God is alone with him.
>
> The angels ask one another, "What's the Holy One doing now?" The answer comes: "He's with His favorite."

This applies even to someone who complains about his material poverty. It is especially true for the one who complains to God: "Why don't You love me more? *If You really loved me,* You would draw me closer and help me to be a better Jew." This kind of prayer is *the most precious prayer in the world.*

EVEN CLOSER

Once a peaceful, loving atmosphere exists between you and God, your words of hitbodedut can take on a more intimate tone. There are many times when there's something you want, another bit of intimacy that you wish to have with the Creator. Of course He's interested, but He's not just giving it away, either. Should you just "roll over and go to sleep," or is there a way to get what you want?

Rebbe Nachman reminds us that God is happy when we best Him. Not just that—we should "sing to the One Who rejoices when conquered" (*Pesachim* 119a; *Rabbi Nachman's Wisdom* #69). What does this mean? It means that even when there's a breach in your relationship and your attempts at reconciliation are being spurned, don't despair. If you keep pursuing God's company and beg Him to favor you, you can "overcome" Him and get your heart's desire. It's not impossible. In fact, there's a woman who did just that, a woman we can all learn from—and do.

Chanah, the mother of the prophet Shmuel, was barren for many, many years. The hitbodedut she had in order to have children was so extraordinary that in many ways it became the paradigm for formal prayer (*Berakhot* 31a).[67] Although Chanah had her husband's unqualified love, she wanted God to show *His* love for her. So she "seduced" Him, bargaining with Him, pointing out her virtues, teasing and threatening to force His hand until she got what she wanted: a son whose whole being—from before conception!—and life would be dedicated solely to God's service. That was how she expressed her love.

> Chanah prayed with such intensity and ecstasy that others thought she was drunk. She was—drunk with love. ❋

Human needs are many. I don't mean the physical, animalistic ones, but the ones unique to the human race. These needs are listed and discussed in psychology texts, self-help books and religious tomes. You might refer to such works to give those needs a name, but you don't need them to tell you what they are: You feel them in your heart, in your gut, in your soul. Ask God to fill the holes in your heart—of loneliness, of emptiness, of having what to give and no one to give it to. God is the Creator of all that you lack, and of everything needed to sustain and maintain you.

With what words can you "embrace" God?

As he was eating the dairy kiddush on Shavuot morning, Rebbe Nachman heard the cantor singing the *Akdamut* poem. He commented to those sitting with him, "Jews are so accustomed to good, they don't realize how exalted *Akdamut* is… *Akdamut* is a love song."

Make your hitbodedut a love song and *sing out*: "I love You, God!" Get closer to your Partner by taking the time to consider all the good He does and has done for you. Don't recap your life events as some dispassionate, philosophical exercise—*really feel* that the softness and sensitivity you've experienced in life has been orchestrated for *your* maximum benefit; the strength and

---

[67] The holy Zohar also comments on the greatness of Chanah's hitbodedut (2:274b). Reb Noson points out that her very name implies prayer (*CHaNah – l'hitCHaNen*).

power that you've borne the brunt of has been orchestrated for your maximum benefit; and *all* the sections of the orchestra—strings, brass, percussion—are playing in harmony. Step up to the microphone and sing!

God's taking care of your life. Embrace it! Connect to it. But don't let your joy be only one-way, relishing the care that He heaps upon you. Let God be joyous too. Tell Him that you appreciate His constant invitations to unite with Him—the mitzvot. Sure, you do some of them, and sure, you're going to add more to your repertoire. And yes, we did discuss using mitzvot to feed your hitbodedut.[68]

Here we're talking about taking it to another level, beyond doing and beyond appreciating mitzvot. We're talking about cherishing them for what they are—an opportunity to hold your Dear One. Let the names and the words of the mitzvot roll off your tongue. Swirl them around in your mouth and savor their taste. And as you caress the mitzvot with your words of hitbodedut, remember to save an extra squeeze for hitbodedut itself: "And with His right hand He embraced me"—this is prayer (*Shir HaShirim Rabbah* 2:6:1).

FIRST KISS

As exciting and comforting as it feels, an embrace or a warm hug touches only the outside of your Lover. You want to be in love not only with what He *does*, but with *Him*. You want to be more personal, to share and feel more of His "insides," to put more of yourself within Him and more of Him within you. You want a "kiss."

What's in His breath? What sort of spirit does He have? What is He thinking and what motivates His actions and directions? At times you should focus your hitbodedut on this intense longing with a cry, loud or soft: "I want to *know* You!" Your hitbodedut

---

[68] See page 111.

words, if honestly spoken, will be coming from a more essential place within you. They will be a cry, obvious or subtle, that you want *all* of your heart and *all* of your soul to be given over to God—that you want to be one with Him.

> The height of hitbodedut is when, because of your great longing to unite with God, you feel your soul bound to your body by no more than a single strand (*Likutey Moharan* II, 99).

The more you examine the mitzvot and study the Torah from which they spring, you will realize that your Beloved has given you a treasure worth more than all the riches of this world. As you contemplate the holistic genius of the Torah—her intellectual, artistic, altruistic, practical, spiritual, accessible gifts—and start to feel her sweetness, as King David did—"How sweet Your sayings taste to me, sweeter than honey" (*Psalms* 119:103)—you will be moved to respond in kind. Then God will say back to you, "My bride, your lips drip sweetness" (*Song of Songs* 4:11).

> Just by "daydreaming" about the unique opportunities that you as a Jew have been granted to "embrace" and "kiss" the Divine, your ecstasy can approach that of Moshe's when he ascended Mount Sinai to receive the Torah. ❀

Reb Noson writes that the sweetness of your hitbodedut song to God is a tikkun-unification of your body and soul, and of Earth and Heaven.

FIDELITY

Be forewarned: Intimacy is neither a game nor a mere "experience." It is a mission, a trust and a sacred goal.[69]

Don't fool yourself. If you want a relationship with the Shekhinah, it's going to have to be monogamous. If you want Her

---

[69] This room of hitbodedut is called "The Bedroom." We need to be both discreet and frank. A narrow passage on an already very narrow bridge.

to be intimate with you, you are going to have commit to fidelity, to foreswear looking at other deities, and to go cold turkey on flirting with other spiritual paths. And ix-nay on the promiscuity.

If you are to take any real, long-lasting steps on your spiritual journey, your adherence to self-restraint in sexual matters cannot be tentative. "You shall be holy, for I, God your Lord, am holy" (*Leviticus* 19:2). "The God of Israel hates promiscuity" (*Sanhedrin* 106a). In Kabbalah-speak, the sefirah that is paralleled in the human body by the procreative organ is called Yesod.[70] The literal definition of yesod is "foundation." Being sexually well-behaved in speech, thought and deed has nothing to do with being prudish or repressed. It has to do with cleaning and clearing the totality of your being so you are able to maintain a constant openness to receiving Divinity. The place where Earth kisses Heaven is, as it were, the bosom of the Divine (*Shir HaShirim Rabbah* 1:13:1).

What do sexual habits have to do with one's spiritual journey? In a general sense, being in command of your sexuality develops the physical and mental toughness necessary to be a spiritual athlete. This toughness is needed to properly address or respond to situations which may test your endurance.

Specifically, the challenge of properly channeling sexual energy is all-encompassing because the entirety of body and mind is used in the sexual act. The successful culmination of the act is called orgasm for a reason—there is no greater physical pleasure.[71] One who can control, master and tame the sexual desire opens the entirety of his or her body and mind to receiving a different sort of thrill.[72] Keeping the body pure allows for God's living touch to be upon all one's limbs.

---

[70] Although Yesod is typically and correctly understood as being primarily male-oriented, the lessons it conveys certainly apply to female sexuality in an analogous fashion.

[71] See Rashi on *Psalms* 27:10 that this pleasure distracts even the greatest of tzaddikim from focusing on God.

[72] The Maggid of Mezeritch, successor to the Baal Shem Tov, compares prayer to intimacy with the Shekhinah. The Baal Shem Tov himself gave a similar teaching. See *The Light Beyond* by Aryeh Kaplan (Moznaim Publishing, 1981), 6:29 and 6:2.

Countless times Rebbe Nachman battled his passion, until God helped him and he was able to subjugate his impulse completely. The Rebbe finally destroyed the fiery chamber of this universal desire completely...

The Rebbe said, "The forces of evil were willing to concede me everything if I would only go along with this. I, however, would concede everything else, but this I would surmount completely."

This is actually how the Rebbe began. At first he directed all his effort toward this goal, to annihilate every vestige of sexual desire. He totally ignored such pleasures as eating, making no effort at all to subdue them. Indeed, he ate very much, more than most people. He said, "At that time, I drew all my desire into my appetite for food." Later, even this appetite was subdued.

Though there are exceptions,[73] the holy Zohar teaches that sexual temptation is the most daunting challenge a human being faces. Be prepared, not scared. Faint heart never won fair Shekhinah. ❀

---

[73] Being addicted to something harmless is worse than falling for a major desire, because the addiction makes you oblivious to other desires. A stubborn infant can literally bang his head against the wall to spite his mother. Some people exhibit the same stubbornness and lack of self-control. They give up every pleasure because of some obstinate, over-powering desire.

⊢— 4 • UNION —⊣

Since God is incorporeal, He is neither male nor female. In fact, no adjective really applies to the Creator. Nevertheless, out of kindness for His creatures, He allows us to use adjectives in order to communicate with Him. We call God "He" when we describe His power to create and supervise the world. We call God "She" when we talk about how God's presence (the Shekhinah) feels our pain and comforts us in exile.

Life can also be said to have both masculine and feminine characteristics. The "feminine" side of life is the part that deals with death. Everything that "dies," that passes out of existence or that loses some of its vitality or utility, even temporarily, squarely confronts the "feminine" side. She must deal with the pain, the logistical setbacks and the aesthetics that have been marred, so that life not only continues, but flowers again and again. Sadness is a major occupational hazard.

It must be emphasized quite clearly that when the Kabbalah teaches that "woman are from the side of death," it does not mean that women have the cooties. Nor does it mean that women are in some way bad or evil. On the contrary, the fact that the "feminine" side of life has to deal with death shows that it is very good, since the Angel of Death himself is described as being "very good" (*Bereishit Rabbah* 9:10).

The job of the "feminine" side is to draw out the good from a bad situation. The brunt of this work typically falls to the women of the world because they are the ones who manifest the "feminine" aspect of Creation. But kudos to them as well, for they bring all of Creation to testify to and trumpet God's existence. Without the "feminine" side doing its job, no more than half of Creation (i.e., those who are so naturally inclined) would acknowledge the Divine.

The "masculine" side of life is the part of you that is "in His presence," that takes its sweet time imbibing what it considers the ultimate of joy. This joy is not granted; it is hard-earned. Finding a spouse, earning a livelihood, exerting control over nature and going out to war all call for overcoming inertia and leaving the comfort of one's four walls. Any time you must impose your will upon an indifferent or antagonistic situation, you tap into your masculine side. Pursue, says Rebbe Nachman, pursue that which is broken in your life and don't rest till you've caught it and transformed it into a source of beneficial joy. Reb Noson writes that this extends to moving earth to make crops grow and to bending metal in order to measure and control time. The truest joy, the joy that will be enjoyed in the Ultimate Future, is the joy "man" has worked to achieve.

This joy and the buoyancy it begets are not for hoarding. Keeping them away from the "feminine" is a mulish, contraceptive decision; the only thing it perpetuates is sterility. The goal is union, to absorb the "feminine" within the "masculine," to turn death into life and sadness into joy.

The fundamental emotion that ought to fill the Bedroom of hitbodedut is joy. Cheer is a prerequisite for being in God's presence. "Smile" needs to be the operative word. Why? Being upbeat allows you to hear the song that cues you to sing your (*plural!*) song, your hitbodedut, the song that brings you closer when you thought you were already as close as close can be.

> "Hey, Ozer! I'm still not sure what should I sing about. Got any suggestions?"
>
> Sure. I can't tell you specifically what to choose, but pick something that you've done or experienced that makes you glad you're Jewish, that gives you hope for the future and brings a smile to your lips and heart. Now try to make it fit the music of a song you like. (No, it doesn't have to be a Jewish song. It does have to be a song you like.)
>
> Still need something more defined? OK, I'll tell you what I sing about when I'm facing a "clean up the mess" situation. I rephrase some

biblical verses, Talmudic sayings or pieces of Rebbe Nachman's teachings and sing them to whatever folk tune or song melody that pops into my head. Sometimes I cast the Shekhinah as the heroine of a love song, like "Always on My Mind."

Odds are you don't sing worse than I do, but even if you do, Rebbe Nachman says to sing away when you're by yourself. You choose the lyrics, you choose the music — you get closer to God. It's that simple (*Rabbi Nachman's Wisdom* #273). ❧

Now, there is the distinct possibility that the opposite may happen — that the darkness of mishaps and life-gone-wrong might smear the bright spots of your existence with soot, staining your mood with melancholy tones. This is unavoidable. You must — and Rebbe Nachman emphasizes this many times — draw on all your resources, internal and external, to pluck a chord of cheer so as to elicit even a hint of a smile. You need to stretch the definition of good[74] to allow more of your experience to qualify as cheerful, and to magnify the greatness of the cheer.

WORDS THAT HEAL

Even before mankind ate from the Tree of Knowledge, good and evil were entwined. The eating was a result of miscommunication. Words not clearly expressed and ideas not fully explained caused good and evil to become entangled. To undo the knot of entanglement, the words you speak in the hitbodedut-bedroom must be employed in a positive way.[75]

"Life and death are in the hands of the tongue... One who finds a woman finds good" (*Proverbs* 18:21-22). The Midrash teaches us that words that are false or harsh can literally kill (*Yalkut Shimoni*

---

[74] Always making sure to stay within the realm of the kosher.

[75] The name of the first woman, *CHaVaH*, the mother of all life, is related to the Hebrew word for speech, as King David says, "Night to night speaks out (*yeCHaVeH*)..." (*Psalms* 19:3).

Tehillim #768). Words that are "feminine," that bring healing and forgiveness, are not just "very good," but boundlessly good (ibid., *Mishlei* #957). Everything that you partake of in life is entangled with good and bad. Use your words of hitbodedut to pull and gently tease apart the cords and strands, and to identify them. Your words of hitbodedut have to interpret what you are experiencing, to bring out the good so that your Jewishness can live in a more healthy and holy way.

Just as lovers' bedroom talk is not always passionate—even when the goal is passion—your hitbodedut-bedroom words will not always be words of passion. They must be spoken lovingly, but they must always be gauged to your heart's current emotion. The passion will follow.

Often your words will pour out motherly love, speaking to the infant heart to exercise its abilities or see the wonder of life. Speak, too, to the child heart that meets harshness outside the home and seeks reassurance that the world can still be a friendly place. And shower the adult heart that feels desolate and forlorn with holy words of hitbodedut that evoke beauty and hope. Your words of motherly love, spoken in the bedchamber of hitbodedut, are holy, pure and simple.

It's absolutely critical to speak words of love when your heart is in "adolescence," experiencing the pull and confusion of immature thinking together with the screaming storm of a youthful body. The lack of God-awareness, combined with the tug of alluring, temporary pleasures, teases you towards false satisfaction. Yet the glimmer of something nobler, more valuable and genuinely satisfying, pulls you as well. Then your loving words must be those of a significant other, convincing your heart which suitor it must reject and which it must choose.

With words, you can bring a smile to your Lover's lips and win Her heart before union. Which words? The holy Zohar suggests we note what Adam said to Chavah: "You and I are of the same bone and of the same flesh; the light we share is One."

Ideally, in the Bedroom of hitbodedut you will come to two conclusions. One is that God's love for you is unconditional. No matter what you've done, He's waiting for you to make up with Him, and He's been trying to get you to give your love back to Him and to Him only.[76] The other conclusion is that your love for God will be unconditional. No matter how He treats you, you won't leave Him: When God disciplines me, I sing His praises; when God applauds me, I sing His praises (*Psalms* 56:11).

Let your will melt into His. The major objective in the Bedroom of hitbodedut is to relinquish your grip on your ego.[77] This sounds like a colossal task. It is. Yet it is accomplished step by step with the asking of a simple, direct question: "Is *this* what my Beloved wants me to do?"

As important as it is, the answer to the question is not the point. It's the honest asking of it, and the genuine willingness to abide by the answer.

In return for your readiness to leave the safety of your ego and its familiar pleasures, hitbodedut offers you protection and security of a higher order. Hitbodedut offers you refuge in the Shekhinah. Come inside. Let Her give you shelter from the storm. ❀

---

[76] Because what could be better?

[77] Don't worry, you won't vanish into thin air.

⊢ 5 • TRANSCENDENCE ⊣

G od fills and surrounds the Bedroom and all of Creation (*Zohar* 3:225a). This applies not only in a spatial sense (i.e., that God is in every place), but in every event and every emotion as well. God fills and surrounds them all. Whatever you feel you need to address with your Partner, He's already there, waiting to show you the love from which it stems.

It's true you can't always see it. That's because too much has gotten in the way. The pain or disappointments might be too many or too much for you to now appreciate or acknowledge the love, but it *is* there. Tell Him you don't feel it. Ask Him to show it to you.

> We all have good days— the days when you feel God's love automatically. We all have bad days—the days when you think it's love's opposite that's being shown to you.
>
> Bad days are like "not putting on tefilin," days when you neglect to bind your actions and thoughts to the awareness that God, Who cared enough to interrupt history and take us out of Egypt to deliver us to a new and holy life, is part of your own personal history and is trying to deliver you from your own Egypt.
>
> When you are mindful to "put on tefilin" in this manner, you start to rise above the limitations of immediate experience and emotion and cut to the chase, the bottom line of love that is the sweet core of the experience. ❋

That's when you begin to realize that the love you *share* is transcendent. The hurts, the mistakes, the winks, the smiles are all messages, signs, that you *are* one, that there is no thing and no event that can separate you. The two of You/you are, as it were, of a piece.

Sometimes you will sense that a certain aspect of this love does not depend on anything; that it is not and cannot be summed up by any thing or gesture; that this love just *is*, and is beyond expression. It does, however, wait to be expressed, to be presented and gifted in a lower form in our finite world, which was created for whatever "reason" there is for Creation to exist.

Surpass the old love with a greater new love, whether "within" or "beyond" the Bedroom. Have we said this already? Yes. But there is no end to the depths of the love of God. ❀

The beggar waited near the bank entrance, hoping to be noticed by a rich gentleman as the latter would leave the building. If one did, it was possible—never definite—that he would give some alms.

Then it happened! It was not merely a rich man coming out of the bank—it was none other than His Majesty, the King.

The King stepped lightly and elegantly, smiling warmly at our beggar. "How fortune smiles on me today!" thought the beggar. "Who knows what gift the King will give me?!"

The King put forth his right hand and asked, "What have you for me?" A kingly jest—to ask a beggar for a gift! Our beggar was confused, unsure of how to respond. Slowly he reached into his bag, selected a morsel of what he had and placed it in the King's palm.

At day's end, our friend returned to his miserable hut and inspected his meager earnings. There, among the pickings, was a morsel of gold. He fell to the floor and cried bitterly, wishing with all his heart he had given the King his all. ❀

ROOM 4
THE NOPLACE

God said to Moshe, "There is place with Me" (*Exodus* 33:21). It is the Blessed Holy One Who is the Place of the universe, not the other way around (*Bereishit Rabbah* 68:9). ❀

1 • FOUR KINDS OF SILENCE

You might well expect that a room called "NoPlace" must not have much to say about it. After all, what more can you say that hasn't already been said—if you can say anything? In truth, the enormity of NoPlace is such that nothing *can* be said about it, other than that it exists. And it is because this dimensionless realm exists that it must be talked about. We want to enter it, even though our visit will perforce be extremely brief.

The NoPlace is an Ocean of Awareness. It is a state in which you experience with total clarity the truth and existence of God. In that state, God has no name by which He can be called, and there is no word or words with which He can be described. There aren't even letters to help you begin to approach Him! In the NoPlace, only God exists. There is no need to name Him, to distinguish Him from some other. There is no "other" there to call to Him or to praise Him.

It is the languagelessness of the NoPlace that renders clear communication about it impossible, even with yourself. Only upon your return can you begin to formulate—somehow, somewhat— what you experienced. Even then, the best you can do is to point towards the NoPlace.

There are many ways we describe silence. It can be ghastly, peaceful, eerie, friendly, deadly, respectful, meditative or deafening. We speak about "a wall of silence," "a companionable silence" and the silence of dumb animals.

The ticket to the NoPlace is silence, and it comes in four flavors. I know, I know. Earlier we said that hitbodedut is about words. At the same time, though, we also said that hitbodedut is not about words at all. Hitbodedut is not only about words because words are only a tool, and sometimes not the most effective one. There is definitely a silent side to hitbodedut.[78]

We must also define a word that comes up often on the way to the NoPlace: bitul. Bitul refers to the state of nothingness, to coming to that state and to remaining in that state. It is used not only in relation to its mystical aspects (as here), but also in halakhah, vis a vis kashrut and finance.[79]

STOPPING THE PAIN

When the going gets tough, the tough get smart—they make themselves vanish. This is the first vehicle of silence which Rebbe Nachman described to Reb Noson:

> Rebbe Nachman once told me, "If things get very bad, one has to make himself into nothing." I asked him, "How does one make himself into nothing?" The Rebbe replied, "Close your mouth and your eyes—bitul!"

Sometimes you just can't win. The pressures are too great; too many people are asking you for more than you can give. God wants something from you, you want something from yourself, and let's not forget our constant companion, the evil inclination.

Reb Noson continues:

> Sometimes you may feel overwhelmed by the evil inclination. You are confused by evil thoughts and are otherwise very bewildered,

---

[78] Rabbi Nachman Goldstein of Tcherin, a second-generation Breslov leader, wrote: "The word hitBoDeDut is a cognate of the Hebrew word BaDaD, meaning 'seclusion' or 'oneness,' as in, 'They shall be one-to-one (bad b'vad)' (Rashi on Exodus 30:34). You must strive to become 'one' with God to the extent that all sensory awareness ceases and the only reality you perceive is Godliness. This is the mystical meaning of Ein od milvado— 'There is nothing but God alone'" (Zimrat Ha'aretz 52).

[79] In the kashrut laws, bitul refers to the loss of identity that occurs to a forbidden food (e.g., a slice of bacon) that falls into a container of kosher food. If the forbidden food cannot be recognized, and there is a sufficiently large amount of kosher food in the container, the identity of the non-kosher food is nullified and the mixture is declared kosher. (The proportion of kosher to non-kosher food needed to effect bitul is generally 60:1.) In finance, bitul refers to the active devaluation of property (usually chattel) so that it is considered ownerless and/or subordinate to other property.

finding it impossible to overcome your evil urge. You must then make yourself vanish.

Your goal, as always, is to improve your Jewishness. But this time you're backed into a corner, conflicted, torn between *Yotzer* (the Creator) and *yetzer* (the evil inclination). You can no longer withstand the stress and are about ready to commit treason and go over to the other side. WAIT! Remember what you are here for, what destiny truly has in store for you—and disappear.

By closing your mouth and eyes, you temporarily give up your identity and place your soul into the Ohr Ein Sof, the Infinite Light, the NoPlace. It is from here that you begin to understand that all suffering, even spiritual suffering, is ultimately for the good. It is from here that the Torah originates, from here that you may able to gain the strength necessary to overcome your challenges.

Again, Reb Noson:

> By closing your mouth and your eyes, every thought is banished. Your mind ceases to exist. You have nullified yourself completely before God.

Rebbe Nachman teaches that anyone can do this, at least sometimes, if he genuinely wants to. You may think (and rightfully so) that you are not yet spiritually strong enough to let go of your identity and self forever. Nonetheless, you can do so, at least momentarily. The crux of the matter is: Do you want to? Are you willing to let go of your most precious possession, your self, to be loyal to God and do His bidding? For no matter how little you are physically capable of doing or resisting, you can always *want* to align your will with the Divine Will. When you vanish and only God is here, His Will certainly will be carried out.[80]

---

[80] A caveat: When the bitul is over, your troubles may seem more overwhelming. To prepare for that contingency, buoy yourself with simcha and study Torah using the new enthusiasm and new insight that you can still taste.

While this silent hitbodedut is definitely meant to be used for sudden emergencies, you don't have to wait for the last moment to practice it. If the forecast calls for storm winds and high waves, you can spend at least some of your regularly-scheduled hitbodedut time on this flavor of silence and bitul.

> The voice of the shofar is a silence, a wordlessness, because you have no words with which to defend yourself—*nolo contendre*.
>
> It happens with every first step you take. When you take your first step to approaching God—not just your initial commitment to observe Shabbat, for example, but your next step closer, your umpteenth first step—your misdeeds, recent and of long ago, raise a hue and cry: "Away with him! He does not deserve to approach!"
>
> You are struck dumb, left muttering and stuttering, because the impurity of your heart impedes it from sending words to the mouth.
>
> At such Rosh HaShanah-like times, when your past self is doing the talking and is hurling accusations at you, silence is the necessary choice. Do not mention your sins! Let loose a shofar-like scream from the depths of your heart! Let your voice carry up your yearning for closeness.
>
> This scream may never pass your lips, but it burns with the fire of shame and awe/fear. This scream can carry you to complete teshuvah, to Keter, the higher-than-speech silence. ❧

OPENING THE HEART'S GATES

It is impossible for anyone to tell you what the shine of NoPlace is like or feels like. The reason is given by the holy Zohar's explanation of the verse, "Her husband is known in the gates" (*Proverbs* 31:23). Each person's awareness of God (the "Husband" of our souls) is unique, proportionate to the gates of his own heart. If, when, how often and how long you enter the NoPlace will depend on the gates of entry you make in order to allow God to enter your heart.

Don't think that your heart is so stuffed or thick or stony or shallow that a gate opening into it would be meaningless. Everyone has within his heart the capacity to house God. Much of the work you do in the other rooms of hitbodedut will free and expand that capacity, directly or indirectly. Actually accessing that space and expanding it requires the powerful, second vehicle of silence—of contemplating God's greatness.

> How large a gate? Does it have to be the size of a hangar door? No—in our day and age even a pinhole will suffice. Make it and God will rush in, as if you had made the most humongous gate in the world. ✤

You certainly know that God cannot be seen with the physical eye. Nor can He be seen with even the most intellectual of eyes. God can only be "seen" with the heart.

> The opposite of talking is not "waiting to talk." It is silently listening. ✤

Even prophetically, God cannot be seen! Even Moshe, the greatest of our prophets who spoke to God "face to face" (*Numbers* 12:8), could not see God (*Exodus* 33:20). He could only hear God's voice.[81] This is true of all the other great prophets and sages—and of ourselves as well. Hearing implies the silence that facilitates hearing. Our Sages teach that hearing depends on the heart's desire to listen. So some of your hitbodedut must occur silently in your heart.

You can only know God by His actions, not by what He actually is. Sometimes your focus may be the wonder of concrete

---

[81] "When Moshe came to Ohel Moed to speak with Him, he heard the Voice speaking to Him from above the Cover that was over the Ark of Testimony, from between the two cherubs, and He spoke to him" (*Numbers* 7:89).

experience. Other times it may be the wonder of transcendental mystery. How much and how carefully you think about His acts—towards you, your people and the world, currently and through history, balancing the kindness that He gives and wants to give with the justice and limitations that He metes out—will determine how well you know Him.[82] This God-consciousness comes only from meditating on His greatness—"her Husband is known in the gates." "May...*the thoughts of my heart* be favorable to You..." (*Psalms* 19:15).

Another reason why you can't speak about the NoPlace is that while you are "there," you are unaware of yourself. In the NoPlace, a person is cognizant only of God. Though a person cannot express it at the time, upon returning from the NoPlace he understands that he has realized that God is good. In the NoPlace, one is like a "child" of God, gaining an awareness and realization of the Divine that cannot possibly be expressed in words. For the NoPlace is not only a realm that exists prior to space; it is a realm that exists before words and before letters. It is languageless.

Thus, anything said about the NoPlace is said only in "return" mode. Whatever words of praise you may speak are only an approximation of what is felt and left in your heart.

The great ocean[83] of expressible God-awareness contains "hands"—clues and allusions to something far greater than that which rational thought can comprehend. That "something" can only be hinted at. If one's teacher is a tzaddik, or a student of a tzaddik, there will be many lessons that he teaches and transmits by the merest indications and cues. Watching the way a tzaddik speaks, gestures and conducts himself can infuse you with an

---

[82] "God is fair in all His ways, kind in all His deeds" (*Psalms* 145:17). Rebbe Nachman commented that if one looks at God's ways from afar, He seems only fair. However, as one gets to see the whole picture, he realizes that God is also quite kind.

[83] *Psalms* 104:25. The entire psalm serves as a wonderful introduction and guide to meditating on God's greatness.

awareness of that which is beyond words. That knowledge will save you from wrongdoing, so that you may come to bitul.

Even after reminding yourself of the goal of growing your Jewishness and being aware of God, and even if you have tasted bitul many times, there are no guarantees that the taste will remain. The challenges have not disappeared and one may forget the taste or even deny the reality of what he experienced. Therefore, one needs to return again and again to the NoPlace. One setting that is conducive to entering a state of bitul is Shabbat. The quiet of Shabbat, provided by refraining from the forbidden activities[84] and ceasing to think of weekday concerns, together with the additional prayers that focus on the greatness of God's work, produces a great calm and yishuv hadaat. And Shabbat comes every week.

"The entire world is filled with His glory" (Isaiah 6:3). The more the light of bitul is opened for you and shines into your heart's gates, the more you are able to shine to others to let them know of God's greatness. One who knows, and knows how, needs to *speak*—to inform, instruct and share with others that God's glory is everywhere and is available to anyone who sincerely seeks it. Even if you cannot say the words, your aware presence is itself a lesson for anyone seeking to learn.

A WORD OF CAUTION

You will do well to read the following two cautionary tales. Why two? Because where we plan to venture is an area in life where the stakes are high.

> A venerable chassid, well-versed in all facets of Torah and years older than Rebbe Nachman, approached the Rebbe and asked, "Would the master please teach us the path with which to serve God?"

---

[84] Did you think the forbidden activities were meant to tie you down? They're meant to set you free!

Rebbe Nachman answered with mock surprise, "'To know Your way *in the earth*'? (*Psalms* 67:3). Why are you seeking a way, a path, when you are still so immersed in earthiness?"

The NoPlace at which we hope to arrive is not a spiritual journey of a day or two. Getting our tickets, passports, vouchers and visas requires a lot of patience, time and grunt work. We can't presume that it is our birthright to enter such an exalted level as the NoPlace. In fact, even those who were able to go, weren't necessarily able to return safely.

The Rabbis taught: Four Sages entered the *Pardes*.[85] They were: Ben Azzai, Ben Zoma, Acher[86] and Rabbi Akiva. Prior to their ascension, Rabbi Akiva instructed them: "When you come to the place of pure marble stones, do not say, 'Water! Water!' for, 'He who speaks falsely shall not stand before My eyes'" (*Psalms* 101:7).

Ben Azzai gazed (at the Divine Presence in the *Pardes*—Rashi) and died. Concerning him Scripture says, "Precious in the eyes of God is the death of His pious ones" (*Psalms* 116:15).

Ben Zoma gazed and was harmed (he lost his sanity). Concerning him Scripture says, "You found honey? Eat only as much as you can, lest you be overfilled and vomit it up" (*Proverbs* 25:16).

Acher cut down the plantings (he became a heretic). Concerning him Scripture says, "Do not let your mouth bring your flesh to sin, and do not say before the angel that it is an error; why should God become angry at your voice, and ruin your handiwork?" (*Ecclesiastes* 5:5).

---

[85] The PaRDeS (orchard) can also be read as an acronym of four Hebrew words: *Pshat, Remez, Drash* and *Sod*. These are four progressively deeper ways of analyzing a Torah text in the tradition of our Sages. *Pshat* refers to the simple, straightforward understanding of the words or events being described. *Remez* refers to the level of "hints" which the text points to. *Drash* is the homiletic level at which Torah anecdotes or teachings can parallel other important lessons. *Sod* is the level of "secret"—the Kabbalah, the mystical interpretations which these four Sages were trying to access.

[86] Elisha ben Avuya, who was called Acher ("the other one") because of what he did after he left the *Pardes*.

Rabbi Akiva entered in peace and left in peace. Concerning him Scripture says, "Draw me, let us run after you; the King has brought me into His chambers" (*Song of Songs* 1:4).

Commenting on this story, Reb Noson explains that the "wine" of bitul can both enlighten a person and, God forbid, impoverish him. It can take away one's life in this world and the next by ruining his perception of and ability to function in the present. Three out of four of the greatest tzaddikim did not return safely from the NoPlace. Should we forget about the whole thing? No, but we need to know what we're facing. When you need to make a decision, you can rethink the matter—and re-pray for Divine guidance.

The Wisdom of Silence

Throughout your journey, with all its stops and starts, and in your entire practice of hitbodedut, with all its ups and downs, there has been one constant: You have become more aware than when you began. The progress may have been unfelt, often unseen, frequently baffling, but at certain points along the way, you've realized that you are better off than when you started.

You've worked at your hitbodedut, for just a short time or a long while, and you've captured some of that elusive, invisible chakhmah—the wisdom of who you are and the self-control that goes with it. You've tasted the wisdom of what a better place this world can be and how you can help make it so, the wisdom of God's kindly presence always at your side, the wisdom to talk about all this, and much, much more.

But you've also discovered something else about this chakhmah: It's endless! It just goes on and on and on. Even when you pause to absorb one of its answers, it points in many different directions with a question for each and every one. You pick one (or does it pick you?) and start to follow its lead—surely the resolution of *this* mystery will bring you to the top of the mountain and the ultimate clarity that comes with the view.

Aha! You discover and re-discover that this is not at all the case. While it's true that wisdom begets wisdom, it's also true that one good question leads to another. Is there any way to resolve this paradox, that the chakhmah you seek should ultimately provide an answer, *the* answer, rather than just questions, frustrations and doubt-inducing objections? Is there a way or a tool with which to trap and tame the genius of chakhmah to make it productive rather than destructive, so that it produces fruit rather than runs amok?

Rabbi Akiva says: The fence for wisdom is silence (*Avot* 3:17).

Although it seems that intellectualism is the mainstay of wisdom, this is not the case. Silence is the prerequisite for gaining and maintaining genuine wisdom. If a person has achieved silence, it can truly be said of him that he is wise (*Midrash Shmuel*).

From time to time, perhaps within the same session of hitbodedut or perhaps quite rarely, the endless ocean of your chakhmah will need to be stilled and tamed in the third vehicle of silence. If not, your chakhmah may turn itself around, wrap itself around your heart and squeeze the living faith out of you. Not a pleasant prospect.

Rabbi Akiva[87] was a master of silence. From the beginning of his career as a Torah student, after he made sure that he correctly understood what he had been taught, he would organize every insight he received from his masters, filing away the insights into neat, intellectual compartments.

When Moshe, the greatest of all prophets, ascended Mount Sinai, the place of the greatest revelation, he noted that God was placing crowns on the letters of the Torah. To transmit His Will and knowledge to the human mind, God dressed them in letters. Any higher form would not be humanly accessible. Even letters, the most accessible vehicle of transmission, contain only the lowest level of communication. The crowns of the letters contain both insights and behavioral laws for coming closer to God that are deeper than the letters themselves.

---

[87] Rabbi Akiva is considered the "father" of the Oral Law. His five disciples, Rabbi Meir, Rabbi Elazar, Rabbi Yehudah, Rabbi Yossi and Rabbi Shimon, were the codifiers and editors of the Mishnah, the Midrash and the holy Zohar.

Moshe asked God about the purpose of the crowns. Could they actually become meaningful to any human being? God showed Moshe that in the future, Rabbi Akiva would understand and teach to others the meanings of these crowns. "If You have someone like him, why are you giving the Torah through me?" Moshe asked. God's reply: "Quiet! This is what I thought!"

In response to Moshe's question, though, God did show him a vision of Rabbi Akiva's flesh being sold in the marketplace after he was tortured to death by the Romans. Moshe exclaimed, "This is Torah and this is its reward?" God's reply: "Quiet! This is what I thought!" ❀

Shema Yisrael: God is One, He is the only one—nothing else exists. God is beyond the mind's grasp; He is the NoPlace.

We can't live like that; our minds can't grasp such a reality. We must be "down to earth" and realize that God is very much right here, right now. He runs and rules the world.

This is the "Barukh Shem" that follows the Shema. It is said in a whisper, intimating the silence of, "Quiet! This is what I thought." ❀

To where do you flee to tame the chakhmah that chases you? Rebbe Nachman teaches that hitbodedut must now be silent. Make Shabbat in your mind and wait in silence.

What do you do while you're waiting? What do you think? Just wait. You're not "doing nothing," being passive or inactive. Instead, your waiting in silence is an emphatic statement: In God I trust.

As you sit silently, letting your accumulated chakhmah present itself in your mind, thought by thought ticking by, appearing and disappearing, you are actively giving witness that the world's direction is *not* in your hands, but in God's. The wisest thing anyone can say is, "I don't know." So you wait for God to make the next move and complete what needs to be done, because you are wise enough to be truly humble. You wait for the moment that you know is the right time for *you* to act. You can wait for either, or both. You have to wait. This is Shabbat; this is Keter-silence.

Keter is waiting, active waiting, as Elihu told his friends, "Wait a bit while I collect my thoughts" (Job 36:2). It is the sign of a vigorous trust—a trust that behind all that takes place in your life and in the world at large, there stands an involved, concerned, positive Will. What is that Will? "I don't know." What is behind all this? "I don't know."

This waiting and this silence bespeak your affirmation that there is a Will greater than your will. All the forces of Creation, including the forces that you have within you—your energy, potential, wisdom and creative ability—are all subject to a higher Will. This Will demands that you cease and desist one day a week—Shabbat—so that every expression of your active and creative will becomes an expression of It.

> "I have to wait for this Will to exercise Itself. Perhaps It will manifest through me in another moment or day, next week, next month or next year. Perhaps It will manifest through another agent, another part of Creation, or perhaps through Itself. I must wait for this Will. *Perhaps* it will fill me and tell me what to say or do."

This is the answer: What do I do? What am I thinking? I am just waiting, yielding my will to a higher Will. Shabbat.

What else do you do while you wait in silence during your hitbodedut? What else do you think about when surrounded by Keter-silence? There really is so much to keep you busy as you sit silently.

Don't stop thinking of doing good. Should any harmful, destructive or worthless thought declare itself to be chakhmah, reject it and replace it. In Keter-silence you are able to access absolute compassion. This is true wisdom; anything else is foolishness.[88]

> Queen Esther knew how to be silent. She told no one of her origins nor her plans. From where did she acquire this trait? From her modesty. ❧

---

[88] You can choose your thoughts. Where God is, there is joy. As we wrote many pages ago, holy thoughts are more easily accessible when you are upbeat. It's part of your choice.

Shabbat continues, for you have not yet mastered control over your chakhmah. There is much to speak about after the silence, because now there is more to say. In fact, your chakhmah, your words, are born and reborn after Shabbat because all words are drawn from Shabbat. Shabbat is supernal-silence and is higher than speech.

This is why your Shabbat talk needs to be different from your weekday talk, with all your "weekday" talk (i.e., non-Torah words) silenced. Shabbat is only for words that are directly related to Torah and tefilah.[89] The Torah herself confirms this: The most sacred enterprise, the construction of the Mishkan that would house the presence of God, was suspended in favor of Shabbat (*Exodus* 31:13).

Silence also serves as the womb for words in another, more basic way. Rebbe Nachman teaches that Elihu's silent waiting was a return from falling out of the awareness of living with God. When you gather your thoughts in silence, you are preparing to *be*. Now you must be silent because you abandoned your humanness—your daat, the awareness that being in God's presence calls for a different manner of living, thinking, speaking and doing that is much more refined and sacred—and instead acted sanctimoniously.

> Even King David, the personification of prayer, had a silent side (*Psalms* 56:1). Silence surrounds Mashiach, his descendant, as well. The announcement of Mashiach's arrival has not yet been made in Heaven and his origins are hushed up.
>
> This is not just a nifty factoid about the Mashiach. This is a clue to *your* salvation. You don't know when your salvation will arrive; therefore, never despair of its coming—*anticipate* its arrival! You may have many skeletons in your closet, but somehow each of them contributes to the birth of your salvation. ❧

---

[89] One is permitted to pledge tzedakah on Shabbat, but may not speak about business activities—even if he intends to donate the profits to tzedakah (see *Shulchan Arukh, Orach Chaim* 307).

Having withdrawn into silence and reviewed life from an "on all fours" perspective, you realize that you have not yet begun to live; you are just now preparing to *be*. It is this aspect of Keter, of "wait a bit while I gather my thoughts," that births the daat anew, enabling you to speak words that convey that daat.

From top to bottom, the root of speech lies in thought, the silence of Keter, the root of Chakhmah. Only when the silence forms speech—when you think before you speak—can you cling to God via words.

BEYOND KETER

Reb Noson writes:

> The Rebbe once saw a book that contained writings of the Arizal not found elsewhere. This work spoke of the levels of development before the Universe of Emanation contained in the World of the Garment.[90] I was very surprised to hear this when the Rebbe mentioned it. I had thought that there was nothing higher than the World of Emanation, and was astonished to discover Kabbalistic teachings speaking of higher levels.
>
> I expressed my surprise to the Rebbe and he laughed. Then he said, "Don't scientists think that knowledge ends with the stars?" Even in knowledge of the transcendental, there are levels upon levels, higher and still higher, without limit or boundaries, because "His greatness is unfathomable" (*Psalms* 145:3). This cannot be expressed in words.

Broadly stated, our purpose here in this world is to wage war against sense-desire and confusion, so that our minds can always be attached to God. At some time you will want to come to the point at which you are clearly aware that the only being that exists is God. This is a level called Ayin (Nothingness). This is the level that we are calling the NoPlace.

---

[90] Kabbalistic names for very basic and primary spheres of activity in the creation and maintenance of existence.

The level of Ayin is so called because there are no categories with which a human being can intellectually grasp it. Since it is unfathomable, it is Nothingness and NoPlace. The more you praise God, the closer you come to this ideal, this fourth vehicle of silence. The highest praise of God is silence, since, in fact, nothing can really be said about Him. God is infinitely higher than any praise we can offer. As King David said, "To You, silence is praise" (*Psalms* 65:2).

Can a human being get to such a level, a level that is languageless because the concept of language and even the concept of "twoness" (the existence of something other than God) does not exist? Yes.

Then the blind beggar spoke. "I remember all these events—and I remember Nothing" (*Rabbi Nachman's Stories* #13).

One can experience many, many levels of existence—of closeness to God and perceptions of the unity of Creation—even while living an average, normal life. To do so takes years of dedicated practice of hitbodedut, improving one's character and refining one's thinking and behavior,[91] but it can be done.

At this level of bitul, one experiences the reality that God is all there is; there is no other. It means experiencing the realization that there is no evil.[92] Even to those who are intellectually comfortable with the concept, and who have faith galore, it still borders on the obscene to say (or hear) that "there is no evil"—particularly when viewing the results of wanton, premeditated violence.

Rebbe Nachman did not harbor even the slightest bit of animosity towards any of his opponents or enemies. He achieved this level of love and awareness during his stay in the Holy Land (*Likutey Halakhot*, Tefilin 5:17; *Likutey Halakhot*, Matanah 5:28-29). ❊

---

[91] It may also require the grace of God.

[92] Although there is certainly pain and suffering, which we are duty bound to alleviate and eliminate.

King David expressed this truth when he said that no matter what happens, he praises God (*Psalms* 56:11). God's names may be many, but He is One and always deserving of praise.

The best time to pursue and achieve this state of bitul is at night, when the world is asleep and taking a break from its constant pursuit of sense-pleasure. "Night" in this context also means your own voluntary reduction and elimination of the pursuit of sense-pleasure as a motive or goal for your behavior. The pain and suffering of the world, which so many dread and try to wish and pray away, is also "night," as it helps you to shut your eyes so that you can focus on the unity of Creation rather than its scatterbrained distractions.[93] The latter type of "night" gives impetus for bitul; the first is the most conducive setting in which to achieve it.

> The reading of the Shema is an exercise in bitul. You are proclaiming that God is One, as in, "On that day God will be One and His Name will be One." You are stating and imparting to the depths of your being a glimpse of bitul, that everything is One, everything is good, for "God is our Lord, God is One." ❧

> The times for reading the Shema are defined by sleep. The time for the nighttime reading begins from when people normally head for bed; the daytime reading must be finished by the time people ordinarily awaken. Between these poles, the world somewhat slows down its pursuit of the light proffered by sense-pleasures, making it easier to access the light of bitul. The Shema must be read with care not to slur or to swallow any of its letters or words. Each letter and each word is a vessel intended to hold a certain measure of Divine light and energy.

> The light and energy can burn and destroy if you don't control or contain it properly. This is because sense-pleasure also contains a kernel of good. The light that you tapped into during bitul may end up being attracted to the light of the sense-pleasure in an inappropriate way. A measured reading keeps your energy under control. ❧

---

[93] The purpose of pain and suffering is to heighten our awareness that the only thing that has any value in this world is oneness with God.

To give respite from the judgments[94] of "night," God gave the gift of sleep to all His creatures.[95] Sleep has two aspects. The first is "closing your eyes" against the transient goals and pleasures of material life. The second is "nullifying your thoughts," letting your mind think without being prompted by your ego or your desires. The holy Zohar teaches that when you "sleep" like this, you are standing on God's mountain.

As with many of his teachings, Rebbe Nachman educates us with a koan: *If you want to see, close your eyes.* If you want to stay focused on the Destiny of the Universe, the great and ultimate good that will be experienced, close your eyes to the trivial and transient in this world. Then you need never suffer, no matter what happens, because you will see and experience even the unfolding of life and history as good and part of that ultimate good.[96]

Obviously, to achieve such a state of closeness to God, your love and yearning for Him must be so great that you are willing to die. "You will love your God with all your heart and all your soul"[97] — even if He chooses to take it away. ✿

---

[94] The judgments include not only your pain and suffering, but *all* the obstacles in your path.

[95] Including animals.

[96] Please remember that not everyone is deemed worthy of achieving such a level, despite the genuine effort and sincerity he or she invests.

[97] From the Shema (*Deuteronomy* 6:5).

┌── 2 • Connecting with God ──┐

What is it to pray, to do hitbodedut in a manner that your entire prayer is whole and one, not a solitary unit among units but a fabric that interweaves every aspect and strand of Creation to which your soul is connected? Rebbe Nachman teaches that such a prayer is like a calm, attentive stroll through a beautiful meadow abounding with fragrant flowers that capture more colors than a rainbow.

The sweet, ambrosial fragrance that arises from clinging to God in bitul is a pleasure of the soul, a pleasure of Eden, a delight of the Future World. You can't wrap your mind around experiencing God; you can only get a whiff of it.

United Under God

Knowing that all is one and united, and that all is good, enables you to unify your entire prayer into one piece. Even though there is a level of prayer at which each letter you speak grabs your soul with passionate love, that is not the highest level of prayer. "One-ing" your prayer is higher.

You cannot make your prayer one without being totally focused on the ultimate destiny of Creation. You cannot attain or maintain that focus without totally and absolutely "shutting your eyes" from looking at this world. When you are in bitul you are unaware of all creations, including yourself.

It would be better if each of us would be able to achieve bitul in response to whatever suffering he might endure. For the vast majority of mankind, however, this simply is not possible. For those of us who constitute that majority, there is a much more pleasant alternative: mitzvot. Each mitzvah that you do, as well as each word of Torah, prayer and hitbodedut that you speak, allows you to access the light—the insight—from the residue of bitul achieved by Moshe and other tzaddikim. In addition, when you reach your "critical mass" of holiness, you are prepared to "do some bitul of your own" if you should ever suffer, God forbid.

> For one who knows how to approach bitul, the obstacles of judgment filter the Light. For one who knows not how to approach, those obstacles are a barrier. ❀

The light of insight and the ability to attain it are drawn from what is known as the Ohr Ein Sof, the Infinite Light. If you make the vessels, the light will come. You are human, so you can make the vessels. As mentioned before,[98] angels and animals are on automatic pilot. Only human beings have free will. The vessels are made every time you choose correctly.

> Everything you do, including plying your craft, is meant to be done properly so that all that you use of the material realm should also receive from the Infinite Light. ❀

> Here are some Blind Beggar suggestions for your self-bitul:
>
> For today, go off-line and don't read any newspapers or magazines. Stay home. This will help you keep your eyes from roaming. This is what makes home-hitbodedut so powerful.
>
> But as in Noah's Ark—where there was no place to go, nothing to see— have a window facing the sky. This adds to your daat and so reduces judgment (Sefer Aleph-Bet). ❀

---

[98] See page 186.

ACCESSING HUMILITY

"Gee whiz! How can I make God 'the only thing' and myself 'nothing,' and still be something, still be me, doing the things 'me' is supposed to do?" A splendid halakhic query if there ever was one. After all, how can a piece of pork that fell into a pot of kosher food become permitted through bitul? It's still in there, isn't it? The answer is: It can be there and yet not be there.

In your search for God, asking, "Where is He?" is really a type of bitul. Asking the question implies that you know that He *is* somewhere; quite possibly, most likely, *here.* Your admission that you don't feel His presence is an acknowledgement that God's existence transcends every sort of description and definition. Any difference in feeling or not feeling His presence is solely dependent upon your perception. The more *you* are there, the less *He* is there, and vice versa.

It's completely impossible to achieve bitul without humility akin to that of Moshe. You must have the willingness, if not the ability, to give up your self, your soul, your very name, for God.

> Earth is earthiness; it is also the ultimate of humility. One who doesn't reach the ultimate degree of humility in life needs to be buried in the ground so that his remaining "earthiness" can reach total humility. Death and burial are bitul. ✻

The bulk of repentance, of restoring Creation to its tikkun-rectification, is the humility that goes hand in hand with bitul. Without humility, without totally forgoing your honor, there is another presence—yours. Therefore, there cannot be bitul. To the extent that you insist on "you" being there, you are blocking God's presence. That is tantamount to idolatry.

> At the level of bitul, God's Attributes of Compassion and of Judgment are really the same; there is absolutely no distinction or separation between them. ✻

The slow, often hard, often frustrating process of stripping yourself of materiality in order to attain bitul means making sure that your decision-making process is unaffected by cold, heat, thirst, hunger, ambitions and dreams, paychecks, applause, awards and rewards, threats and promises, love or hate. Your focus on God should be total and absolute. At such a point you are unaware of your own existence. This state must be temporary; you must force yourself to return to an "ordinary" state.

Not everyone achieves bitul. It is not available to everyone— even to those who want it. It requires a great deal of sanctification, total self-mastery over one's sense-desires and negative attributes (such as greed, impatience, etc.), and revealing to a tzaddik what one has done wrong.[99] Rebbe Nachman teaches that there are three steps one must take in order to have any chance of reaching bitul:

> Step #1: You must see the face of the tzaddik—i.e., understand the inner intention of his teachings and advice, as well as put his advice into practice.

> Step #2: You must provide the tzaddik with the wherewithal to continue teaching, so that more and more people can become more and more mindful of God.[100]

These two steps enable you to totally eliminate your desire for material pleasures together with your bad character traits. However, they do not offer you direction, showing you where *you* must go. This requires the third step:

> Step #3: You must confess your mistakes to the tzaddik. This gains you entry to bitul.

---

[99] Having to admit your wrongdoings to another being of flesh and blood wrings out of you another level of humility. Such an admission can only be made to a tzaddik who will not be adversely affected by what you tell him, and who will be able to re-form your words of misdoing into positive direction for your future.

[100] For this reason, many Breslov chassidim, beginning with Reb Noson, assumed the financial burden of publishing and reprinting Rebbe Nachman's works.

Most of what we eat grows from the ground (e.g., grains, fruits, vegetables). All that grows from the ground starts through a process of bitul, as the seed totally dissolves itself into the earth and loses its own identity.

Therefore, when we eat such foods, we can meditate on that essential quality and transform it into tremendous longing and yearning for the highest possible levels of closeness to God.

And like the seed that was, we can grow into something lush and thriving. ❊

On a number of occasions, a Jew kindles the silent flame of light—to usher in Shabbat or a Jewish festival, to illuminate the reader's lectern for communal prayer, to kindle the Chanukah menorah. In each of these settings one is shining into mankind the Infinite Light, so that we all may better realize that God is One and that all our experiences, whether painful or pleasant, are good and leading to the ultimate good.

The granddaddy of all these lights is the light of the Menorah, which was lit in the Holy Temple. The Menorah was situated near the entrance to the most sacred chamber of the Temple, the MostHoly. Only once a year did one person enter the MostHoly— the kohen gadol on Yom Kippur. The highlight of the Yom Kippur service that he performed there was bitul. The light that remained after his bitul shone from the Menorah.

The MostHoly was the location of the Foundation Stone. Every place in the world is rooted in the Foundation Stone. It is where Earth kisses Heaven. ❊

⊢— 3 • AFTER BITUL —⊣

Notwithstanding the loftiness of bitul, the truth is that God desires your worship more than your bitul. The experience of bitul will open your eyes to the reality of a Unity in which all is good and everything that happens is good. But you can't yet live in that Unity all the time. It would be like trying to buy a house with a futuristic currency—this is not the time or the place where it can be spent.

The point of bitul is the return from it. As important as "getting there" is, coming back with something good and living right as a result is even more important. When you come back from that state, you can take the light and fashion it into proper measures and vessels. The goal is the running to bitul *and* returning from it with an awareness of God that the residue of bitul enables.

Rebbe Nachman provides you with an idea of what degree of awareness your post-bitul life can have. He tells you that the NoPlace is right here. You can get there with hitbodedut.

> Your mind can withstand any temptation. It is written, "God gives wisdom to the wise" (*Daniel* 2:21). Every person has the potential for wisdom. This potential must be used. With it alone you can overcome all temptations. But God also gives wisdom to the "wise"—this can bring you even greater strength.

> Certain impurities in the mind must be subdued. When you do this, you will not want for anything in this world. *Everything will be the same to you.* It is written, "When you walk it will guide you, when you lie down it will watch over you, and when you awaken, it will champion you" (*Proverbs* 6:22).

> When you have purified your thoughts, there is no difference between this world, the grave and the next world. *When you only desire God and His Torah, all are the same.* In all three you can grasp onto God and His Torah.

But if you grasp at this world, there is an agonizing difference. This world is spread before you, while the grave is a tight, cramped place. *If you purify your mind, all will be the same.*

So, you've finished your hitbodedut for the day and you come back from bitul. Where are you going to put all that Infinite Light? Into the Torah. Rebbe Nachman teaches that those who succeed in reaching bitul return with a residue of the Infinite Light. As we wrote earlier, God is beyond human ken; no mind can be wrapped around what He is. Only through bitul can He be apprehended. The crux of revealing God's presence in the world depends on securely protecting the memory of that experience.

The Torah you learn will give you the ability to protect and retain the light that remains from your experience of bitul in your intellect and emotions. When you study the Torah with renewed enthusiasm, viewing it in a new light and using it as a springboard for further hitbodedut, you will complete and perfect your bitul, just as you begin to get ready for the next go-round.

The experience of bitul is exhilarating, to say the least.[101] You may be tempted to downplay the importance of trying to "bottle it" within the letters and words of Torah. After all, you *saw* the light. True enough, but one can still forget something he saw.[102]

> Because memory protection is so critical, you must be vigilant about further sanctifying your mind, rejecting the evil and the unholy so that your brain remains a proper Ark in which the Torah can rest. Without proper sanctification, her great light cannot be contained. And then you forget. ❧

How much Torah must you learn to retain the experience of bitul? Reb Noson points out that a Torah scroll that lacks even one

---

[101] Or the most.

[102] The classic example is the tragic case of the Israelites in the desert. They made the golden calf a mere forty days after hearing God speak to them directly.

letter is invalid because it cannot and does not fully hold the light. Therefore, the more holy words of Torah that you speak, the more letters you possess with which to contain the residue of bitul. The more words of Torah that you learn and the more prayers that you speak, the better you will remember what you experienced and the more you can reveal Godliness. Therefore, speak as much Torah as you can.[103]

> It is impossible to know God without complete and total bitul, which requires sealing one's eyes from "looking"—i.e., from valuing this world and its goals and pleasures. (Of course, you must engage in doing all the human stuff, such as eating and having a family. You just have to do them in a holy way.) When a person is experiencing bitul, he is on a plane higher than daat, the integration of knowledge and emotion that becomes part of one's being. One can have daat only when he has returned from bitul-mode.
>
> Most people do *not* experience bitul. This is not surprising, because bitul is an experience within the Ohr Ein Sof, which is higher than the sefirot, higher than all the Names of God. All the sefirot and God's Names, as well as the Thirteen Measures of Compassion, come from the *residue* of the Light.
>
> That which the prophets and sages grasped, and the *entire* Torah we have from Moshe, and *all* the teachings of the tzaddikim in each of the succeeding generations, come from the "glow" provided by the residue of their bitul! Hence the daat of ordinary folk only stems from the Torah that the tzaddikim provide them.
>
> Whether your experience of bitul is firsthand or vicarious, if your awareness of God (i.e., the residue-Light) is only in your brain and not in your heart, *then you know nothing whatsoever of God*. Even when it is in your heart, it is still fragile and must be protected. ❊

Bitul is neither a place visited only once in a lifetime nor a permanent residence. It is like a home base which one needs to visit every so often, in a back-and-forth manner:

---

[103] There is no particular or recommended post-bitul curriculum. You just need to study what interests you in a manner commensurate with your level.

You make vessels to hold the light.
You touch it and step back.
Repeat.

Rebbe Nachman warns that each time you come back from bitul, equipped with the capability of making the world a better place, the challenges you face will be more difficult and painful, the suffering more intense. Because bitul redirects your focus to the ultimate good that lies behind everything, your return can come as quite a shock, magnifying the problems of this world even more. You must ensure that your *joie du Judaisme*—the joy that results from your experience of realizing that all is good—is in proper working order in order to survive and succeed. The greater the suffering, the stronger the bitul must be. When it was necessary, Moshe was willing to go so far as to sacrifice every trace of his existence.[104] ❀

One of the Rebbe's followers was speaking to him about a marriage proposal he had received. He told the Rebbe, "There is no place for me there."

Rebbe Nachman answered, "When a person has a Jewish heart, he has nothing to do with space. The heart is Godliness, and the world is located within God." ❀

Even though you may fall to such an extent that all your spiritual work has been ruined, there remains forever a residue of light from every single thought and effort that was invested in producing it. Therefore, *do not despair!* ❀

---

[104] When God threatened to annihilate the Israelites for the crime of the golden calf, Moshe argued with God to forgive them. If God wouldn't, Moshe said, "Erase me" (*Exodus* 32:32).

HITBODEDUT
IDEAS

— 1 • One-Minute Hitbodedut —

Instructions

Set a time during the day when you know you will be alone and fully available for *just one minute.*

1 • Stop what you're doing.

2 • Take a deep breath.

3 • *Thank* God for any two things in your life—one current, the other current or past.

4 • *Ask* God for two *material* things—one related to *today,* one related to the future.

5 • *Ask* God for two *spiritual* things—one related to *today,* one related to the future.

6 • *Ask* God to help the Jewish people in two ways.

7 • Either:

(a) Ask God to talk again tomorrow and say, "Thank You," or

(b) Keep talking. When you finish, go to 7a. ❋

⊢— 2 • HITBODEDUT OF THE JEWISH SAGES —⊣

From the few recorded samples of hitbodedut of our Sages (*Berakhot* 16b), and from many of the formal prayers, you can take a cue on how to formulate your own prayers and what you might pray for.

MINI-HITBODEDUT OF TALMUDIC SAGES

Lord, our God, may it be Your will:

- that love, brotherhood, peace and friendship be our lot
- that we have many students
- that we have a good old age in which we see our hopes fulfilled
- that our portion be in the Garden of Eden
- that You better us with a good friend and the good inclination
- to help us to start the day early, with our heart's desire focused on doing Your will.

Please provide our needs and wants.

REBBE ELAZAR

God—
See our shame and suffering, and respond with compassion, strength, kindness and favor. Please, always act towards us out of goodness and humility.

REBBE YOCHANAN

God—
Help us to not sin—spare us the embarrassment. Help us not to be ashamed in comparison to our ancestors.

REBBE ZEIRA

God—
May Torah be our craft; may our hearts not know hurt; may our eyes never be dimmed.

REBBE CHIYA

God—
Please grant us:

- long life, a life of peace, good, blessing and prosperity
- "settled" bones, fear of sin
- a life free of shame and disgrace
- prosperity and honor, and love for the Torah
- awareness of the Divine
- a life in which You fulfill in a beneficial way all our heart's desires.

RAV[105]

God—
Save me today and every day from:

brazen people / defamation / bad people / the urge to do the wrong thing / bad friends and influences / bad neighbors / accidents / the evil eye / gossip and slander / snitches / false testimony / the hatred of others / libel / an unnatural death / debilitating, chronic illness / mishaps / Satan—the Destroyer / severe judgment / harsh opponents, whether Jewish or not / and the judgment of Hell.

REBBE YEHUDAH HANASI[106]

God—
Please make peace in Heaven and peace on Earth—including in the Torah community. May all who engage in Torah study do so for the right reasons.

RAV SAFRA

God—
Please situate us in a place of light, not in a place of darkness.

RAV ALEXANDRI OR RAV HAMNUNA

---

[105] This is the communal prayer said on the Shabbat preceding the beginning of each Jewish month.

[106] This prayer is part of the daily liturgy, said immediately after the Morning Blessings.

Master of the Universe—
You know we want to serve You. You know what holds us back? The "leaven in the dough" (i.e., the evil inclination) and the servitude of exile. Save us from them and we will turn ourselves around to wholeheartedly do Your will.

RAV ALEXANDRI

God—
Before I was created I wasn't worthwhile, and now that I've been created, it's as if I wasn't created. I am dirt when alive, and certainly after my death. I stand before You, a vessel filled with shame and disgrace. Lord, my God and God of my ancestors, may it be Your will that I never sin again. In Your great compassion, erase my wrongdoings, but without subjecting me to troubles or serious illness.

RAV HAMNUNA[107]

PRAYERS, THANKS AND REQUESTS

Our Sages formalized prayers, thanks and/or requests for the following gifts:

> sight / clothing / shoes, belts and hats / the ability to stand and to walk / sleep and being refreshed and recharged / wisdom, intelligence and insight / a heart inclined to Divinity / trust in God / forgiveness / redemption / healing / livelihood and prosperity / Jewish unity / an honest judicial system / freedom from depression and anxiety / an end to traitors and treachery / the rebuilding of Jerusalem and the Holy Temple / being granted an audience with the Listener of All Prayers.

Our Sages also formalized prayers for:

> being granted a body that functions, and a pure soul / safe travel / joy, happiness, friendship and camaraderie, brotherhood and peace, and a happy marriage / food and drink we're about to eat, and after we've eaten, and the Land of Israel / pleasant smells and natural wonders (like the Grand Canyon and the Alps), and more. ❁

---

[107] This prayer is part of the Yom Kippur confessional.

┣━━ 3 • Everyday Opportunities ━━┫

Shabbat Candle-Lighting

After lighting the Shabbat candles and reciting the blessing over them, the woman of the house traditionally utters a few personal prayers for the welfare of her family and of the Jewish nation. Now is also a ripe time for hitbodedut:[108]

"Dear God,

"Thank You for allowing me the honor of opening the doors to let Shabbat enter my home.

"With something so simple and easy, You've shown me that I can determine the value and holiness of time, for myself and others, and that the simplest and most ordinary things in life can be so holy if Your light shines on them.

"Please help me and my husband/children/parents to allow the light of the tzaddikim and of the Torah to shine wherever we may go, now and in the future. May we bask in Your light and may You bask in our light."

Kissing the Mezuzah

"God, thank You for helping me to do this mitzvah, for making it so easy. I hang it up once and I'm keeping it 24/7. Let me be cheered by the sight of it, knowing that You've helped me accept Your invitation to be part of my home.

"I've heard that our Sages teach and Rebbe Nachman re-emphasizes that the mitzvah of mezuzah can help me overcome my acquisitive desire and not be jealous of others. Help me to remember that every

---

[108] Care must be taken not to speak between the lighting and the saying of the blessing. This follows the general principle that no interruption should be made between the recital of a blessing and the act that accompanies it. You could engage in some hitbodedut before lighting the candles, but you may get so caught up in your prayer that you forget to light till it's too late—Shabbat has already begun! Therefore, Jewish women traditionally offer their "Shabbat-candle prayers" after they light and recite the blessing over the candles.

so often, so I can own my possessions, instead of the other way around. Help me to undo my thoughts of jealousy and the things I did wrong as a result. May such thoughts never again hold sway over me.

"Please protect my body, soul, money and possessions from all harm and damage, from theft, robbery and loss.

"May the holiness of the mitzvah of mezuzah become part of me as I come and go. May its merit protect me wherever I travel, so that I leave home and return home in peace and safety.

"May I be inspired by the mitzvah of mezuzah to holiness and generosity, and may that holiness and generosity bring a long, joy-filled life in their wake.

"May they also save me from disagreements, both spiritual and material, and from enemies, and may there be peace in the world."

WEARING TZITZIT

"Dear God,

"May the corners of my tzitzit become wings, shielding me from temptation—in particular, the mirage of sexual consumption—and allowing me to become holier.

"May the corners of my tzitzit become wings, carrying me closer to You. May my newfound holiness help me recognize and refuse bad advice, advice that is ultimately harmful and destructive. Help me and protect me from smooth talkers and good-lookers, even if their intentions are innocent.

"Let my mind be clear, unencumbered by the transient things of life, so I can understand correctly the advice of tzaddikim, so that the choices I make will be true and intelligent."

ANGER AND TEMPTATION

The words of hitbodedut that you speak—the ones you give birth to from your deepest emotions—are the ones that love you best in return. When you really, really know and finally spit it out that you've got a problem with a particular emotion (e.g., anger or jealousy) or temptation (e.g., chocolate), then the next time you're about to lose it, those hitbodedut words will rush to your side and help you realize what's in danger of happening.

"God! My fuse is way too short. Almost every least little thing sets me off and ruins my equilibrium. What's worse is my reaction! Words that shouldn't be said, tantrums that shouldn't be had, throwing stuff. I break things and ruin my relationships with people, some of whom I actually like!

"Please help me. Remind me that You are in charge of the world, not me. Remind me that You've got a plan and that You're in the details; that it's OK, or even better than OK, if things don't go my way.

"I'm not a baby anymore. Help me to be mature and to behave maturely."

* * *

"God, how come my sister can get away with anything, and I get yelled at for stuff I didn't even do? It's not fair!

"She makes a mess, I have to clean it up. She wants something, Dad gives her his credit card. If I want something, it's, 'What? Am I made of money?' IT'S NOT FAIR!

"I'm just a kid. It's hard for me to see her enjoy everything at my expense. Sometimes I have these dark fantasies about her going away for a long, long time, but I know that's not right.

"I don't know if my parents or my sister can change. They don't even realize there's a problem. So, please help me deal with it. I don't know how, but show me, somehow, some way, how not be destroyed or upset by her victories, and please help me to enjoy whatever You give me."

* * *

"What can I tell you, Lord? I'm a normal, healthy, red-blooded male. I have drives. I have urges. And everywhere I go, everywhere I look, those drives and urges are being teased, stoked and stroked.

"Sex sells. It's on TV, in the movies, in newspapers, magazines and billboards. Not to mention the porno machine—I mean the computer. It's even on the cell phone!

"Lord, I feel like a bobble-head doll, a ping-pong ball. I can't help myself—*but I want it to stop!* My eyes are bugging out and my mind is a cesspool. I CAN'T STAND IT ANYMORE!

"I don't expect the world to change any time soon, but if You want me to be aware of You and not of them, You're going to have to help me, big time. Maybe we can start by..."

You might not actually put down the frying pan the next time hubby upsets you. You may curse under your breath the next time your sister comes home with a new dress. You might not actually avert your eyes or attention, but you're already better, and better off. ✺

Appendix A
⊢—— PRE-HITBODEDUT SELF-QUIZ ——⊣

Before you get started in hitbodedut, or at any point along the way, it's a good idea to tune into and clarify your desire for more Jewishness and a closer relationship with God. The questions presented here are suggestions. They are meant to help you rate your Jewishness and create your goals, and prevent you from shooting yourself in the foot. Use only the ones that you think will work for you. You can ask and answer before hitbodedut, during hitbodedut or both. If you're doing it before hitbodedut, it may be worthwhile to write down your answers now, rather than interrupt your hitbodedut to record them. Keeping a "hitbodedut diary" can be quite helpful to get and stay organized, as well as provide yourself with encouragement.

SELF-AWARENESS

1. If you were to live your life as Jewishly as you would like, what is the first change you would try to make?

2. What aspects of Jewishness do you want MORE of in your life? (Make a list.)

3. What do you love about Jewishness? Which part of you really loves that?

4. What aspect or practice of Jewishness would you incorporate into your life if you knew you would not fail at it?

5. What aspect or practice of Jewishness can you work on now that would make the biggest difference in your life?

6. Name one change to your Jewishness that would give you more peace.

7. What's the one Jewish thing you would love to do before you die?

8. What's the biggest impact that would result from achieving your Jewishness goal(s)?

Certainly not all is bad. Rebbe Nachman teaches that you should always look for—and find—what's right about you. So:

9. In what way is your Jewishness currently perfect?

10. In what areas of Jewishness are you succeeding?

11. What else can you find to be grateful for?

PERSONAL ROADBLOCKS

1. What are three things you do regularly that run counter to your goal(s)?

2. What do you wish you had less of, because it interferes with your Jewishness? (Make a list.)

3. What frustrates your Jewishness? Which part of you really hates those frustrations?

4. What's your favorite way of sabotaging yourself and your goals? What can you say to yourself when you realize you're doing this?

6. Do you find yourself focusing on aiming towards something, moving away from something, or both?

7. Does your current attitude help or hinder your progress?

GOAL-SETTING

For each goal that you would like to reach, ask yourself these questions:

1. How will you measure your progress towards this goal?

2. What will happen (i.e., what will it cost you) if you don't do anything to progress towards this goal?

3. Is now the right time for you to make a commitment to achieving this goal?

4. If it is the right time, what are three actions you could do this week that would make sense?

5. On a scale of 1 to 10, how excited do you feel about taking these actions?

6. What would increase that score? (For example: overcome fear, define the steps more clearly, ask a friend for support, pretend it's fun.)

Taking the Next Step

1. What *is* your next step?

2. What Torah study or advice could help you find the next step?

3. Do you have a friend (or a friend of a friend) who could help you illuminate this issue?

4. Whom should you be associating with, or what group could you join, so that achieving this goal becomes more attainable? (Do you know people who are already doing it?)

Remember, impulses to grow and to do new things come and go. Use hitbodedut to keep the momentum going.

By the time you finish this quiz, you should have a better idea of what you want, why you want it, how much you want it, and how you're going to try to achieve it. ❈

Appendix B
⊢—— TWO APPROACHES TO THE SAME GOAL ——⊣

TEASE YOURSELF

Sometimes it's hard to believe that you can make dreams come true. Even after you've worked through the process of defining a goal, you may not be convinced that you can really achieve it. Here's a technique you may enjoy to strengthen your inner resources and nudge your goal towards fruition.

In hitbodedut, address yourself as if you have already accomplished your goal. Imagine answering your phone and hearing someone say, "Hello. May I ask how you manage never to lose your temper? How did you manage to make your home kosher and give up eating at non-kosher restaurants? Please, tell me your secrets."

At this point you may feel a little smile coming to your lips. Why not? Your goal has been spoken out loud. It is that much closer to becoming real because you have made a vessel which God can fill with His kindness.

"I've been searching everywhere for someone who has a similar background to mine, who knows how hard it is to maintain self-control. Can you please help me?"

Even a tiny taste of what it might feel like to live your dream can be a powerful motivating force to keep you enthusiastic and on track.

AN EXERCISE

Even if the goal you envision is huge and may not even be accomplished in the near future (if at all), practice interacting with the world as if you've already achieved it. Here's one scenario:

"You ask why it doesn't bother me at all that you're screaming at me in front of all these people? Well, it's because the yishuv hadaat I've gained in hitbodedut helps me to stay calm and unflustered."

Tease yourself with your goal!

TAKE YOUR GOAL AWAY

Here's a method that comes from the opposite direction.

From time to time you may face a period of self-resistance. You may become extremely frustrated to hear yourself saying that you can't take the next step, or restating the obstacles instead of looking for solutions to overcome them. Maybe you'd really rather play it safe and stick with the familiar and unsatisfying, rather than take another step forward on the narrow bridge.

Sometimes this desire to be safe can suck you into thinking that you really are stymied, when in fact you're just not admitting to yourself what's truly important or that you're truly afraid.

After the umpteenth time of progressing towards a certain goal and failing, it's time to try a different strategy: Admit that right now, you're just not interested enough to really go for it.

Here's a hitbodedut I had one morning:

"OK, God, what would You say to someone who always wants to show up a little bit earlier for Shacharit, but never seems to manage it?

"You would ask him what he really wanted? Well, what if he mentioned some obstacles, like he works late into the night. So, You would ask him if he could cut back his hours three or four nights a week, and come early to shul on the following mornings?

"What if he answered You that he has to work late because he has a mortgage to pay. Ah. You would ask him if he's willing to show up early at least on Shabbat? Well, I know what he's going to tell You. He's going to tell You, 'Oh no, I can't do that. I need some time to relax and be with my wife and kids.'"

After about three minutes of really not enjoying this, I said:

"I know what he should do! Tell him this is the plan: Keep working late till the mortgage is paid off, pretend that even on Shabbat you have no time for yourself, and then, when you're seventy years old, look back and wonder what could have been had you made a real effort to solve your problems instead of rationalizing them!"

I sat stunned for a few moments, and then blurted out: "That's a terrible plan!" And then I mumbled to myself, "Yeah, well, isn't that the one you're working with?"

AN EXERCISE

Look in the mirror, at the person who wants to be different but keeps complaining about how he or she can't do it because there are too many obstacles. Suggest to that person that it's time to throw in the towel, give up, and just continue in the same old rut. "Sure, why not keep coming late for services till the day you die? Why not continue seething with anger and busting a gut from stress? When you've got one foot in the grave, then you can think of what might have been." Say it seriously, as if it were really a valid option.

If you find yourself resisting a goal, pretend it's almost too late. Maybe feeling yourself squirm a bit will propel you forward. Enjoy! ❈

Appendix C
—— COURAGEOUS HITBODEDUT ——

Courageous hitbodedut is the most important thing you can do for your spiritual growth. It can free you from your demons and improve your relationships with others.

Your relationship with God is greatly affected by your relationship with your fellow human beings (*Avot* 2:1, 3:13). Use courageous hitbodedut to improve your relationship with others—and with Him.[109]

What is courageous hitbodedut? It's the hitbodedut you don't want to have. In fact, your best hitbodedut is probably the one you haven't even thought of having.

Think for a minute. What's the hardest hitbodedut you can imagine having? What's holding you back from having it? When you think you know the answer, keep reading.

The kind of hitbodedut we're talking about is the one that can transform your relationship with God—or with another person, perhaps even yourself. It may free you from bad habits and bad traits. It will certainly clear the air.

Would you like some examples of what it take guts to say? I thought you'd never ask!

- "I've hated you for leaving me."

- "I stole $2,000 from you twenty years ago."

- "I don't have a license to practice, and would like to become legitimate."

---

[109] Rabbi Chanina ben Dosa would say: One who is well-liked by people is well-liked by Heaven (*Avot* 3:13).

- "We've never said, 'I love you' in this family. I love you."

- "Will you marry me?"

- "I'm not enjoying our love life."

- "I had an affair five years ago."

- "I really gave you a hard time at school, and I'm sorry I hurt you."

- "God, I'd like to feel You acknowledge me for all the hard work I do."

- "I'm angry at how You treat Your children."[110]

To know if you're ready for some courageous hitbodedut, here are a few clues to look for: How is your relationship with God? Your partner? Family? Co-workers?

If your relationship(s) is less than wonderful, chances are you're holding back something—something that, once expressed, could allow your self-awareness and Jewishness to grow.

Here are other clues that you need some courageous hitbodedut: You're angry at or avoiding someone. You're ashamed of something you did or scared that people will find out about it. You're worried about the consequences of such a hitbodedut session or feel uncomfortable thinking about it. Another important clue is that the trigger for such a session of hitbodedut happened a long time ago, but still resurfaces in your mind every now and then, maybe as you're reading this.

The best clue is that you don't want to have hitbodedut about *that!* This is a sure sign that you're avoiding something. In a nutshell, you probably haven't had the courageous hitbodedut yet because you're afraid of the outcome you imagine will result: loss, discomfort or change.

---

[110] Warning! Addressing God in an overly aggressive manner may be hazardous to your health (*Taanit* 25a, *Sukkah* 53a). Be courageous, be daring—but be respectful too.

Why Dig Up the Past?

Shouldn't it be buried? Isn't the past just the past? The answer to that depends on your feeling about digging it up again. If you have absolutely no negative reaction when you sit down and think about what happened—assuming that you've already honestly appraised what you did and its outcome—then you may not need to readdress it in hitbodedut. On the other hand, if you're immediately plagued by feelings of guilt, anger, sadness or love—any unexpressed emotion—then give it some time in hitbodedut.

Your sessions of courageous hitbodedut will show you where your barriers are, where you're most frightened.

It's certainly easier to stay in a cocoon. Yet if you are serious about making progress, sooner rather than later you'll have to beat your wings against the walls of your cocoon in order to explore new realms of your joyous flowing self, to live unafraid, to be you.

Skeletons in Your Closet

Courageous hitbodedut is the best way to rid yourself of another pariah: the skeleton in your closet. Everyone has at least one. A "skeleton in the closet" is anything you did in the past that you feel was wrong, that gnaws at you, or that you would like the world never to know about. You can choose to continue walking chained to your skeleton, weighed down by your heavy fears. Or you can choose to be courageous, to come clean and decide that living an honest Jewishness is the most important thing in your life. If you are genuinely willing to risk everything you hold dear to tell the truth, your growth and peace will be unsurpassed.

Let's start with some easy examples: What do you regret, but have never apologized for? What are you still feeling guilty about? Who are you avoiding because you feel uncomfortable about some past interaction? What are you afraid that people will discover about you?

Think about it. Is there anything about you or what you have done that you want to hide from? Pause now for five minutes and make an inventory. If it's not Shabbat or a Jewish holy day, put it in writing. It's worth it.

Then there are the more difficult examples: Have you ever stolen something valuable? Have you had an affair that is still secret? Are you terrified that others will find out you're not the wonderful person they think you are? Did you ever exploit anyone? What lies have you told that you pray will never be exposed? You know what you have been carrying around; add it to the list.

No matter how small or how big, you can be free of it. If you find the matter too big to clean up right now, or if the fear has too great a hold on you, it can be handled a couple of ways. It can all be over five minutes from now—albeit with shallow breath and sweaty hands—or it can be a process.

When you clear something up, it always works out in the long run. The more fearful you are, the greater the potential for growth. If the consequences are not to your liking, then there's a chance for even more growth. So get on with it. Identify a skeleton. Start with a small one to build your muscles, if you like. Or start with a big one and work down. Make your lists (the ones mentioned above)—and start talking.

THE AFTEREFFECTS

The peace you gain as a result of courageous hitbodedut won't go unnoticed. Others will feel it as well, without your having to say a word to them. Your courage to become stronger can have an amazing effect on other people.

As a result of one courageous hitbodedut that a friend of mine had, he called an old acquaintance of his to say, "I thought of the fight we had and how we stopped collaborating. I want you to know that I was going through some rough times. It wasn't your fault." His acquaintance had watched several of his other friendships go sour in a brief span of time, and was despondent. It meant the world to him to hear someone tell him that it wasn't his fault. My friend told me, "The hitbodedut that got me to make that phone call was worth a million bucks."

Some people justify not having courageous hitbodedut by saying, "I'll just move on," or, "It's enough that I know about it." "It might upset her" is another way to avoid facing up to a session of courageous hitbodedut. Rebbe Nachman teaches that doing hitbodedut only in your head isn't enough. It's in the speaking that the transformation occurs.

Your courage also might be contagious. Imagine how fearless others might become once they've seen your example. Your courage can ripple out and change the world. People have told me, "You know, after you called me, I started to think. So I picked up the phone and called…"

THE RISKS

However, there are no guarantees that the immediate results will be exactly what you pray for. Even when the ultimate outcome is positive, it may be accompanied by a calamitous price, perhaps worse than the one you feared. If that happens, remember that the true outcome is your Partner's doing. You had been squeezing the calamity into a box in order to avoid it. Now it's time to trust God and let Him run the universe as He will. As Rabbi Akiva said, "Everything the Merciful One does is for the best" (Berakhot 60b).

Perhaps this is a good time to say that having courageous hitbodedut can lead to bankruptcy, prison, death or even worse. The spiritual warrior realizes this, puts truth and love above all, and accepts the outcome with grace. You're fully responsible for any actions you take as a result of reading this book. In fact, that's kind of the point! (If acting on your courageous hitbodedut could have legal or medical consequences, I recommend consulting a lawyer, doctor or other appropriate professional first so you know what you are getting into.)

There are things that should not be said to other people, even if they should be said to God. If and when you do decide to clear the air, take care to minimize others' hurt feelings. You have a responsibility to speak with compassion and to speak responsibly. Take responsibility for what you have done. Avoid blaming.

No matter how compassionately or gently you share the truth, the other person may feel pain. That may be unpleasant or gut-wrenching, but that's not necessarily a bad thing. Maybe that's meant to be. If you speak honestly and not vindictively, it usually does more good than harm.

It's important to note that "It might upset him/her" ranks high on the all-time list of excuses for wimping out.

FIVE STEPS TO HAVING COURAGEOUS HITBODEDUT

1. Admit to yourself that you don't feel 100% wonderful or complete with God, other people, or yourself—but would like to.

2. Identify the kernel of truth that you want to express. If you were to die today, what message would you leave in your ethical will? What work would you like your spiritual children—those whose lives you've influenced—to finish or continue on your behalf? What mistakes would you exhort them to avoid?

3. Imagine the worst outcome that a session of courageous hitbodedut could produce. For example: You'll have to quit your job, divorce your spouse or be publicly disgraced. Accept that possibility.

4. Remember, you're allowed to feel uncomfortable, or even terrified! Even so, your vocal cords should still function. The more frightened you feel, the more fearlessness you need to summon. Life is a very, very narrow bridge. You must cross it. You can! Don't be scared!

5. Now start talking, and talk honestly. Whatever needs to get said will be said. ✿

Appendix D
⊢—— COMING CLEAN ——⊣

As unsullied as you may appear, with purer vision, you'll see it isn't so. As clean as you are, there's always cleaner.

Rebbe Nachman often refers to two parallel categories of people. One is the ger (convert); the other is the baal teshuvah (returnee to the faith, penitent). The latter category really includes everyone, because all of us have to "return" some previously unclaimed aspect or area of our lives to sacredness.

"For this every chassid should pray to You, for when it is needed" (*Psalms* 32:6).

The Talmud (*Berakhot* 8a) asks what "it" refers to. The Talmud offers a number of answers and singles out "a readily accessible toilet in time of need" as being the best.

This teaching underscores something that is absolutely vital for your spiritual growth. Often, if not always, your approach to goodness and holiness—your attempts to improve your Jewishness—will be blocked by hurdles and walls. This is especially true when you've already begun and seem to be making progress. It might even happen after you've been working on your Jewishness for years with various practices, including hitbodedut, and have actually detected improvement. Suddenly you'll face a setback. Thoughts and desires of immense and frightening proportions may envelop you. The source of this torrent is your own filth, what Rebbe Nachman terms, "the soiled garments." The source of this mess is euphemistically referred to as "the sins of youth," or "sowing one's oats."

The soiled garments translate into all kinds of obstacles of varying degrees of intensity that keep one out of the realm of the sacred. Even a person who has improved significantly in her outlook may suddenly find herself confronted with lusts and doubts more powerful than she ever encountered before. Not everyone has the gumption to keep forging ahead, trudging on through the morass. To provide us with encouragement, Reb Noson offers an analogy:

> Wheat is grown so that we may have nourishment. We must expend great effort to plow the ground and sow the seeds. The fully ripened stalk is a great step forward to the goal, but certainly not what we seek. It must be reaped, winnowed and threshed. The result is closer to what we want, but it is still not usable. Now we need to grind and sift the grain.
>
> Yet even this fine flour cannot nourish. So we draw water, add it to the flour and knead it into dough. Dough, still, is inedible. So we stoke the oven until it is sufficiently hot and bake our loaf of bread. Even then, however, it cannot serve our purpose, for we cannot swallow it whole. We cut the bread into slices. We chew. Then we begin to be nourished.

So although you are growing all the time, relative to what you can accomplish you are still raw material, unfit for the ultimate, desired goal. All the dirt, pebbles, chaff and bran that are sticking to you must be removed. This is done, at every stage, by studying and applying Torah teachings. As Rebbe Nachman taught:

> A pot of water may seem perfectly clear. Yet when it is placed on a fire and begins to boil, all its impurities rise to the surface. One must stand by and constantly remove these impurities. The original purity is merely an illusion. With a little heat the impurity surfaces; when the impurities are removed, the water is truly pure and clear.
>
> The same is true of a person. At every stage that he begins to serve God, good and evil are completely mixed together within him. The impurities are so closely united with the good that they cannot be recognized. When a person begins to study Torah and prays to apply it to his life, he is touched by the heat of purification. All the evil and impurities come to the surface. He must remain vigilant and constantly remove the dirt and impurities as they appear. In the end, he is truly pure and clear.

Purification requires agitation and confusion. One starts out totally immersed in the material. He then begins to come close to God. It would seem it is possible to remove the dirt and impurities at once, but the mind is completely intermingled with the mire. Were it to be removed immediately, the good of the mind would also be discarded. Therefore, one must be purified little by little. ❋

Appendix E
— DON'T LOSE YOUR HEAD —

In a slaughterhouse, animals lose their heads. In our world, too, something causes people to lose their heads and get caught in the thicket of confusion and the vortex of illusion. What drives us to distraction? We lose our heads over a coin.

Money—not only for pursuing luxuries, but even for maintaining the bare necessities—takes hold of us. Wherever one goes—academia, sporting arenas, boardrooms, bedrooms, street corners—everyone has money on his mind, some version of gelt on his lips.

Of course, it's always for something "good," like dream kitchens, dream vacations and dream cars, and often for something noble, like ridding oneself or others of misery or solving society's ills. "If only I had a million dollars, I'd…"

This is how money gains control of our heads. It plants a feeling of emptiness, a sense that "what I have is not enough and not good enough." This puts us in a dissonant place, making our minds a perpetual-motion machine of negative craving. Once the mind's eye is focused on "what's not there" and on "what they have," it can never be satisfied.

God is fullness, wholeness, shalom. Idolatry represents the opposite—it is a lacking, a deficiency. Idolatry is not an emptiness that needs to be filled, but an emptiness that consumes even what is there, making it impossible for you to enjoy even what you possess. Money, Rebbe Nachman teaches, is the idolatry that embraces all other idolatries.

The "it's not enough" cancer spreads to other parts of your life as well: Your food and diet aren't right, your wardrobe is all wrong, others have the power and respect that "belong" to you, and one partner (or at least the one you have) is not enough.

Can you buy your head back? Can you put a stop to the pursuit of material happiness before you go over the brink into a bottomless pit? Thank God, the answer is yes. The answer is to turn your mind to Shabbat—to think nothing.

The Torah describes Shabbat in this manner: "Six days shall you work, and the seventh day is an eternal Shabbat, holy to God..." (*Exodus* 31:15). The Talmud asks, "Can one finish all his tasks in six days? No; but when Shabbat arrives, as far as *you're* concerned, all your work *is* done" (*Beitzah* 16a on *Exodus* 20:9). On Shabbat, you're "retired." You have no more pursuits to concern or haunt you. Your mind is liberated. You can devote your thinking and focus to keep it liberated seven days a week.

The ability to stop thoughts is not an option, nor is it a skill reserved for super model Jews. It is a necessary skill for every Jew at every stage and step of Jewish growth—for reining in your lusts and confusion, hushing your emotions (even positive ones[111]) and keeping your intellect in check.

Part of the quieting of the mind includes forgetting. Once something has passed, let it go. Don't focus your hindsight on it. Yes, you may spend some time in hitbodedut to review whether or not a *decision* you made was correct or not, so that you don't repeat a mistake, but do so without any "would've, could've, should've." What's done is done. Forget about it. ✳

---

[111] For example, not allowing regret over past mistakes to snowball into feelings of failure, which could lead to despair.

⊢—— GLOSSARY ——⊣

AKDAMUT—liturgical poem recited in synagogue during Shavuot morning prayer services

ALEF-BET—the Hebrew alphabet

ARIZAL—Rabbi Yitzchak Luria (1534-1572), Jewish scholar and founder of the modern study of Kabbalah

BITUL—negation, nullification. In a mystical context, refers to total nullification of the ego.

BRIT MILAH—covenant of circumcision

CHAKHMAH—wisdom. When capitalized, refers to one of the sefirot.

CHAG SAMEI'ACH—literally, "Happy Holiday," greeting offered on Jewish holidays

CHASSID (pl. CHASSIDIM)—a member of a chassidic group (see Chassidut)

CHASSIDUT—a Jewish revival movement founded in Eastern Europe in the eighteenth century by Rabbi Yisrael ben Eliezer, the Baal Shem Tov, Rebbe Nachman's maternal great-grandfather. One of its core teachings is that God's presence fills all one's surroundings, and one should strive to serve God in every word and deed.

CHESSED—kindness

CHUMASH—the Five Books of Moses

CHUTZPAH—nerve, audacity

DAAT—knowledge, awareness. When capitalized, refers to one of the sefirot.

DAVEN, DAVENING, DAVENER—Pray, prayer, one who prays

EITZAH (pl. EITZOT)—suggestion, advice. In Breslov parlance it refers to a spiritual practice, usually one recommended by Rebbe Nachman.

GOD—the Creator and Sustainer of life. God is neither He nor She nor It. God just is. However, since God interacts with the world as both giver and taker, and giving is considered a masculine attribute while taking is considered feminine, God, Who does more giving than taking, is classically referred to in the masculine. (In the Torah, God is, in fact, referred to by feminine pronouns on occasion.) This book uses the classic formulation.

HALAKHAH—Jewish law

HITBODEDUT—literally, "self-seclusion." Rebbe Nachman uses the term to refer to a daily practice in which one sets a time and place to speak to God. In a certain sense, hitbodedut is prayer; in another sense it is unstructured, verbal meditation.

KABBALAH—body of esoteric Jewish wisdom

KASHRUT—Jewish dietary laws

KETER—the highest of the ten sefirot.

KIDDUSH—reception or buffet following Shabbat and holiday morning prayer services; alternately, the blessing recited over a cup of wine at the start of a Shabbat or holiday meal

KOAN—a puzzling, paradoxical statement; used in Eastern thought as a means to spiritual awakening

KOHEN—a member of the Jewish priestly class, a patrilineal descendant of Moshe's brother, Aharon

KOHEN GADOL—high priest

KOTEL—the Western (or "Wailing") Wall in Jerusalem

KRIAT SHEMA—the recitation of the Shema Yisrael

MAARIV—the evening prayers

MASHIACH—the Messiah, descendant of King David

MENORAH—seven-branched candelabrum used in the Holy Temple of Jerusalem. When lowercase, refers to the eight-branched candelabrum used to perform the mitzvah of lighting the Chanukah candles.

MEZUZAH (pl. MEZUZOT)—small parchment containing the verses from *Deuteronomy* 6:4-9 and 11:13-21, which is attached to the doorposts of a Jewish home

MIDRASH—homiletical Rabbinic teachings

MIKVEH—a special pool of water used for ritual purification

MINYAN—quorum of at least ten men required for a communal prayer service

MISHKAN—the Tabernacle, the portable sanctuary containing the Tablets of the Law, which traveled with the Jewish people during their forty-year sojourn in the desert

MISHNAH—the redaction of the Oral Law which forms the first part of the Talmud, redacted in the second century C.E.

MITZVAH (pl. MITZVOT)—a Torah precept or commandment; a meritorious act

NESHAMAH—soul

NUDNIK—one who is a nuisance

OHR EIN SOF—God's Infinite Light

OLAM HABA—literally, "The World to Come" or "The Next World," the realm designated for receiving reward for the good one has performed in Olam Hazeh (This World). A utopian ideal.

OLAM HAZEH—literally, "This World," the realm designated for preparing oneself for entry into Olam Haba (The World to Come)

PURIM—holiday commemorating the salvation of the Jewish people after they were threatened by a royal edict in ancient Persia

SEFIRAH (pl. SEFIROT)—Divine emanation

SHABBAT—the Jewish Sabbath, extending from Friday sunset to Saturday sunset

SHABBAT SHALOM—literally, "Sabbath Peace," the traditional greeting offered on Shabbat

SHACHARIT—the morning prayers

SHALOM—peace, wholeness. Also used as a greeting for "hello" and "goodbye."

SHAVUOT—Biblical festival commemorating the giving of the Torah at Mount Sinai

SHEKHINAH—the Divine presence

SHEMA, SHEMA YISRAEL—a declaration of faith in the oneness of God and a commitment to fulfilling His commandments, comprised of verses from *Deuteronomy* 6:4-9 and 11:13-21, and *Numbers* 15:37-41. Recited daily during morning and evening prayers, and before going to sleep.

SHEMONEH ESREI—literally, "Eighteen," the silent devotional prayer which is the focus of the three daily obligatory prayers. So named because it initially consisted of eighteen blessings; an additional blessing was added later.

SHLEP—pull, drag

SHOFAR—ram's horn, traditionally blown during Rosh HaShanah morning prayer services

SHUL—synagogue

SIDDUR—prayer book

SIMCHA—happiness, joy. B'SIMCHA—upbeat.

SUKKAH—a thatch-covered structure used as a residence during the festival of Sukkot

SUKKOT—Biblical festival centering around the symbol of the sukkah, commemorating God's benevolent care of the Jewish people during their forty-year sojourn in the desert and His continuing providence over material blessing

TALLIT—prayer shawl

TALMUD—the Jewish Oral Law

TEFILAH—prayer

TEFILIN—mitzvah of wearing special leather boxes on the head and the arm during morning prayers (except on Shabbat and Jewish festivals); the boxes themselves, which contain Biblical verses declaring the oneness of God and the miracles of the Exodus from Egypt

TESHUVAH—repentance, returning to God

TIKKUN—correction, repair, rectification

TIKKUN HAOLAM—rectification of society and the world at large

TORAH—the Jewish Written Law, given by God to Moshe on Mount Sinai

TZADDIK (pl. TZADDIKIM)—righteous person; one who has spiritually perfected himself

TZEDAKAH—charity

TZITZIT—mitzvah of attaching tassels to a four-cornered garment; the four-cornered garment with the tassels; the tassels themselves

YISHUV HADAAT—a settled mind

ZITSFLEISH—ability or patience to sit still

ZOHAR—the greatest classic of Kabbalah, a mystical commentary on the Torah authored by Rabbi Shimon bar Yochai, a Mishnaic sage, in the second century C.E. ❈

Rabbi Ozer Bergman is a talented and engaging teacher of Breslov themes for over twenty-five years. He teaches Jews of every stream, from as old as four years to as young as eighty, in English, Hebrew and Yiddish. He is also a writer and editor whose lessons on the weekly Torah reading can be accessed at www.breslov.org/parsha.html. He and his wife Udel and their family live in Jerusalem.

A practitioner of hitbodedut for nearly thirty years, Rabbi Bergman welcomes questions on this subject. Write to him at www.breslov.org/earth-heaven.php. ✽

✻ ✻

MAY IT BE HIS WILL
THAT WE MERIT PRACTICING
HITBODEDUT PROPERLY,
AS HE DESIRES.

✻ ✻

⊢——— ONEG SHABBAT ———⊣

Made in the USA
Middletown, DE
31 August 2020

16911124R00166